Winning Elections in the 21st Century

Winning Elections in the 21st Century

Dick Simpson and
Betty O'Shaughnessy

Foreword by
US Congresswoman Jan Schakowsky

University Press of Kansas

Published by the University Press of Kansas (Lawrence, Kansas 66045), which was organized by the Kansas Board of Regents and is operated and funded by Emporia State University, Fort Hays State University, Kansas State University, Pittsburg State University, the University of Kansas, and Wichita State University

Library of Congress Cataloging-in-Publication Data

Names: Simpson, Dick W., author. | O'Shaughnessy, Betty, author.
Title: Winning elections in the 21st century / Dick Simpson and Betty O'Shaughnessy ; foreword by US Congresswoman Jan Schakowsky.
Other titles: Winning elections in the twenty-first century
Description: Lawrence, Kansas : University Press of Kansas, 2016. | Includes bibliographical references and index.
Identifiers: LCCN 2015044257
ISBN 9780700622139 (hardback)
ISBN 9780700622764 (paperback)
ISBN 9780700622146 (ebook)
Subjects: LCSH: Political campaigns—United States—Handbooks, manuals, etc. | Campaign management—United States—Handbooks, manuals, etc. | BISAC: POLITICAL SCIENCE / Political Process / Elections. | POLITICAL SCIENCE / Government / Local. | POLITICAL SCIENCE / Government / National.
Classification: LCC JK2283 .S55 2016 | DDC 324.70973—dc23 LC record available at http://lccn.loc.gov/2015044257.

British Library Cataloguing-in-Publication Data is available.

Printed in the United States of America

10 9 8 7 6 5 4 3 2 1

The paper used in this publication meets the minimum requirements of the American National Standard for Permanence of Paper for Printed Library Materials z39.48–1992.

Contents

....

Tables and Figures

Tables

Figures

Foreword

....

Imagine for a moment if every person who is eligible to vote actually did. If that happened, the policies that govern our country would be quite different. Politicians and policy makers would have to be far more responsive to the wishes of ordinary American voters, including all those families that struggle to make ends meet, afford college tuition, or retire comfortably.

It is obvious that there are far more everyday people than corporate CEOs, Wall Street moguls, and multimillionaires and billionaires. The superwealthy have done quite well under current laws and regulations they helped write.

I have run for office fourteen times and won thirteen elections. I tell aspiring candidates that in many ways my first losing race for Cook County commissioner in 1986 was the most important because I learned so much about how to do it better. I regrouped, ran, and won for Illinois state representative in 1990, where I served until running for Congress in 1998. After nine elections, I am still privileged to be there.

Before being elected, I was a community organizer and consumer advocate. Since that time, I have always believed that *people power CAN trump big money*, but only if you act on the lessons you will learn in *Winning Elections in the 21st Century*. I was a national cochair of the presidential campaign of my friend Barack Obama when few thought he could ever be elected, but "Yes we can!"

You will find that there is no magic bullet to conducting successful election campaigns. The good news is that it is a learned craft, and you can learn it.

This book will teach you how to take full advantage of all the new technologies, including use of social media, small-donor online fund-raising, targeting outreach to voters, vote analytics, and how technology can improve direct voter contact both door to door and on the phone.

Although we must take full advantage of all the new technologies, remember that *personal contact* is still the greatest predictor of whether a potential voter goes to the polls, mails her ballot, or votes online. According to academic studies, there is nothing more effective. It is the face at the door, the neighbor on the phone, the candidate personally asking for the vote—person-to-person contact is ultimately the best.

You can learn how to win elections here. Coauthor Dick Simpson, a friend and colleague for many years, writes from real-life experience. Dick Simpson was a nonmachine Chicago alderman in the days when the Daley machine ruled. A winner in a city that invented the term "politics is not beanbag," he knows what he is writing about. Earlier versions of the book became the standard handbook for participatory campaigns such as mine around the country. This new book, coauthored by another political scientist and former officeholder, Betty O'Shaughnessy, provides the definitive guide for citizens in our battle for a better future.

Winning Elections in the 21st Century is the book I recommend for candidates, campaign staff, volunteers, and citizens. There are few experiences more exciting or challenging or important than working in a competitive election for a candidate you believe in—and maybe that candidate is, or someday will be, you!

—*US Congresswoman Jan Schakowsky*

Preface

....

Campaigns today have new technology available, but the most successful ones merge that technology with proven techniques from the past. In the same way, this book rests upon the foundation of our earlier work. Author Dick Simpson, after winning his election as a Chicago alderman, published the first *Winning Elections* book in 1972. It has been in print continuously since then. Author Betty O'Shaughnessy was elected as a township trustee and has written on elections in books such as *The Keys to City Hall*.

Yet, the last edition of *Winning Elections* was published in 1996. The vast changes in electioneering since required an entirely new book. Too much has changed.

We have tested the new chapters and materials on our students at the University of Illinois–Chicago and Loyola Academy, where we teach. Their comments and questions have helped us hone the examples and explanations we provide here.

Techniques such as voter analytics, social media, and effective use of the Internet developed by presidential campaigns are now available to candidates in state and local elections. In *Winning Elections in the 21st Century* we describe campaign methods as old as Cicero's Roman campaigns two millennia ago and Abraham Lincoln's campaigns before the US Civil War. However, these techniques are merged with the latest whiz-bang technologies now available.

In our book we also seek to help candidates, students, and citizens consider the opportunities and challenges these campaign tools provide. To harness them properly, new laws are needed but also a greater awareness of their potential to either promote or undermine democracy.

We write primarily about participatory campaigns, in which the maximum number of citizens participates, as opposed to campaigns funded by a few wealthy individuals and interest groups with the money and expertise to buy elections. We explain how people power can prevail with the right candidates, issues, and support.

In short, we hope to inspire and empower readers to dive into the fun and excitement of electoral politics. For those already engaged, we show you how to win elections.

In creating this book, we are indebted to many people. We were taught the craft of running and winning elections by folks such as John Kearney, Sherwin Swartz, and Milton Rakove. We worked with leaders such as Robert Houston, Don Rose, Tom Gradel, and too many others to mention.

Chapter 9 was originally drafted as a student paper by Elise Doody-Jones and fact-checked by campaign manager Erica Sagrans and candidate Will Guzzardi.

The staff members at the University Press of Kansas have made the book infinitely better. We are especially indebted to Fred Woodward, who masterfully guided it from acquisition to publication; to Larisa Martin, the production editor; to our copy editor, Melanie Stafford; and to all the others who brought this book to you.

Winning Elections in the 21st Century is about participatory politics, in which citizens find candidates they want to elect to office and then, with or without party support, put together a voluntary campaign that wins. It is written to help citizens win campaigns over party machines, big money, or high-tech manipulation of voters. It is meant to provide you the tools of democracy, but you have to decide to use them.

*Winning Elections
in the 21st Century*

Chapter One

The Beginning

....

A campaign is composed of individuals and their decisions. There is the choice by a candidate to run, choices by leaders and participants to work, and the strategic decision by the candidate and campaign leaders to take public stands on some issues and ignore others. There is as well the selection of a campaign theme and basic principles and the decision by each voter whether to vote for a candidate. Each choice has consequences both for the person making the decision and for the outcome of the election. A campaign is finally won or lost by specific decisions made by individuals.

This book inevitably focuses upon mechanical and generalized aspects of running a winning campaign. Whether a campaign is a local race for city council or school board or a national campaign for member of Congress or president, it is composed of individuals and their choices. This chapter focuses upon these personal decisions, which breathe life into an otherwise mechanical process, making each campaign unique.

Everyone in the campaign makes a decision to devote time, talent, and money. For the candidate and key campaign leaders, this decision is of a different magnitude than that required of volunteers, workers, and contributors. Not only do the candidate and key leaders risk more of their time and fortune but also they risk more of themselves. Ordinary citizens provide the support necessary for victory, but the candidate and campaign leaders must launch the campaign.

Democracy is not possible unless some citizens willingly decide to become candidates for public office, campaign staff members, and volunteers. Committed individuals must decide to become involved in politics from candidate to volunteer if democracy is to flourish.

Deciding to run for public office is an especially important choice. A candidate risks her name, must pay debts incurred in the campaign, and may be ridiculed by the opposition. Most of all, a candidate must ask people to elect her to office. She may find it distressing to stand in front of stores shaking hands or to go to friends and associates asking for money. Yet candidates are their own best fund-raisers and workers. A candidate simply must learn to ask people to support her if she is to run a good campaign.

No candidate is really drafted. Some friends or citizen groups may ask if she is interested in running, but, at some point, she must decide to run and begin to seek the help and support necessary to win. If she decides to run, the campaign is launched. If she refuses or hesitates, the campaign is lost, and someone else steps forward. The decision of one person—the candidate—to risk all on the bid for public office is the most important decision of the campaign and one that only the candidate can make.

There are many concrete reasons for a candidate not to run—it will mean time lost from her family, take her away from the profession she has spent years building, and cost a lot of money. The positive reasons to run seem terribly abstract—her election will give the community a strong representative and spokesperson, she can make government more efficient, and she can pass legislation to improve her community. In addition, she can bring integrity, leadership, dedication, and experience to public office.

Personal ambition and ego also enter into the decision. A candidate may run in order to serve as a spokesperson, to get into the limelight, to get paid a better salary, or to prove to herself that other people really love her. These motives may seem shallow or selfish. However, some combination of public and private reasons that differs for each candidate must overcome all the practical reasons not to run. After the decision to go ahead is made, the other decisions about how to mount the most effective campaign are simpler.

Timing is also key. There is an old saying: "In politics, timing is everything." You can be involved in politics, learn the craft, and make a positive impact, but like a sailor in a small boat, when the winds of change are at your back you will move forward more easily. When there are no winds, you will be dead in the water.

Thus the decision to run for an office is not an abstract one. It is not a question of "Should I ever run for office?" Rather, it is "Should I run for *this* particular office in *this* election under *these* particular, unique circumstances?"

It is easier to win an open seat than to run against a popular incumbent. It is best to run for office when conditions are favorable. Yet, to make an impact you sometimes have to run for office or support a candidate when it is not clear that she will win. In the end, the decisions of the candidate to run and of staff and volunteers to support her are critical.

Key campaign personnel also face difficult decisions. To
bers, people might have to take leaves of absence or inter
work on the campaign full time. Like the candidate, staff
hours of work and separation from their families. They str
tions of whether they can do the job and whether they are
necessary sacrifices. It is one thing to support a candidate, to give a few hours
or to donate a few dollars to the campaign, but serving as a campaign leader
requires dedication, and usually, personal commitment to the candidate.

The sacrifice required of others is in many ways the greatest burden a candidate undertakes. A campaign will disrupt many people's lives and require
their contributions of time and money. This places on a candidate the responsibility of conducting the campaign in a fashion that will make it worth these
sacrifices—and of continuing the campaign even though a candidate might
sometimes wish to back out. All those who take a leadership position in a
campaign undertake an action with great consequences both for themselves
and for their community.

After the decisions to run and to support a candidate are made, campaign
leaders must still decide upon a general theme and take positive actions that
will symbolize to the press and to the community what the campaign is all
about.

In Dick Simpson's first campaign for Chicago alderman, he proposed a citizen ordinance to the city council to limit the power of the mayor in school
board appointments. This made it clear that if elected, he would not be a "rubber stamp" alderman for Mayor Richard J. Daley. Such actions on the part of
a candidate create the enthusiasm and support necessary to win. Thus, a candidate and staff must find creative ways of dramatizing the campaign. Unless
they do, even personal appearances by the candidate, paid political ads, creative use of social media, and precinct work are likely to be insufficient.

Existential choices, controversial issues, bold action—these are some of the
human stuff of campaigns. The campaign structure and hard work in the precincts provide a base, but good campaigns embody issues and actions that
cannot be completely planned in advance. They require the same personal
courage and careful decision making as the original choices to stand for election and to staff the campaign.

Winning Elections in the 21st Century draws from campaigns around the country. Our own campaigns enable us to give you the feel of campaigns from the inside, so we use frequent examples from campaigns in which we have been directly involved. In addition, we use examples from other states and other campaigns to illustrate diverse campaign choices and methods.

We make two basic assumptions in *Winning Elections in the 21st Century*: (1) This book describes participatory politics, which means there are a large number of volunteers involved in a campaign; and (2) the candidate is well qualified for the position and has a genuine platform on which to run. Otherwise, without massive resources or unusual circumstances, most candidates will not be able to win.

Of course, no book can substitute for experience. On our website, http://pols.uic.edu/political-science/chicago-politics/how-to-win-elections, we provide a variety of Internet resources in which experts discuss the various aspects of local campaigns from precinct work to fund-raising.

We recommend that after you read this book you work on a campaign—*preferably a winning campaign*. When you reread the book afterward, you will understand many elements that eluded you the first time through.

The Next Step

Many of you have positive goals, such as an end to poverty and racism in the United States. To realize such aspirations requires reforms to the political system. To do that we must elect leaders who support these goals and develop a constituency to support these leaders.

Instituting new values, electing new leaders, evolving new procedures of greater participation, and developing a constituency of conscience can certainly be pursued at the national level. The ultimate success of such strategies, however, depends upon the creation of an informed constituency and capable leaders in local communities. That is why *Winning Elections in the 21st Century* focuses primarily on local elections.

We seek to provide an introduction to innovative campaigning both for students of politics and political practitioners. During the past several decades there has been a tendency to divorce political science from real politics. Our book brings them together.

We make recommendations as to how to win elections, how to achieve your goals, and how to alter our political system. *Winning Elections in the 21st Cen-*

tury is an introduction to the study of electoral politics in the United States as it is actually practiced and as it can be improved.

Our book sets out the requirements for winning campaigns against strong opposition. Its message is simple: you can fight city hall and win.

Chapter Two

Choosing Sides

....

Just as the journey of a thousand miles begins with a single step, major political reform begins when a single citizen commits himself to winning elections, changing public policies, and opening up the political process. Reform begins with each of us fighting campaigns in our own communities and winning our own victories. Many of your neighbors, coworkers, and people you have met only casually feel the same way you do about the need to reform politics and government. They are waiting for someone to take the first steps—to offer viable candidates and proposals for new government policies.

Getting into Politics

"Politics is such a dirty business! You are too good to get involved with all those liars and cheats! In a position of responsibility like yours, you just cannot afford the time. And, you do not know anything about politics, anyway." Friends and family will use these and similar arguments to dissuade you from major political involvement. We have come to consider citizenship a passive thing— read the paper, watch television news, gripe to friends, tweet a snarky remark or post one on Facebook, vote on Election Day, and decry the results. Many of us believe it is the duty of a good citizen to vote, but few of us believe it is also our duty to undertake those actions necessary to make the electoral process meaningful by actually participating.

Of course, the opposite ideal is just as absurd. Not everyone can be involved passionately, completely, and only in politics. There are many aspects to life. The artist more dedicated to politics than art becomes a "social realist" or a reactionary demagogue. Workers more concerned with politics than their jobs become essentially patronage workers, employed for the sake of their work done in precincts at election time.

Groups as divergent as Occupy Wall Street and the Tea Party have recently called for changes in our "politics as usual."[1] Our governments from local city halls to state capitals and the national government in Washington, DC, face major crises. As a people, we face decisions that will affect our lives for decades to come. Surely, this is a time to get involved in politics.

Unfortunately, in recent years political participation has been on the decline. Many Americans show little trust in the political process. This trend is found especially among young people and the disadvantaged.[2] Consequently, some of us must become active participants in order for more passive citizens to have any meaningful role in shaping their government and society. There is a strong relationship between participation and positive traits such as a sense of political efficacy and personal effectiveness.[3] People with a greater sense of efficacy and effectiveness and less alienation, anomie, and cynicism are more likely to participate actively in politics.[4] Participating actively is important for society, and in turn, this reinforces our positive personal attitudes. For the ancient Greeks the quality as well as the quantity of activity was considered crucial to our personal development. As Pericles said of Athens: "Our citizens attend both to public and private duties, and do not allow absorption in their own various affairs to interfere with their knowledge of the city's. We differ from other states in regarding the [person] that holds aloof from public life not as 'quiet' but as useless."[5]

There are good reasons to be involved in politics. We face the necessity of renewing our entire political process from top to bottom, of reorienting personal and societal priorities so as to place the value of people before property and concern for our fellow citizens on par with concern for ourselves. If we lose this battle, our society could deteriorate into a closed one, an eternal battleground of increasingly violent factions, or into a complacent, greedy culture.

To paraphrase Abraham Lincoln, it falls to us in our time to renew our democracy so that government of, by, and for the people shall not perish from the earth. A part of this task of renewal is becoming involved in the electoral process. Participating in the public life of our communities can help us ensure that our governments promote justice and democracy for all.[6]

We all like to be recognized for what we do and desire the respect and esteem of our fellow citizens. In this sense, those of us who go into politics have political ambitions. There is nothing shabby or immoral about such ambitions, but politics has an amazing ability to corrupt. Therefore, although the desire to best serve the community is legitimate, expecting a "payoff"—especially an immediate and tangible payoff—because of political involvement is wrong.

Becoming a legitimate political person is difficult. To be political, a feel for the use of power is necessary, but not enough. A politician must first and foremost be a person of honor, sensitivity, integrity, and creativity. He must also be responsive to the needs and concerns of others. An outstanding political leader must first be an outstanding person. Max Lerner put the point this way: "I don't hold it against a [person] that he has spent his mature life in politics, provided there is more to him than politics. The question about Richard Nixon is whether there is this 'added dimension' (as he likes to call it) or whether the politician has eaten up the man."[7]

Thus both personal and altruistic reasons for political involvement—self-interest and honest concern for the community—must coincide. Only then will the political leaders necessary for the creation of a modern, participatory, inclusive, and positive politics emerge.

Joining a Political Organization or Campaign

Individuals decide to join a political organization or back an individual candidate based upon their particular situations. Most people begin by backing a candidate they admire and want to see elected. They then go on to join a more permanent political organization or party.

We recommend that you *not begin by running for office yourself.* Work on another candidate's campaign and learn the craft of politics. After you have direct campaign experience you will be able to make wise judgments about which staff to hire and how to run your own campaign if you choose to do so. No matter your personal circumstances, start first by working in other campaigns to learn about politics and government, and then get elected to local offices to learn how to govern. Studies have suggested wealthy candidates without political experience may not govern well, even if they have the resources to buy the best campaign staff.[8] After hands-on experiences, you will be ready and qualified to run for a major office.

People who participate in political campaigns decide to support specific candidates for a variety of reasons. Here are four reasons campaign volunteers gave for backing Bernie Weisberg, a qualified candidate for delegate to the Illinois Constitutional Convention:

> Because he is independent, which is most important to me, especially in a city like Chicago where the Democratic machine is so strong. (Student)
>
> There are people in this world that aren't getting a fair shake—black people, poor people, young people, and I'm trying to help remedy that situation. (Journalist)

I got sick and tired of having other people make the decision for me. I wanted to have a hand in making the decisions that affect my life, myself. So I became involved in independent politics. (Professor)

As a private citizen, I have to do more than just gripe about bad government. I think we all have to work very hard to change it. I have added personal reasons in that I am a clergyman, and I feel if I really take seriously my concern for people and human problems and doing something about it, then I feel I have to do more than preach sermons on Sunday. And so I'm getting involved and what I'm most pleased about is that large numbers of my parishioners are beginning to take seriously what it means to be religious people and to do something about their government by working for a good candidate such as Bernie Weisberg. (Catholic priest)[9]

Volunteers were attracted to work for the Obama for President campaigns of 2008 and 2012 for many of the same "idealistic" reasons. In 2008, they wanted to change government, support a variety of reforms such as healthcare and energy policy, and elect an African American as president of the United States.[10] In 2012, they continued to support change and reforms such as defending the Affordable Care Act (ACA), gender equality in marriage, immigration reform, and a higher minimum wage. Likewise, conservatives were attracted to work for the Republican and Tea Party candidates in these same years because of patriotism, cutting government programs, rolling back the deficit, and defeating Barack Obama's health care program ("Obamacare"), which they saw both as intrusive and socialistic.[11] In all these instances, campaign volunteers were attracted by their concern for other people, dismay at the failures of the political system, and a desire to be part of crucial decisions that affect all of our lives.

There can be, however, many other reasons people work on campaigns. They might do so to get some benefit, such as a job or government contract, or they might be more ideological, wanting to change how government works. Some have a direct self-interest in getting a particular law enacted or repealed. Others join because campaigns are a great way to meet people, expand their social lives, and make new friends. More than any other single factor, most people get into politics because someone they respect asks them.[12]

Campaigns can be exciting, and people join because of that excitement. Of course, other factors such as a sense of civic duty, of being a good citizen, of paying back to the community some of what you have been given by society, also play a role. You must decide for yourself which combination of ideological and personal motivations cause you to get involved. Not all volunteers work for the same reasons, so to recruit others successfully, you have to learn to "sell" the campaign to them on their terms.[13]

Working in Elections

Because participatory politics is so issue oriented, many people want to dive immediately into issue battles waged separately from campaigns. Paradoxically, beginning with a clearcut and exciting election is easier than fighting a separate issue battle. The best way to deal successfully with issues may be through electoral politics. With an election, it is known well in advance that the decisive event will be on a certain date and that the result will be determined by a majority of the votes cast. The last date for citizens to register, the rules of campaigning, and the myriad procedural details are not only established but accepted. The public sees participation in elections as a familiar and proper activity.[14] In contrast, in an issue campaign, it is hard to know who can make the decision you desire, much less the rules by which the decision is to be made. Major business and political leaders with decisionmaking power are relatively isolated from the public. Thus, it is difficult to pressure them directly. Issue campaigns are possible. However, they are harder to fight and harder to win.

During the campaign, your candidate can address critical issues while articulating his perspective on current problems. However, if your candidate takes stands, especially extreme stands, on every issue facing your community, he will make too many enemies, be counted an extremist, and be defeated at the polls. Instead, during the campaign, he can dramatize two or three concrete issues as examples of the steps he would take if elected. In a community where not many issues have previously been debated or resolved, this action is not a limitation but a major beginning.

In Dick Simpson's campaigns for alderman, he raised issues of better and fairer delivery of city services, an end to "machine" domination or boss rule in Chicago, and the right of citizens to have a direct voice in decisions made by local government. In his later congressional campaigns, he raised the issues of congressional reform, abortion rights, a smaller defense budget, national health-care reform, economic development, and saving jobs in the district.

Betty O'Shaughnessy, in contrast, campaigned as part of a team made up of all the township office candidates slated by the local Democratic Party. In their campaign, these candidates did not raise ideological issues but rather emphasized that they shared the local concerns of their neighbors and took an interest in the well-being of the township. In that spirit, the team emphasized specific issues such as fair and efficient property assessment, providing transportation and general assistance for the township's elderly and needy, and maintaining roads in unincorporated township areas.

When a candidate wins an election, then supporters will be able to have an effect on the issues raised during the campaign. After winning, the candidate can introduce legislation supporting the solutions for which he campaigned and can easily get the publicity needed to bring it to public attention. Therefore, begin with elections, and after your candidate wins you can turn to fight your issue battles.

Certain themes or issues are more basic to the outcome of the campaign than others. In Simpson's first campaign for alderman, he developed a general appeal that transcended ethnic and interest groups by running as a reformer against a Democratic machine candidate. Simpson pledged that, if he were elected, (1) citizens would receive their government services as a matter of right rather than as partisan favors because he would open a full-time alderman's office to serve all the people, (2) citizens would have a representative on the city council who would vote according to his conscience and his constituents' interests rather than simply rubber stamping the mayor's legislation, and (3) citizens would have an opportunity to participate directly in government policy making through the creation of a ward assembly with representatives from every precinct and every community organization. The ward assembly would hold monthly meetings open to the public rather than continue policy making by a handful of party leaders. His stand, in favor of a more participatory and fairer system of local government, placed the issue of the type of government we should have squarely before the electorate. In O'Shaughnessy's campaign, she and her team members ran on a platform of "experienced, caring community leaders," fiscally responsible neighbors who would continue to provide service to the community. Because some of the candidates on the slate were incumbents, the team could show that it had expanded services for seniors and low-income residents while keeping township taxes among the lowest in the state.

Issues such as those we raised in our elections do not by themselves attract enough voters to win, but they point up the importance of an election to both campaign workers and voters. They are an example of the kinds of policies that ought to be at stake in all elections.

A final warning: some people will encourage your candidate to run an "educational campaign." They mean that he should take strong stands on issues even if such stands will cause him to lose. Such candidates make beautiful speeches. Unfortunately, even though educational campaign enthusiasts are right about campaigns being educational, they fail to understand what is taught. When a candidate gets only 10 or 20 percent of the vote, *the electorate concludes that it is stupid to back such a candidate or cause because their votes are just being thrown away.* When politicians see such a result, far from being convinced to take a more courageous stand, it reconfirms their belief that they should not heed such political radicals because they have no support in the community.

A political campaign should be run to win, thereby educating the electorate to the fact that good people can be elected. If you have a good candidate, organize well, and work hard, winning should be possible. You will not win every election, but you must make a credible try. Such campaigns, to a much greater extent than any educational campaign, will convince more people to pay attention to issues, join in the political process, and help bring about desired policy changes.

Initiating Candidacies

Initiating a viable campaign is easiest at the local level. If you are part of the dominant party in the local community, the process is simple. An open endorsement session is held, and would-be candidates present their credentials. Party members then vote for the candidate they think best represents their political views *and* has the best chance of winning the election. Parties are inevitably pragmatic about this. They are in the business to win but usually reward political loyalty; if a longtime party worker and a newcomer are both asking to be "slated," party leaders will trust and endorse their party worker. Existing political party organizations can support reform candidates even though participatory campaigns also develop support by nonparty groups and individuals of such candidates. Too often, however, existing party organizations represent the status quo and are not open to greater citizen involvement.[15]

NONPARTISAN CANDIDATE SELECTION

If a political party is closed to candidates who would better represent the community, then a "citizens' committee" can be created to screen local candidates for city council, school board, county board, or state legislature. Such a citizens' search committee should consist of leaders from all community, economic, ethnic, political, and religious groups that might support a reform candidate. A strong citizens' search committee will both locate a worthy candidate and lay the foundation for a broad-based coalition capable of mounting an effective campaign.

Some local elections, such as for some village, school, or library boards, are nonpartisan. In these elections, there is often a caucus that interviews potential candidates and selects those its members feel would do the best job if elected. This slate is then formally endorsed by citizens attending a town meeting. Sometimes the town meeting rejects some of the candidates chosen by the caucus, resulting in a new set of candidates running for office. These elections, though nominally nonpartisan, can reflect factions in the town or school district that act like local parties. These elections can be an excellent "first" election for citizens who would like to get involved in electoral politics and later run for higher office.

DECIDING TO LAUNCH A CANDIDACY

When a candidate runs for a higher office than city council or school board, campaigns are launched differently. A few people—the candidate, some advisors, and friends—determine if a campaign is feasible. Factual considerations are involved. For example, how many votes did it take to win the last several campaigns for this office? How much money was spent? By what margin did the incumbent or dominant party candidate win? Which groups came out to vote? In most districts, only 60–70 percent of the potential voters are registered. Of those, probably fewer than half vote. And the winning candidate gets only 50–60 percent of the votes cast. Thus, in a district of 60,000 people, your candidate can win the election with fewer than 9,000 votes. In a congressional district with 600,000 people, a candidate can win the primary election with 10,000–50,000 votes depending upon which party primary is entered. Thus, some simple facts must be examined in deciding whether to run.

This process of deciphering election statistics is called "picking your target number" by Lawrence Grey in *How to Win a Local Election*:

> The election statistics will tell you the results in the last four or five elections, the total number who voted, the number who voted in your race, the number who voted in similar races. With this information, you come up with an average number of people who are likely to vote in your race. Divide that by two, and you have your target number.
>
> Once you have picked your number, you have to sit down with your campaign people and decide how you are going to get that number, precinct by precinct.[16]

In addition to voting patterns, demographics of the district and public opinion poll information can help you decide whether a particular candidacy might be viable.

After picking your target number, studying demographic and public opinion poll information, and developing a general strategy, two other principal facts need to be considered. It is easier to win an "open" seat than to run against an incumbent. If there is an incumbent, it is easier to run a successful campaign in a newly redistricted constituency rather than in a district that has elected the same incumbent a number of times. Obviously, an incumbent has greater name recognition than a challenger, and citizens who have voted for a candidate before are more likely to vote for him or her again.[17]

Suppose after collecting the facts and consulting with advisors and knowledgeable campaign leaders, your candidate still wants to run for office. How do you proceed?

One more reality check is critical before rushing to announce a candidacy. Can a viable campaign be run? At this stage, the easiest way to answer this question is to find out if the key resources necessary for a successful campaign can be raised. These resources include: (1) campaign leaders and staff, (2) endorsements by recognized political or community leaders that will lend credibility to the campaign, and (3) money.

The number of paid staff members in a campaign varies by the level at which it is run and the campaign budget on which it is run. A low-key campaign, say for suburban school board member, will have no paid staff and a total budget of a few thousand dollars at most. There will still need to be a "campaign manager," but he will serve without pay or with minimal reimbursement. The campaign might get help from experienced campaigners from a party or independent political organization who can perform some of the staffing functions that require more paid staff members in larger campaigns.

In larger local campaigns, such as for city council and state legislature, or for citywide offices in smaller cities, there will be at least three paid staff members. These will usually be a campaign manager, office/volunteer manager, and public relations coordinator. Often the budget for this type of campaign will range from $100,000 to more than $250,000. A congressional, county, or major mayoral campaign needs at least half a dozen staff members and a campaign budget of more than $1 million. Contested senatorial and gubernatorial campaigns can cost tens of millions of dollars. Campaigns at different levels demand that different resources be raised.

At the most local level, a sufficient base of support might be the agreement of a knowledgeable campaigner to serve as campaign manager. Then, the endorsement of a handful of key community leaders and, perhaps, the endorsement of a local political or community organization usually involved in such elections will be sufficient. These are the easiest offices for which to run, but some minimal level of support is still necessary to run a successful campaign. These minimal resources need to be committed before a campaign is launched.

Midlevel campaigns (for city council or state legislature) require the commitment of at least one experienced staff member and several thousand dollars to begin. Then, the endorsements of at least a couple dozen campaign activists, political officials, and community leaders are needed. If that level of commitment cannot be raised before beginning the petition drive to get on the ballot, the resources necessary to win will not be raised later. It is better to withdraw and back the best of the other candidates who have the requisite resources than to lose by a wide margin.

By the time a candidate decides to run for Congress, the necessary resources have to be more substantial. He should have won at least a local election and served in government so that he has name recognition among the voters and campaign and governing experience. He should have recruited several key campaign staff members or campaign consultants signed up to run the campaign, at least $10,000–$50,000 in the bank or in pledges, the firm commitment of several dozen experienced campaigners to coordinate different aspects of the campaign, and the promise of endorsements by a number of elected officials. A party endorsement would also be helpful, but party endorsements often have to be won in party primaries or caucuses as a part of the campaign. Party leaders can certainly be helpful, but they are less likely to support reformers proposing to change the political process and government.

Before deciding to launch a candidacy, establishing basic resource goals is important. If minimal resource goals cannot be met in the beginning, they are unlikely to be met later. After the campaign has begun, an exact fund-raising plan, public relations program, and voter contact plan will be needed to set forth targets for later stages of the campaign. If early resources are present, you will be able to mount a solid campaign with a chance to win.

Creation of a Campaign Citizens' Committee

A campaign needs a citizens' committee to endorse, support, and legitimize a candidate in the eyes of the media and the voters. It also needs a finance committee to help raise money. In a small campaign there may be only a single committee with both functions. In larger campaigns there will probably be at least two distinct committees with subcommittees for different fund-raising events.

The campaign citizens' committee headed by the campaign chair (and perhaps several well-known honorary chairs) is simply a list of people who have given written permission to use their names as having endorsed your candidate. Certainly, every endorsement that might convince other voters to vote for your candidate should be collected and used in some fashion, even if it is only in letters and cards mailed to the endorser's friends and home precinct members. A citizens' committee often consists of hundreds of people and may never meet as a committee during the entire campaign. Yet, all campaign literature and advertising will have a box to check off such as:

☐ Yes, you may use my name on the Smith for School Board Citizens' Committee.

A finance committee is even more critical to the success of the campaign. It is the job of the finance committee to raise the funds necessary for a winning campaign. Because most people do not like to raise money, one of the difficult jobs in beginning a successful campaign is to convince a number of supporters to take on this task. Members of the finance committee provide names of people to solicit for funds and invite to campaign fund-raising events. They also host small fund-raising events such as breakfast meetings, law firm gatherings, or cocktail parties where the candidate and the host solicit larger campaign contributions.

A final test for your campaign is the ability to recruit campaign and finance committee chairs along with other key volunteer campaign leaders. In addition to the staff and candidate, volunteers must be willing to commit significant time and money to make the campaign a success. If they are not recruited early, the campaign will probably fail.

Decisions of Candidates and Their Families

A good candidate decides much more readily to run if there is a chance to win, and a good candidate runs independently of political parties only if there are independent organizations to provide a base from which to launch the campaign. Any candidate needs financial resources and committed volunteers to win. If raising the money or recruiting experienced staff and volunteers is not possible, a realistic candidate decides not to enter the race.

The candidacy of Bill Singer for alderman on the north side of Chicago illustrates the importance of knowing that the resources will be available. A citizens' committee was formed to search for a candidate, and Singer's name was one of many suggested. At the same time, the Independent Precinct Organization (IPO—a grassroots reform organization) needed to raise money as an organization. Singer and ten other people were called together at a luncheon and asked if they thought a viable alderman race was possible. They were then asked to write out checks to keep IPO alive until the election, and a significant sum of money was raised. When Singer saw money raised so easily, he knew a tough campaign could be financed. When fifty representatives of community organizations showed up at citizens' search committee meetings to select a candidate, he knew community support could be found. When IPO workers went door to door with petitions to get him on the ballot, he knew a campaign organization could be built. This kind of demonstration of support was necessary to get an able young lawyer to run against a Democratic machine candidate in a district in which no independent had ever been elected. Good candidates want to know the race, if they enter it, will be a serious one, and they will get enough support to wage the kind of battle necessary to win.[18]

In 2011, Will Guzzardi, a new resident of Chicago, decided to run for Illinois state representative against the incumbent who was the daughter of a powerful Cook County politician. He lost by only 125 votes. With this close race against an entrenched political organization, Guzzardi was encouraged by many of his grassroots supporters to run two years later for the same office and against the same incumbent. They took another look at their close but losing campaign, considered the odds, and decided Guzzardi had a chance but would have to run on a shoestring budget. The candidate loaned his campaign startup funds, collected money on the Internet, and found a small office. With his name recognition from the first campaign, Guzzardi brought in both enthusiasm and campaign donations from the community and defeated the organization's incumbent candidate in the primary. He then won the November 2014 general election. He would not have had a chance against such an incumbent if he had not built up name recognition, experience, and the community contacts he needed when he ran the first time.[19]

Weisberg, a candidate for Illinois Constitutional Convention delegate, said about his candidacy that even though a man might hold a position of considerable prestige in his profession, even though many sacrifices might be required, saying "no" will be difficult if a group of citizens asks him.

> I never thought of running for office, and I could easily see that becoming involved in the campaign would involve kind of a major disruption in my working life as a lawyer, my family life; and I wasn't sure that I really had an appetite for it. The more I thought about it, the more negative I was, really. I could see it taking a tremendous amount of time, costing a pretty substantial amount of money, and I was pretty much on the verge of saying definitely no until I suppose really two things began to weigh in my con-

sideration. One was that I felt I really wouldn't feel very good saying no for the reasons that I mentioned already because it seemed to me that those weren't consistent with the idea of having some share in the responsibility that we all have really about government. And secondly, the more I thought about it, the more I was impressed with the suggestion . . . that running for office can be an educational experience which you really cannot get in any other way.[20]

Even if a potentially great candidate knows the minimal resources are present to run a strong campaign, there are still other real considerations. First, a candidate should not run for an office he does not really want just for the sake of positioning himself for some higher office. There is always a significant chance of losing. If a candidate wins, serving in an office he hates could be a terrible experience.

Second, no one should run for any significant elected office if he or she is afraid of possible negative campaigns by the opponents. Any serious candidate must expect negative campaign ads, nasty direct-mail pieces, social network notices, and scathing blogs from their opponents even if those do not occur in every campaign. Moreover, after the candidate enters office, criticism by opposition political leaders and common citizens who believe every public official is a crook is inevitable. If there are major skeletons in a candidate's closet, he should not enter the public arena unless he is willing to have them exposed. Even if a candidate has nothing to hide, desperate opposition candidates will distort his background and positions on issues.

Third, the pressures on candidates and their families are immense, and they usually intensify if the election is won. For six months to two years, a candidate has to campaign day and night. The pressures of campaigning, especially winning and serving in a high-profile office, are enough to weaken or destroy marriages. Campaigning means not being around as a parent much during this period. This is especially hard if the children are young. Thus, any decision to campaign must be an informed family decision—another reason it is useful to have campaign experience before you decide to run for higher office. This is not a step to be taken lightly.

Voter Decisions and the Challenge to Democracy

Traditionally, a voter's decision as to whether to vote and for whom has been influenced by his socioeconomic position in society and by his identification with a political party.[21] Recently, more elections have become candidate centered;

consequently, a voter's decision can be determined by a candidate's character, personality, and stand on issues.[22] Thus, one of the primary tasks of participatory politics is to reorient voters toward voting for the person and the issues, not just the party label and economic self-interest. Unless people get involved in politics, find qualified candidates, and build strong campaign organizations capable of fielding an army of volunteers to talk with the voters, political parties and powerful special interests will continue to control our election decisions. Political reform begins with a single citizen's commitment. Political stagnation continues only because you and I fail to act.

Today there is an additional challenge. Despite advances in social media and the amount of information available on the Internet, money is having a particularly deleterious effect on politics.[23] This imbalance of money in politics has worsened with the *Citizens United v. Federal Election Commission*, *McCutcheon et al. v. Federal Election Commission*, and later court decisions, which essentially allow corporations and wealthy individuals to give an unlimited amount of money to political candidates who favor their agendas.[24]

As seen during the Guzzardi campaign, discussed further in Chapter 9, the candidate with the most money does not always win. Another example is that the superPACs opposing President Obama's reelection in 2012 wasted $600 million supporting Mitt Romney and various conservative Republican congressional candidates to no avail.[25] However, the sheer cost of campaigns has grown exponentially when running for alderman in a big city can cost from $100,000–$250,000 and running for Congress costs more than $1 million. Such high costs mean that many well-qualified candidates with great ideas for improving government are discouraged from running, and we are all left with fewer good choices on Election Day.

The dominance of the Republican and Democratic Parties, which are facilitated by biases in election laws, mean that third parties such as the Green Party cannot really get a foothold. This is in spite of the fact that some of their issues such as "green" or renewable energy might be popular. Often their issues are co-opted by the majority parties, so voting for third-party candidates often seems like throwing your vote away.[26] When their issues are picked up by the dominant parties, they do have an impact, but it is rare that minority party candidates win elections.

Despite these challenges and flaws in our political system, the decision by candidates to run, and the decisions by others to staff and volunteer in their campaigns, are critical to our democracy and to the improvement of our society.

Chapter Three

Organizing a Campaign

....

Recruiting, funding, and organizing a virtual army of volunteers is the first priority of a participatory campaign. It begins with the citizens' committee that selects the candidate or launches the campaign. It is augmented by a candidate's own personal contacts, enhanced by the wise selection of leaders, shaped by the evolution of a campaign structure, and completed by direct personal solicitation, political house parties or "coffees," social media, and campaign events. Every campaign activity must help to recruit the hundreds of volunteers and raise the thousands of dollars necessary for success. If a volunteer army can be raised and equipped, election battles can be fought and won. If not, your political war is over before it has begun.

Each participatory campaign differs, yet many principles and techniques remain the same. City council campaigns, state legislative races, congressional contests, and presidential runs provide examples of campaign techniques to demonstrate the differences between them at various levels of government.

In Chapter 2, we looked at the decisions a candidate and a candidate's supporters must make in order to determine whether to run in a particular election. In this chapter we want to consider how a campaign must be organized to succeed. We begin with the story of Dick Simpson's alderman campaigns and those of other independent candidates fighting the Democratic Party machine for control of Chicago's governments in more recent years. Next, we will relate the tale of Betty O'Shaughnessy's suburban campaign for township trustee, which used some of the same principles.

Just as it is reasonable for schools to teach the basics of reading, writing, and arithmetic before moving to sonnets and calculus, it is best to study smaller campaigns before leaping to the more high-tech, expensive methods of congressional and presidential campaigns.

In 1970–1971, Simpson ran for alderman. In his case, a citizens' search committee had been looking in Chicago's 44th Ward for a strong aldermanic candidate. The 44th Ward was a community of 60,000 people and about 30,000 voters on the north-side lakefront of Chicago. The search committee had been unsuccessful in locating a suitable candidate. Simpson met with several of the committee members, and they asked if he would be willing to move from the neighboring ward to run as an independent, anti–Mayor Richard J. Daley candidate. Dick and his wife then met with the entire search committee of about fifty people. They were enthusiastic, pledged to work on the campaign, and raised some of the money necessary to begin it.

It was nearly Thanksgiving in 1970 when his campaign began. Petitions to get on the ballot had to be filed in a few weeks, and the election was less than three months away. Thus, at least two rules of campaigning were violated by his first campaign: (1) run only in an election district where you have lived for some time, and (2) build a successful base of campaign support over months, if not years. However, Simpson had two major advantages. He was running for a vacant seat in a district without an incumbent and in a district that had a history of electing independent candidates. Thus, a base of campaign volunteers and voters had already been established by previous campaigns.

In 1971, Daley was still the boss of the last great city machine. The 1968 Democratic National Convention in Chicago, with its riot and police crackdown, had demonstrated how authoritarian his reign had become. So, by the 1970s the political battle lines were drawn between proDaley and antiDaley forces. The lakefront liberal wards were breaking free of machine control election by election. Simpson's campaign was a frontal assault against the power and control of Mayor Daley; therefore, the machine would do all it could to defeat him. To his advantage, this guaranteed media coverage along with financial help and volunteers from other parts of the city to support his candidacy.

The O'Shaughnessy campaign was a much less controversial affair. It was a local suburban election without major issues but still used many of the same strategies as those of the Simpson campaign. O'Shaughnessy had lived in West Deerfield Township, part of Lake County, Illinois, for several years. She was a high school social studies teacher and a lifelong Democrat. Although Lake County historically had maintained Republican victories in local elections, West Deerfield Township was showing an increase in voters asking for Democratic ballots in recent primaries. Consequently, in the 2005 township election, the Democrats decided to field candidates for the township trustee offices, resulting in a Democratic victory and a West Deerfield Township board with a Democratic majority.

In the next township election in 2009, O'Shaughnessy ran for the township board. She was well known in the community, had volunteered in the 2008 Obama campaign, and had been active in getting her students involved in politics and government. With this record, the West Deerfield Township Democrats slated her. Although this was her first run for trustee, the other trustee candidates and the supervisor were incumbents. Often in small elections a slate of candidates will run as a team, and this was the case in the 2009 West Deerfield Township elections: all the Democratic candidates for township office decided to run together. With O'Shaughnessy as the only new candidate, the "Your Democratic Township Team," as they called themselves, ran on a record of good service and fiscal responsibility at a time when the economy was in terrible trouble. They got help running their campaign from the West Deerfield Township Democratic committee, whose chair served as an informal campaign manager, and the 10th Dems, a grassroots group made up of Democrats from the Illinois 10th Congressional District.

Campaign Structure

Even if a campaign is local and noncontroversial, like that of the West Deerfield Township team, it is best that candidates do not serve as their own campaign managers. They should turn campaign direction over to trusted volunteers (on a local level) or preferably paid staff members in larger campaigns. Alderman Bill Singer, who ran two successful Chicago aldermanic campaigns, a valiant race for mayor in 1975, and later a victorious campaign for Chicago School Board, discovered this in his first campaign.

> The candidate must have confidence in the staff's ability to run the campaign, as he cannot run it himself. Likewise, the staff must have confidence in the candidate and his ability to see the issues and the problems of the campaign. The candidate is not going to be able to select all of the campaign personnel, and this should be particularly the job of the Campaign Manager, who will select the persons responsible for running various aspects of the campaign. Of course, the Campaign Manager should consult the candidate on these selections. But the candidate should and must select a few key persons upon whom he is going to have to place great reliance, and this must be done early in the campaign. From that time on the most important thing for the candidate is exposure and personal contact. This can't be done from his office or on the telephone working out campaign problems.[1]

Many campaign workers play important roles in a campaign. However, because of the nature of participatory politics, a dilemma arises. Decisions often have to be made quickly, and instructions have to be followed exactly by campaign workers if a campaign is to be successful. Still, workers have a right to share in decisions they are called upon to implement, and they can make perceptive contributions to campaign decision making. A balance must be struck between the authority of campaign leaders and the right of workers to be part of decision making. Creating a more participatory democracy can begin with the campaign itself. Key campaign leaders and staff members will undoubtedly make executive decisions, but the total campaign leadership should meet at least once a week. Whereas immediate decisions must be made by key staff, long-range planning involving such areas as publicity, precinct work, and fund-raising should be discussed in the larger weekly meetings. The advice of campaign workers should be heeded as often as possible.

In smaller campaigns there is usually a small campaign committee that includes the candidate and campaign manager. They meet weekly to guide the campaign and to discuss key decisions and the inevitable problems that arise. Catherine Shaw in *The Campaign Manager* advises that committee members "should consist of individuals with different personal strengths and areas of ability . . . [who] must feel safe to speak candidly without fear of recrimination."[2]

In larger campaigns, the campaign committee includes the coordinators for each aspect of the campaign (such as volunteer coordinator, house party coordinator, events coordinator, and most especially the precinct coordinators). In weekly meetings in the evenings or on Sunday mornings, they provide information and advice on key decisions. Often larger campaigns also purchase expert services to design campaign buttons, press materials, brochures, mailers, and paid media ads. These are designed by professionals and not by the committee, but the campaign strategy committee still provides much input and guidance.

There is no perfect organizational chart or set of job descriptions for campaigns because the structure varies according to the size of the campaign to be undertaken, the skills and experience of the leaders, the time volunteers can devote, the number of workers available, and the personal relationships that exist or develop among members of the campaign. However, the organizational chart in Figure 3.1 can serve as an example of a good campaign structure for medium-sized campaigns. It is the model used for campaigns in a district of up to roughly 25,000 voters on a budget of about $150,000. Such campaigns involve several hundred volunteers. Recruiting that many volun-

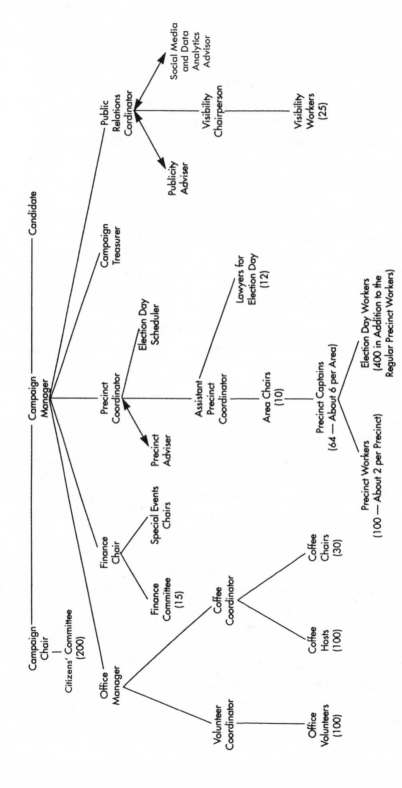

3.1. Campaign Organizational Chart. Courtesy of Dick Simpson.

teers today is much more difficult because employment trends have changed. More women work full time; increasingly, both men and women work more than forty hours a week or have several part-time jobs, leaving less time for volunteer campaign work than in earlier decades.

The full-time, paid staff members in a medium-sized campaign for local office usually include a campaign manager, office manager, and public relations coordinator. All the campaign officials listed immediately beneath the campaign manager along with the candidate and campaign chair on the organizational chart form the campaign strategy committee, which meets weekly.

All leaders in a campaign have more or less explicit functions and are directly connected to the volunteer workers necessary to carry them out. Although there is a need for an explicit, hierarchical structure in order to complete the Herculean tasks of the campaign in time for the election, considerable communication and coordination both within and between structural units is also necessary. The structure should allow for speedy communication within given functional areas so that the precinct coordinator, for example, can relay instructions to precinct workers and receive precinct-by-precinct reports on the progress of the campaign.

Weekly reports by precinct workers, either by phone or e-mail, are critical in reminding workers of the tasks they have to perform, allowing for effective campaign strategy and informed decision making, in providing for better control, and allowing for course correction.[3]

Communication and coordination are needed between the different sections of the campaign as well. That is the reason for the frequent strategy sessions, the weekly leadership meetings, and the occasional training sessions with all campaign workers from the early months of the petition drive until Election Day. All of these structures, meetings, and reports are not meant to stifle but to promote creativity as well as the coordination needed for a successful campaign. The functions of campaign committee members are to determine what jobs have to be done and match those tasks with what the people on an organizational chart agree to do.

CAMPAIGN CHAIR

The *campaign chair* is head of the citizens' committee listed on the campaign stationery and website, and her prominence is used to convince the media and the public that the campaign has broad support. She chairs weekly leadership meetings and is an important fund-raiser as well. However, the job can be much more. Donald Page Moore described his tasks in the Bernard Weisberg for Illinois Constitutional Convention Delegate campaign this way:

The role of the campaign chairman isn't really definable. You've got to do a little bit of everything. You're in charge of hiring and firing people and finding people to do the multitude of tasks that have to be done. I've been involved in public relations, lawsuits, hiring a campaign manager, hiring an office manager; fund-raising takes a lot of my time [and] recruiting lawyers to do poll watching on Election Day. I've done everything from sweeping out the headquarters to holding press conferences.[4]

Sometimes the campaign chair replaces the candidate in chairing internal campaign meetings or in meeting with important people the candidate cannot meet personally because of scheduling conflicts. In larger campaigns, the campaign chair might also serve as a surrogate speaker at events the candidate cannot attend.

In issue-based campaigns such as referenda, initiatives, or votes on bond issues and constitutional amendments, the campaign chair (or cochairs) plays an even bigger role. As Shaw put it, "The messenger is the message. . . . Those people should be noncontroversial leaders in your community . . . with established relationships with other prominent local leaders."[5] They play the spokesperson role that candidates play in other campaigns.

CAMPAIGN MANAGER

Unless the campaign chair has the time to oversee the day-to-day operations, the *campaign manager* has the principal task of running the campaign while the campaign chair helps the candidate with raising resources and getting other members of the campaign to work hard. A campaign manager coordinates the efforts of all the other workers. She designs a winning strategy in consultation with other campaign leaders, ensures that the materials (such as campaign brochures) arrive on time, and makes the day-to-day decisions. As campaign managers jokingly say, a campaign manager works sixteen hours a day instead of the fourteen hours put in by volunteers.

Although the candidate maintains veto power over certain key decisions about the campaign message, spending, and debt, the campaign manager should have authority to make, approve, or reject almost all other decisions. A wise campaign manager will encourage each of the other staff and key volunteers to make their own decisions about details of operation. She will also obtain the advice of professional campaign consultants or experienced volunteers on fund-raising, voter contact, and public relations. Although subject to be overruled by the candidate, the campaign manager must have the authority to run the campaign.

The campaign manager makes sure the campaign strategy is consistent, each element of the campaign fits with all other parts, and responses to changing campaign conditions are quick. A campaign manager becomes a general of the army of campaign workers even in a participatory campaign.

In *How to Win a Local Election*, Lawrence Grey describes the role of a campaign manager in this way:

> The candidate is out front—meeting and talking to people and listening to them. . . . The campaign manager is doing the things behind the scenes that have to be done to assist the candidate. . . .
>
> The campaign manager is involved in all of the aspects of planning—budgeting, research, the campaign theme, mailing, radio, and fund-raising. Once the plan is decided upon, however, his duties shift from being a thinker to being a doer.[6]

The campaign manager supervises all aspects of the campaign, conducts the regularly scheduled staff meetings, and works with the candidate and campaign chair to make sure the campaign is proceeding smoothly. Any changes that need to be made because someone is not doing her job, something is not working, or opponents have taken action are the responsibility of the campaign manager.

In hiring a campaign manager the candidate looks for someone with prior experience in winning campaigns. A campaign manager should be familiar with field operations, fund-raising, a campaign office, and public relations. She may not have done all these things personally in other campaigns, but she should have observed them firsthand before she undertakes to direct these operations. Joseph Napolitan in *The Election Game* offers the following advice:

> My advice to candidates is to look long and hard before selecting a campaign manager, and when you do settle on the person you want, to give [her] the authority to do the job properly, and this includes expenditure of funds. . . . The worst choice any candidate can pick for [her] campaign manager is [herself]. No one—repeat, no one—can do a competent job in a major campaign if [she] tries to serve both roles.[7]

The job of the candidate is to meet people, get votes, and raise money. The campaign manager helps design and implement the campaign plans. A major campaign is governed by the tyranny of the calendar. There is an absolute date on which the nominating petitions must be filed, a last day citizens can register to vote, and only one Election Day. If printing rates are to be kept reasonable, copy must be delivered to the graphic designer and the approved electronic files to the printer on specific dates. Similarly, there must be enough time to prepare for a campaign benefit properly if it is to raise the necessary funds. The campaign manager cracks the whip and makes sure that what must be done is done well and on time. It is not always a popular job, but it is an indispensable one.

PRECINCT COORDINATOR

The *precinct coordinator* (or field director) plays an essential role in any participatory campaign. This person puts the precinct organization together, conducts training sessions, receives workers' reports, and coordinates petition signature collection, voter registration drives, voter canvassing, and Election Day activities.

Local elections are won or lost by efforts in the precincts. Precinct sizes differ around the country, but it is not unusual for them to be about 350–400 voters each. Even in national campaigns, precinct work can be the key to victory, from the first Iowa caucuses and New Hampshire primary to the general election.

Precinct coordinators direct the personal voter contact, which changes votes and motivates voters to go to the polls. In these days of voter analytics to target voter contacts, the precinct coordinator also has to be familiar with data management systems such as NGP-VAN, VoteBuilder, rVotes, or whichever data management system the campaign purchases. Because these data systems develop the "walk sheets" that direct the precinct volunteers whom to contact, they also determine how to make the best campaign pitch. Thus it is important that the precinct coordinator fully understand the data system being used. Then the precinct coordinator can, in turn, properly instruct the precinct volunteers. She also needs to get updates from the data system of reports of voter contacts in each precinct to guide overall campaign efforts.

FINANCE CHAIR AND TREASURER

The jobs of *finance chair, treasurer*, and *purchasing officer* can be either combined or separated. Their tasks are raising the money, determining what expenses can be afforded, and locating the cheapest suppliers of buttons, flyers, printing, posters, and other necessary commodities.

With the change in financial disclosure laws, the job of finance chair has tended to focus more on fund-raising while the treasurer concentrates on reporting contributions and expenses. The finance chair usually works with a committee of a half-dozen people who contribute lists of potential donors, contact some contributors directly, and host fund-raising events such as breakfasts, cocktail parties, or theater benefits.

These days the treasurer is most often a certified public accountant (CPA) working pro bono for the campaign. The treasurer signs the official campaign disclosures, which report the campaign's large contributors and major campaign expenditures. In larger campaigns a bookkeeper may be added, or the office manager may assume the responsibility of recording individual contributions and expenditures.

The treasurer does not usually develop the finance plan or raise the money. The volunteer finance or fund-raising chair, or in larger campaigns, the fund-raising staff member, develops the plan and helps the candidate obtain the necessary contributions. Instead, the treasurer is charged with completing registration forms and finance reports as required by law in each state. If the treasurer is not a CPA, a CPA is usually hired to make sure all of the campaign filings are correct. As Shaw writes, "Your treasurer and the CPA or banker should be sticklers for detail. The opposition will be examining your contributions and expenditures . . . for any mistakes to report to the state elections office. If a mistake is found, it is bound to make the local papers. That sort of damage is totally preventable."[8]

PUBLIC RELATIONS COORDINATOR

The *public relations coordinator,* sometimes called the *press secretary*, supervises the production of all publicity, including brochures, buttons, bumper stickers, posters, news stories, TV and radio appearances, and commercials. June Rosner, the public relations coordinator for the Weisberg constitutional delegate campaign, summarized her job thus: "Basically my job is to get the candidate's name familiar with the voters and build the sort of image for him that will make workers enthusiastic to work in the campaign."[9]

In larger campaigns with substantially larger budgets, several people (staff members, volunteers, and consultants) may be involved in the public relations activities. The public relations coordinator or press secretary provides strategy and coordination. A graphic artist designs all the printed campaign materials (buttons, stationery, brochures, posters, bumper stickers, etc.). These same designs are used in electronic media such as the website.

In better-funded campaigns, a public relations consultant or a public relations firm may propose media strategy. A separate media advisor or agency will often develop television and radio ads essential to major campaigns. Thus, in larger campaigns the public relations staff is bigger, and the candidate, campaign manager, campaign chair, and public relations coordinator become the client when outside professional firms are involved.

As we discuss later in Chapter 7, still other staff and volunteers may develop the social media activities, but they must be under the supervision and control of the public relations coordinator. It is important that all aspects of the campaign be "on message" to reinforce the overall campaign theme.

OFFICE MANAGER

The *office manager* is responsible for work done in the campaign headquarters. This includes keeping records of all potential workers, supervising mailings, photocopying or printing campaign literature, sending e-mails and posting blogs, purchasing supplies, preparing for rallies and training sessions, directing telephone banks, and answering the ever-ringing campaign telephones. The office manager also supervises the computers and trains staff and volunteers in computer and software use.

Ideally, the campaign will have a separate *volunteer coordinator*. She will contact those potential volunteers who sign pledge cards upon meeting the candidate at campaign events or who have volunteered on the campaign website. After the volunteer coordinator recruits them, the office manager greets the volunteers when they arrive, plans the necessary work, assigns them to their specific tasks, answers questions, gets them the necessary equipment or space to do their tasks, and coordinates all the office activities necessary for a winning campaign.

HOUSE PARTY COORDINATOR

A good *house party coordinator* or team of coordinators will, by the end of the campaign, have convinced more than one hundred families to host a coffee, barbeque, cocktail party, or other event at their homes. This is a social event organized by volunteers to which they invite their neighbors and friends. The candidate speaks and attempts to convert those who attend into campaign supporters. Because coffee and cookies are often served, they are sometimes called coffees even when other refreshments are provided. It is equally possible to serve wine, beer, and soft drinks at these events. They then become cocktail parties or fiestas. However, it is important that not so much alcohol is served that they become a debacle that would embarrass the candidate or the campaign. The key to a successful house party is to get voters, along with potential campaign volunteers and contributors, to meet the candidate in a comfortable social situation.

The coordinator sees that the appropriate campaign materials, including instruction sheets and invitations, are delivered to any hosts. Finally, they have to recruit and train dozens of event chairs, develop the schedule, and brief the candidate for each appearance.

These hundred or more small social events are critical to recruiting volunteers, raising money, and meeting voters. In some campaigns a separate coordinator recruits, assigns, and trains the chairs to run the house parties and similar social events.

VISIBILITY CHAIR

Because name identification is so important, a visibility crew, often made up of high school and college students, is created to ensure that hundreds of posters are placed in windows of homes and stores and that yard signs are placed on suburban lawns. They also make sure that lampposts throughout the district are covered with stickers or small posters attached with wire so that they can be removed when the campaign is over. They help distribute and make sure that as many people as possible are induced to wear campaign buttons or place campaign bumper stickers on their cars.

This hardworking crew is coordinated by a *visibility chair*. The members work week by week throughout the campaign. Then on election eve, they do a complete blitz during the night or early morning hours, putting up posters near all the polling places in the district.

AREA CHAIRS

The critical middle management of participatory campaigns are the *area chairs*. The chairs coordinate from four to six precincts each. They recruit many of the precinct workers and provide them materials, instructions, and assistance with problems in the precinct. A critical part of the job is to collect reports from all precincts under their supervision. Area chairs are the key communication links in the campaign through regularly phoning or e-mailing the precinct captains or coordinators. Their reports from the precincts and their suggestions at the weekly campaign leadership meetings are essential to making decisions to alter the direction of the campaign, intensify the effort, or simply proceed with current plans if the campaign is effective.

Recruiting Workers

In West Africa there is a saying, "Nothing can be done without money." Whether a road should be built, a marriage contracted, or a chief elected, the answer is always the same. In participatory politics a more appropriate saying would be that

3.2. WHAT EVERY GREAT COFFEE CHAIR HAS TO KNOW

1. Call the coffee host the night before the coffee to let him or her know that you are coming.
2. Get to the meeting promptly, preferably fifteen minutes before the announced time.
3. Introduce yourself and, while awaiting the gathering of the group, remind the host to have all the guests sign the sign-in sheet as they come in. Set Simpson literature out on the table and give it to guests as they arrive.
4. Call the meeting to order in time for introductory remarks before Dick arrives. (This should usually be done about twenty minutes after the announced time of the coffee.)

These are the principal points to cover.

Background on Dick:

- After redistricting of wards from the 1970 census, he beat Democratic machine candidates to become 44th Ward alderman, serving two terms during which he created the 44th Ward Assembly, Community Zoning Board, and Asamblea Abierta
- Founder of the Independent Precinct Organization in 1968, which merged with the Independent Voters of Illinois to become IVI-IPO in 1979
- Associate professor of political science at the University of

nothing can be done without volunteers. If there are no workers, there is no campaign. Because volunteers are necessary to a successful campaign, recruiting them is a major concern underlying every campaign activity.

Four methods of recruitment are most frequently used. The first, which often goes unnoticed, is direct personal contact. Campaign workers tell their friends and acquaintances about the campaign and sign them up as volunteers.

The campaign leadership also systematically recruits volunteers one on one. When you are an area chair charged with recruiting twenty precinct workers to canvass the precincts you supervise, or a house party coordinator signing up a hundred coffee hosts, you begin with a list of prospective workers. These lists are garnered from friends, acquaintances, supporting organizations, prior political campaign files, and people who have already volunteered to help in this campaign but have not yet been given a specific task. Each prospect is called and assigned a job.

Second, if the original lists are insufficient, then going door to door or phoning registered voters in an area might be necessary to find enough volunteers to get the job done.

Third, in addition to direct contact with friends and people on prospect lists, social events make an ideal occasion for citizens to meet and evaluate a candidate and to be converted into volunteers.

Fourth, campaign websites and social media are used to find, recruit, and coordinate volunteer efforts. In Chapter 7, we discuss how these strategies may best be used for these purposes.

HOUSE PARTIES

Coffees and similar campaign social events have been used so often and so effectively that a more-

or-less explicit formula for success has been developed. They begin with the host or several hosts inviting their friends and *every registered voter* in one or more precincts (see Figure 3.2). Printed formal invitations are mailed or placed in the mailboxes of voters along with evites via e-mail, Facebook, or Twitter. It is still essential that the host *personally* phone and invite as many potential guests as possible. Of those who receive the printed or electronic invitation, only a handful out of a hundred invitees will appear. As much as 25 percent of those called personally is likely to come. Therefore, the telephone calls are essential to a good house party.

To quote Bob Houston, an expert event chair, "No coffee is ever a failure."[10] If only the host and one other person show up, at least the neighbors in the area and the hosts' friends have been invited and know that the candidate has been in the neighborhood to meet with constituents. Moreover, the host and the other person attending the coffee can both be signed up to do precinct work, which can affect hundreds of voters. Regardless of how many people attend a small event, maximizing the result is important. House party results are measured precisely by the number of volunteers and financial contributions collected at the end of the evening.

To achieve the best results, a chair is assigned to the event. She does not need to come from the same precinct or neighborhood where the event is being held, but she will most often be from the district in which the campaign is being waged. As the guests arrive, the chair and the host have them sign an attendance sheet, introduce them to the others in the group, and hand them campaign literature to read. Usually about twenty minutes after the announced time of the coffee, the chair will call the meeting to order, and the

Illinois–Chicago, where he has written and published numerous studies about voting patterns of city council and county board members and city and county budgeting processes
- Former executive director of Clergy and Laity Concerned (CALC), an interfaith peace and justice organization

1. Dick will be running in a new northwest side congressional district that will be created containing the area from about Diversey on the south, Ashland on the east, and the city limits on the west and north. He will run against either Congressman Dan Rostenkowski or Annunzio.
2. One key issue on which Dick is running is the need to reform Congress by limiting terms of members of Congress, providing public financing of congressional campaigns, and requiring more accountability from representatives.
3. Go around the circle asking guests what particular issues concern them most about the district and what issues they would like Dick Simpson to cover.
4. When Dick arrives forty-five minutes after the time for which the meeting was set, stop. The host should introduce him to the group individually, and he should shake each person's hand. Briefly tell Dick what issues are uppermost in the group's mind. After he

speaks, he will answer questions until it is time for his next meeting. Generally, he should not stay more than thirty to forty-five minutes. You may have to help him stop and get on to his other commitments.

5. *You, not Dick Simpson, are the climax of the evening.* When, after answering all questions, Dick leaves, take over. Do not let the group drift apart. Make a pitch for *workers, money, and more coffees* to help wage a successful campaign. Use the volunteer cards to do this. To make a successful pitch: After you pass out the pledge cards to everyone, say that you are not here to persuade anyone to do anything to elect Dick but to explain what they can do if they want to get him elected. Then explain what each item on the pledge card means.

6. Collect all of the pledge cards, contributions, and attendance sheets. We need them returned to the campaign headquarters at 2501 W. Lunt, Chicago, IL 60645 by the next day so we can follow up on potential workers. Use any leftover materials at future coffees or return them to campaign headquarters.

7. Thanks and congratulations. If you have any questions or need additional materials, call our coffee coordinator, Coralee Kern, at 773-111-1111 or campaign headquarters at 773-111-1112.

group will discuss the background of the candidate briefly and review facts about the election such as the date of the election, how many candidates citizens may vote for, who the candidates are, and how citizens may register to vote. If electronic voter registration is legal in the state, unregistered voters are also registered at the event itself.

Then, the guests are asked what particular issues they would most like the candidate to discuss. The candidate arrives about forty-five minutes after the time for which the meeting is set, and the host introduces her to each guest. Unless the crowd is too large, the candidate shakes hands with each guest as she is introduced. The chair will tell the candidate the questions that interest the group. The candidate speaks and then answers questions for about half an hour. In a complicated campaign, such as the election of delegates to rewrite the state constitution, candidates sometimes spend slightly more time at critical events, but it is terribly important that they not stay until all the fire has gone out of the meeting.

A candidate can make from three to five house parties a night if she keeps her remarks brief and to the point. Thus, carefully timed events can multiply a candidate's exposure. In larger districts these social events can even be organized around a candidate's television appearances or candidate debates, thus maximizing a candidate's exposure to a number of voters by multiple, back-to-back parties. Better-financed campaigns will even produce a short video to show at events a candidate cannot attend or by precinct workers to interested voters and their families in their homes. These videos can also be linked to the campaign website and posted on sites such as YouTube.

The chair, however, not the candidate, provides the climax to a successful coffee. His or her pitch for volunteers and contributions is crucial. The coffee chair explains why help is needed, what needs to be done, and urges people to make up their minds by filling out a pledge card and turning it in before they leave. It allows voters to indicate ways in which they are willing to contribute to the campaign. The chair then thanks each person who commits him- or herself, and she judges success by how many workers sign pledge cards and how much money is raised.

The pitch can be a hard sell. Although the people in the room are voters, they do not have to like the chair. That is one of the reasons the chair makes the pitch rather than the candidate. An example of a good pitch was given by Campaign Chair Donald Page Moore at a Weisberg for Illinois Constitutional Convention Delegate coffee, later shown in the *By the People* film (see Figure 3.3).

VOLUNTEER RECRUITING

An important means of finding volunteers is to make every campaign event a recruiting effort. All members and potential members of the citizens' committee should be called and asked to serve in some capacity with the campaign, or at the least to lend their names and their money to the campaign effort. People should not only be recruited to work in the petition drive, but every person who signs a petition to get your candidate on the ballot should receive a personally signed thank-you letter from your candidate, along with a pledge card and a request to join the campaign. The same is true of every person who attends any campaign event.

Every time precinct workers or the candidate go door to door to register people or get their

3.3. CAMPAIGN PITCH BY DONALD PAGE MOORE

The [Chicago Democratic] machine is tough, and we beat one machine candidate by 1,600 votes and the other beat us by 115 votes [in the primary]. . . . So if we're going to win, we can only do it in a couple of well-recognized ways. One, we've got to have money, and we can't shake the money out of people the way the county assessor's office does. It's going to cost us $35,000 [in 1970] to run a decent campaign for Bernard Weisberg. And this leaves us with about $20,000 to raise in the next six weeks. I don't see any point in making a secret about it, those are the facts. We've got fifteen in and we've got twenty to go. And if we don't get the money, we can't win the election because we can't run an effective campaign without money. . . . Precinct work and Election Day work are fundamental. They're vital. They can be fun. You can be part of something that really means something for the future of this town. And we can't do it without it. We can't get by with 850 workers on November 18. If we've only 850 workers on the street we're going to get buried. . . .

And don't listen to this talk that Weisberg's got it in the bag. All that means is we're running up front. We've got a whale of a chance, and they can beat the daylights out of us if we don't keep up the momentum. Now we can do it, but it is not in the bag, and we need help desperately.

We need 1,500 workers on the street Election Day, working in the polling places, passing out literature, helping run the pluses [voters favorable to Weisberg], helping make the phone calls, everything that has to be done on Election Day.

We need at least 1,000 precinct canvassers working in between now [and then], in the odds and ends of their week: on the weekends a few hours, in the evening a few hours. We've got to have it. If we don't have it, we get beat. And all these months and months of work and dedication and hope and all the rest of it go right down the drain. A dying machine is going to get a terrific shot in the arm, and independent politics on the north-side lakefront of Chicago is going to get a kick in the tail that will set it back for five years. . . .

It's terribly, terribly important. People all over this city . . . people in city hall, people in political headquarters all over this city are watching this and one or two other races in the city of Chicago to see what happens. To see if the independents can make it stick or are they going to run out of gas after a couple of cheap wins. That's what they are asking themselves, and the political future of this state to some extent [depends on the outcome]. . . .

Let me just put it to you, will you help? Will you take some personal responsibility to help us here? I've got some cards that I'd like to pass out. They've got

vote, they should look for potential workers to help. Every person who comes into the headquarters to see what the campaign is all about should be put to work in the office immediately and later convinced to help out in the precincts.

When your candidate shakes hands at bus stops or supermarkets, she should take pledge cards to sign up new workers on the spot. Every campaign effort, from stories in the newspapers to rallies in the park, should pay off by recruiting volunteers and by affecting as many individual voters as possible.

Organizing a Winning Coalition

Campaigns occur at many levels. One is creating a winning coalition beginning with an electoral coalition. If the dominant political faction or party in a particular district endorses your candidate, she usually wins. Political scientists have discovered three main reasons people vote for a particular candidate: party identity; candidate personality, persona, or image; and overriding (usually economic) issues.[11] In general elections in which party labels are clear, in the absence of other information on candidates running for lower offices, Democrats vote for Democratic candidates and Republicans vote for Republican candidates. Therefore in any election, building support of established political groups is important.

Links between race, ethnicity, socioeconomic status, and political party identity are also clear. Innercity African American districts tend to elect Democrats, and wealthy, white suburbs tend to elect Republicans. The Latino/a and Asian American votes are also beginning to be overwhelmingly Democratic because of immigration and economic issues. Thus, the party identity of your candidate is often key to winning elections.

Building the proper political coalition to gain the dominant party endorsement is therefore often critical to winning.

In thinking about coalition building, it is important to remember that a candidate only has to win a majority of votes cast on Election Day—not gain the support of a majority of citizens or registered voters. Any political coalition is assembled by appealing to group self-interest.[12] The first questions you need to ask when deciding whether to support a candidate in a particular district are: What groups must support that candidate to win, and what is the likelihood of gaining their support? Thus, gaining the public endorsement of community leaders indicates the breadth of group support for a candidacy and makes it easier to appeal to those groups of voters.

In considering coalitions beyond strictly electoral coalitions, the distribution of race and ethnicity in a district is important. Generally speaking, a black candidate cannot win in an all-white district, and a white will not win in an African American district. Other ethnic and social divisions are less absolute but still matter. For instance, Latino/as and Asian Americans are likely to vote in greater numbers in support of candidates from their own racial and ethnic groups.[13]

Still, Simpson was elected alderman in Chicago's 44th Ward despite the fact that as a white protestant he represented none of the major ethnic or religious groups in the ward. The 44th Ward was heavily Jewish and moderately wealthy on its east side, Hispanic and Catholic in the middle, and German working class on the west side. Luckily, Simpson was more or less acceptable to all of these groups. He won heavily on the east side and gained support in the middle of the district from the young professionals moving in

blanks for your names and addresses, squares you can check off if you are willing to work in a precinct, if you are willing to work Election Day, if you are willing to work in our headquarters between now and Election Day. This is in your spare time. It can be a tremendous experience.

Please join with us. If you can't give time, give money. If you can't give money, give time. If you can, do both. If you can't do either, vote for us.

—Donald Page Moore, in
By the People (film)

because of his liberal stands on social and political issues as well as his opposition to Mayor Daley. Hispanics voted for him because he was the only Anglo politician paying close attention to their issues. Although he did not win the west side, he got votes there as well because he was not as threatening as a black politician would have been to the conservative, older, German community.

Beyond the race, ethnicity, and religion of the candidate and the voters, campaigns assemble the political organizations, former campaign workers, and community leaders to support their candidate. After the candidate's base is solidified, then she reaches out to other constituencies. As a candidate meets with various groups and their leaders, she takes stands on the issues that concern them. Specific ethnic groups often form community organizations to which a candidate can also appeal for support. Just as with other groups, ethnic communities have special channels through which they can be reached. Chicago, for instance, has a daily Korean newspaper, Spanish radio stations and newspapers, Spanish television stations, and many other specialized media that reach specific groups.[14] In larger cities you can use these media to ask for the support and participation of these voters in your campaign.

When a campaign contacts racial and ethnic groups through their community organizations and community leaders, its candidate and workers attempt to understand which issues an organization considers important. Just as you would not assume that a labor organization represents the political view of all working people, do not assume that a Chinese Mutual Aid Association speaks for all citizens of Chinese descent. It might also be necessary to produce campaign literature in the language of a group you hope to reach, using someone fluent in the language to translate it from the English version.

In appealing to different groups, however, it is important that you not make contradictory promises or play to the racism and bigotry of a particular group. Groups have to know that although a candidate is sensitive to their issues and concerns, she can be trusted—that is, she is not telling one thing to one group and then changing her position when talking to another.

There is an old political saying: "Politics is about addition, not subtraction." You have to pick political enemies so that it is clear what you stand for, but politics is basically about accumulating the support of different groups and individuals, not about factionalism and splintering support, as can often happen even within political parties and interest groups.

Campaign strategy is not only about contacting voters individually but also about assembling a winning coalition. Some of these coalitions may last for decades, only to be replaced by new alliances. The assumption that white southerners would always vote Democratic was destroyed by Republican Party victories in congressional and gubernatorial elections across the South after the 1960s. Other coalitions are as easily destroyed. When in power, coalitions must be carefully nurtured and maintained. When out of power, coalitions must be carefully and consciously built group by group.

Starting a Campaign Office

When an election is still many months away, a campaign office might be set up in the basement of a candidate's home, in a home office of a future staff member, or in a supporting organization's office. A campaign at this stage might also be run from the offices of several campaign staff members or consultants in a larger campaign.

Even with these humble beginnings, a campaign office must have at least one paid staff member (even if only part time), a phone with at least one dedicated campaign phone number (whether it is a cell phone or landline), an answering machine, and several computers. Such a small office can be adequate to launch a campaign. Strategy meetings can be held, fund-raising calls made, and early press relations handled with these limited facilities. Research on the district, campaign position papers, press releases, and the first campaign literature can be produced here.

Such limited facilities are adequate as the sole campaign office in only the smallest local campaigns—a local referendum or suburban school, zoning, library board, or a town council race. For all other campaigns this startup office and its operations are meant only to launch the larger campaign. These limited facilities are being used to keep costs down until actual campaign offices can be opened with full staffing. If the computer is donated and the rent is free, a startup office, including parttime staff salaries, might cost only a few hundred or a couple of thousand dollars a month.

The "real" campaign office is large enough for the candidate, at least three paid staff members, and three or four volunteers. It should also be large enough to hold strategy meetings of the staff, key volunteers, and precinct coordinators. When newspaper photographs are taken or a television crew interviews the candidate, it should look like a winning campaign headquarters. Generally speaking, it should be more than 1,000 square feet with smaller cubicle offices for staff and a larger open area for volunteers and meetings. By contrast, campaign offices for presidential or statewide candidates take up as much as a floor of a downtown office building and have room for many more staff members and volunteers.

In a full campaign office, a number of computers will be needed, although both staff and volunteers might supply their own laptops or tablets. Instead of a single phone line, there will be several along with the cell phones brought in by volunteers. There will soon be a leased copier and printer and at least as many desks as staff members. There will also be some big tables at which volunteers work, a coffeemaker, a refrigerator, and a number of folding chairs. The walls should be freshly painted and decorated with maps of the district, campaign literature, and newspaper clippings about the race. Most of all, the office must be staffed by friendly, professional campaign officials who seek to recruit everyone who wanders in the door.

An ideal office is a storefront centrally located in the district, on a major street near public transportation with plenty of parking nearby. Obviously, the rent should be inexpensive so that the campaign's money is spent on reaching the voters. However, because staff and volunteers will be working there at least from 10 a.m. to 11 p.m., the office must be comfortable and attractive. Any media photographs or TV footage taken of the candidate or the campaign there should look like what voters expect a winning campaign to look like. As actors say, this stage set should "look good from the third row." Office space in a rundown slum should not be rented because too much money and time will go into renovating it, or it will be so unappealing that the staff and volunteers will not want to work there. This is especially a safety issue for female staff and volunteers.

The way to plan all aspects of a campaign is to envision what you need to win the election and plan so that you can comfortably grow into that vision. If you are going to need 500 volunteers going door to door or calling voters on the phone, then you have to be set up to coordinate that many people from the office and have the facilities to provide them precinct lists, phone lists, instructions, and campaign literature. This means you will need several phone lines in addition to the cell phones volunteers will use, computers, a Wi-Fi network, plenty of tables and chairs, room to store boxes of campaign brochures, and so forth.

The best way to design an office is to plan for the office(s) you will need at the end of the campaign. Although you might be starting up with a single staff member, at the end you will have three to seven staff members. Whereas one telephone line might be enough in the startup office, at the end you will need a phone bank with more lines, space for volunteers with their cell phones, call lists for all callers, and a single data management system to record the results from door-to-door precinct work and phone calling.

Although you might start small, you need to plan so that each new aspect becomes available just as the campaign requires it. For instance, new landline phones can take weeks to be installed after they are ordered, so you cannot wait until the last few weeks of the campaign to order them. You do not want to learn too late that your computers, servers, and software infrastructure cannot handle the necessary volume and the number of users involved at the end of the campaign.

Campaign Technology

In planning the office it is also important to use the latest technology you can afford. Modern campaigns use some fancy, high-tech tools. It is necessary to understand what is possible, what it costs, and what effect each new tool has on winning the election. Because campaign support services change quickly, it is impossible to give the names of the providers from whom one should order, but we will discuss what is possible in 2016, confident that later changes will mostly be newer versions of the same techniques.

Most high-tech campaign technology has six main uses:

1. Research
2. Office work
3. Fund-raising and financial reporting
4. Press relations
5. Campaign literature
6. Voter contact

RESEARCH

Early assessment of the district mostly involves collecting prior election statistics, census data, and the like. Storing the information and creating a simple data file and perhaps an Excel spreadsheet to manipulate the numbers for strategy and planning might be sufficient. Most documents are readily available in digital form at public websites provided by city and county clerks, boards of election commissioners, the US Census Bureau, and universities. Little special equipment is required to determine if the race is winnable and to plot general campaign strategy.

After a decision to undertake the campaign has been made, a good researcher, a research director (often the campaign manager or the public relations coordinator), and sophisticated computer equipment and software is necessary, but this will often be owned already by the researcher. Opposition research requires the most sophisticated techniques and methods. Opponents' voting records are most easily studied in a computerized form, which at more local levels of government might have to be created from hard copies of legislative journals of proceedings. Opponents' previous campaign contributions (which might well give clues as to conflicts of interest) will often be recorded with the Federal Election Commission (FEC), state board of election commissioners, or county clerk. These data are usually now available in an electronic format and often posted on a public website. Even on the most local level, a lot of information is available online. Various databases make searching for newspaper articles on opponents relatively easy, yet all of this material has to be collected and translated into a form useful to the campaign.

Issue research is also important. It can include data such as the number of factories that have closed or the types of serious crimes in the district. When running against an incumbent legislator, it is also helpful to trace how he voted even in committee and to trace public reaction from all sides toward his position on these seemingly minor votes. After the facts are known, it might be possible to develop important campaign issue briefs for publications such as brochures and press conferences.

Sometimes data can be purchased from private companies that specialize in compiling voting records, campaign contributions, plant closings, or crime statistics. In any case, manipulating this data and sharing it to produce tables and charts for the campaign in the form of illustrations for press conferences, press releases, campaign literature, and campaign websites requires a computer and sophisticated software.

OFFICE WORK

There is an endless amount of office work in campaigns, made easier and more efficient with computers. Some campaigns try to link all their computers into a local area network (LAN). Usually this is a mistake because it takes a sophisticated level of maintenance to keep the system from crashing all the time. Many volunteers will have different levels of computer literacy. If they make a mistake on a single machine, especially if it is their own laptop, tablet, or smartphone, the damage to the campaign is minimal. However, if they are working on a network, they can crash the entire system, depriving the campaign of working computers for the number of days it takes to get a computer specialist to get the system running again.

Most campaigns use standard software such as Dropbox, Google Docs, or simple e-mail attachments in programs such as Microsoft Word to exchange information. They use a single software package such as VoteBuilder, Voter Vault, or rVotes to handle information about voter contacts and contributors. A staff member or volunteer simply copies his or her work into the software program or the "cloud" for the next person to use. In a campaign it is especially important that the level of technology be appropriate to the skills of the campaign workers. It is also critical that everyone be trained to use the software selected by the campaign.

The schedule for the candidate and the campaign will be kept on a computer by the office manager or the scheduler in larger campaigns. Most campaigns create them on an all-purpose scheduling form upon which staff members fill out scheduling requests. After the office manager, candidate, and campaign manager agree on the requests to fulfill, the daily schedule is generated with standardized information. It is then entered into scheduling software, most often Google Calendar, which then automatically syncs with the candidate's smartphone for instant access. In addition, the candidate gets a printed daily and weekly schedule along with briefing sheets about each major meeting. Obviously, campaign staff at the headquarters keep both digital and hard copies of the schedule. A different campaign schedule with deadlines for filing petition signatures, various events, and campaign projects is made available to all the key volunteers who coordinate the different campaign functions.

Computers are used for endless numbers of projects in campaigns just as they are in business and government. They are used to make agendas for staff and strategy meetings, draft letters and instructions for volunteers, compile research, draft publicity, coordinate collection of voter data for analytics, and myriad other functions. These word processing, data, and computational demands of campaigns make it advisable to use compatible computers *and the same software.* The office manager and campaign manager make a choice of computers and software for the campaign office and then make it the standard for the entire campaign except for specialized functions.

FUND-RAISING AND FINANCIAL REPORTING

Campaigns have come a long way. Formerly, the names of potential contributors were kept entirely on handwritten three-by-five index cards, and financial reports required by the government were typed onto government forms. Now software programs easily accomplish both functions and much more.

For congressional campaigns, specialized campaign software platforms such as VoteBuilder store and sort information on voters, volunteers, and contributions and produce personalized letters, envelope labels, and the critical financial reports to the FEC and state election commissions.[15] These platforms allow you to enter fund-raising prospects with their addresses and phone numbers, generate individualized letters to each potential contributor, keep track of all contributions and expenditures, write individual thank-you letters for each contribution, create potential precinct walk sheets, keep lists of volunteers, and produce financial reports. In larger campaigns, a staff member will be assigned to fund-raising, and in smaller campaigns a volunteer will be in charge. In either case, they will use similar methods to keep track of prospects, donors, and financial reports.

PRESS RELATIONS

The public relations coordinator or campaign press secretary will need, at a minimum, a phone to call the press, a computer to write press releases and news assignment memos, and a method such as e-mail to deliver these instantly to the press. A list of press e-mail addresses and a Wi-Fi connection are also essential. Setting up a campaign home page on the Internet on which to put campaign press releases and announcements is also now a standard means of communicating with the press, campaign supporters, opinion leaders, and interested voters.

CAMPAIGN LITERATURE AND COMMERCIALS

The production of campaign literature often occurs outside the campaign headquarters at the office of professional media consultants. A professional graphic artist usually designs campaign brochures after the campaign manager and public relations coordinator develop the copy. After the necessary photographs are taken, the designer will add them and send the brochure electronically to the printing firm, which then provides proofs of the work for approval by the graphic artist, campaign staff, and candidate.

A different technology is employed to make radio or television commercials. Although the copy might be written at the campaign office or on the media consultant's computer, a video camera and a television or radio recording studio will be necessary to produce the finished product. Because the public expects high production values in commercials on television and radio, professionals must be used in all aspects of production. A home video camera held by an inexperienced brother-in-law and an amateur script written by someone's mom simply will not do. Although you can save immense amounts of money if the studio and talent donate their time, commercials must be made professionally. The equipment involved will be rented or provided by the media consultant's firm because no campaign can afford to buy the equipment owned by media professionals and recording studios. The resulting ads can then be posted as well on the campaign website and YouTube.

A key decision for any candidate and campaign leaders is how to spend scarce resources for voters contacted individually door to door, by telephone, by direct mail, or electronically. Should money be spent instead on another round of mass media ads in newspapers or on radio and television? It is a decision with both ideological and practical consequences. Part of the decision making will be guided by what is called *voter analytics,* or more simply by an analysis of the information the campaign has on the voters. This trend in campaigning was made particularly popular by the Obama campaign.[16]

As Jonathon Alter writes in *The Center Holds,* his "contemporary history" of the 2012 Obama presidential campaign, "The old machines ... were run on patronage. ... The grease for the new machine ... was money, of course, but also data—highly sophisticated analytics." He explains that the Obama campaign merged fund-raising and precinct work with high-tech analytics of donors, voters, and targeted media purchases. This allowed its leaders to concentrate on contacting the most likely voters, making the best pitches to potential donors, and making the most effective media buys at the lowest cost.[17]

The key to the Obama analytics effort was the work of the geeks housed in a windowless office called the Cave. In addition to census data and voter information from the 2008 voter contacts and continuing e-mail lists of supporters, the Obama campaign made calls to 4,000–9,000 voters in battleground states each night. Using this and other available voter information, the campaign used predictive modeling and extrapolation to produce a "support score" from 0–100. Any potential voters who scored above 65 were worth contacting, and those above 80 were a must visit.[18]

The VoteBuilder software the campaign used allowed canvassers to skip most houses and knock only on doors where supporters or potential supporters lived. Such data management systems are available in a scaled-down version depending on a campaign's person power, sophistication, and finances.

Participatory campaigns nearly always opt for individual voter contact along with social media and mass media ads. They believe you "get more bang for your buck" with direct voter contact because it is easier to convince voters to support your candidate if volunteers directly persuade them and answer their specific questions. Political science research backs up the claim that in-person voter contact is the most effective of all methods of motivating potential supporters and persuading undecided voters to support a candidate.[19]

There are six principal methods of voter contact used in campaigns: (1) direct contact by the candidate, (2) door-to-door contact by campaign precinct workers, (3) direct mail, (4) telephone, (5) news coverage and advertising in the mass media, and (6) contact through social media and the Internet. The campaign office(s) must be set up to facilitate all of these methods of contact.

Currently, direct voter contact by the candidate requires the least high-tech effort, although computers are used to schedule the candidate's appearances, and voter analytics may be used to target the voters to be contacted. A candidate can meet voters at public transportation stops, factory gates, supermarkets, and parades. She also goes to house parties and attends community meetings, candidate forums, and debates. She appears at campaign rallies and fund-raising events. The scheduling of all these appearances is facilitated by forms and software programs the office manager develops. Staff and volunteers request that the candidate appear at various events, and the office manager, in consultation with the campaign manager and candidate, produces weekly and daily schedules. In all campaigns, the candidate, key staff, and volunteers get a weekly copy of the schedule. The candidate and her driver get a detailed schedule of each event each day. In larger campaigns, the "public schedule" is given to the news media once a week or upon request.

Door-to-door contact is more labor intensive because of the need to prepare the walk sheets, voter lists, training, and reports from volunteers, not to mention the hours put in by the precinct workers going door to door actually contacting the voters. Data-management systems provide a list of all voters in the district, their addresses and phone numbers, how often and in which elections they voted, social characteristics such as age, and their party identification.[20]

Purchasing and preparing this data for the campaign workers is expensive. Usually a campaign staff member or several staff will have to spend a lot of time carefully supervising volunteers and making information available in the most useful form for them. However, if you are going to make an effort to directly contact individual voters in a large district, the costs in time, money, and effort to target the contacts are worth it.

Incumbent officeholders have the additional advantage of computer software that tracks all service requests by their constituents. Thus, they are able to add to their voter data information such as "Mary Jones requested a pothole to be filled and was satisfied with the response from our office."

Three alternatives exist for local campaigns that cannot afford all the hightech expenditures to facilitate direct voter contact. First of all, in smaller campaigns there are cheaper ways to assemble the information. For an election in a single city ward, small town, or suburb in which there are fewer than 30,000 voters, voter information can still be assembled from free maps and poll lists from the local board of elections, reverse phone directories, and Internet searches. By simply copying information cut and pasted from various sources, you can compile voter lists for volunteers for as many as fifty precincts.

A second alternative for a smaller campaign is to hook up with a bigger one. A candidate running for Congress, state legislature, or citywide office might be willing to provide computerized voter contact lists in return for another campaign's volunteers simultaneously distributing the larger campaign's literature when they contact voters. Although the West Deerfield Township election in which O'Shaughnessy took part was a small local affair, the combination of the supervisor, assessor, clerk, and trustee campaigns allowed for a less expensive and more unified effort, with more activities possible in which voters could meet all of those candidates.

Third, political organizations or a group of campaigns can purchase the necessary computer equipment, data, software, and staff jointly. As a twist on this approach, Simpson encouraged a number of judicial candidates to share the cost of a mailing he wanted to send to voters during his campaign for Congress. None of the campaigns could afford the computerized lists and postage to do direct mail on their own, but together their joint campaign mailing reached more voters than any one campaign could afford.

Some campaigns now rely entirely on direct mail, public relations, and mass media ads as their principal method of campaigning. If a campaign purchases software that produces voter lists, it can cut direct mail costs dramatically. First of all, it can do targeted mailings using volunteers. For instance, one can mail a prochoice mailing to women voters below forty years of age or send senior citizen mailings to every voter in the district older than fifty. This means a campaign can tailor its campaign message for particular voters with hot-button issues most likely to win their votes on Election Day. Similarly, with computerized lists a campaign can mail to wealthier sections of the district with a contribution pitch, pledge card, and return envelope. The money received from this mailing can help finance other mailings in the district. A computerized list will also let a campaign send only one letter per household even if five voters live there, and the campaign can personalize the letter.

A form of voter contact campaigns use quite effectively is contact by telephone. This strategy means having as much information about voters as possible so you can target whom to call. Either a professional telemarketing firm can be hired to do the work, or as with most participatory campaigns, volunteers can do the calling. The problem with the campaign workers making the calls is that a phone bank (usually from four to ten phones or volunteers with cell phones) must be set up. The volunteers must be trained and directly supervised by a staff member, although with the new computerized methods it is possible for volunteers to call from home and to enter the response into a special software program. In any case, a careful pitch must be written, and the phone numbers to be called must be generated. This campaign operation is expensive in time and money but can be effective.

The best phone campaign is coupled with other campaign efforts. The most common is to send a direct mail letter to the voter followed by a phone call pitch. This double contact is often more successful than either the letter or phone call by itself. Because voters are solicited all the time commercially, many are now resistant to campaign phone solicitations. They know this is not just a friend or neighbor calling to chat. Professional telemarketing firms have found more and more answering machines are taking the calls and a general unwillingness of people to answer the phone. If a campaign wants to reach voters and does not have the precinct workers to visit their homes (or campaign workers cannot get into residences such as high-rise buildings with security guards), then a phone canvass might still be the best alternative.

Organizing Your Campaign

Campaigns look so much simpler and more glamorous in movies than in real life. In *The Candidate*, Robert Redford's character makes a few speeches, gets covered by the media, and wins the election. The problems of coordinating staff and volunteers, the tension and personality conflicts within a campaign, and the thousands of hours of hard work behind the scenes are not conveyed in movie versions of campaigning.

Organizing a campaign with the right staff members, campaign reporting structure, equipment, and support services is a poorly understood part of winning elections. Neither voters nor the media see the task of recruiting hundreds of volunteers one by one. This is a part of the nuts and bolts of the campaign plan, put into effect months and even years before the successful candidate finally makes her acceptance speech on election night.

Chapter Four

Raising Money

....

Having the best candidate in the world, the best campaign theme, and running against a lackluster opponent are still not sufficient to be elected. You still have to raise money to be taken seriously as a candidate by the media and to deliver your message successfully to the voters. How much is enough? If you have a good candidate and a good campaign platform, you usually do not have to raise more money than your opponents to defeat them. However, a candidate does have to raise enough money to deliver his campaign message. Unless a candidate is independently wealthy, he cannot pay for election costs himself. He has to raise the money from contributors—wealthier individuals and groups such as labor unions or business political action committees (PACs).

It is useful to have a fund-raising committee that can provide the names of good prospects and handle special fund-raising events to which their friends contribute. However, the primary secret to raising money is to have the candidate personally ask prospects himself.

This begins with a letter from the candidate and a campaign brochure. Several hours a day a staff member or volunteer literally places calls for the candidate to the prospects on the list who have received the letter. Candidates hate to do fund-raising calls. It seems to them too much like begging, but they have to make the calls if they want to be elected. Raising money from PACs is much the same—writing the PACs with the information that they require and the candidate calling or meeting with the PAC staff to close the deal.

Fund-raising has always been important, but in the campaigns of the twenty-first century, despite all the fund-raising scandals, it is central to a successful campaign. Therefore a candidate has to allocate at least several hours *every day* to fund-raising, like it or not.

A campaign, of course, also raises money in small amounts on the Internet, from the campaign website, and from individualized e-mail appeals to sup-

Table 4.1. Typical Campaign Budget: Campaign to Elect Will Guzzardi, 2014

Category	Description	Total
Staff	Campaign manager (six months)	$50,000
	Field director (seven months)	
	Deputy campaign manager (seven months)	
Mail/printing	Six to eight planned pieces to be sent to 10,000 targeted households to reach approx. 14,000 voters*	$50,000
Offices, phone, utilities	Short-term lease	$15,600
	Electricity	
	Gas	
	Phone line	
Voter tracking online service	Internet-based voter database	$800
Internet services	E-mail list management (Constant Contact)	$3,400
	Online donation management (Act Blue)	
Phone polling service and strategy	Targeted paid polling	$11,500
Fund-raiser	Short-term staff last four months of campaign	$ 5,000
Postage	Stamps for thank-you cards, postcards, miscellaneous	$ 2,800
Supplies	Cases of paper, pens, clipboards, printer toner	$ 5,000

*Note: A volunteer consolidated the mailing list so that addresses with multiple voters where couples and families were obvious received only one mailer

porters. It can also raise money from special events such as a dinner or a play and can, absolutely, raise money from smaller social gatherings such as coffees or cocktail parties. However, these events and appeals never produce enough money by themselves, especially for the bigger, more expensive races. The candidate must still make personal, individual appeals to major donors.

Just as the campaign recruits workers through personal contact, intimate social gatherings, and campaign events, money is raised in the same way. Nonetheless, before much money can be raised, you have to know how much is needed. To know that, campaign leaders have to know the necessary campaign expenses and make a budget.

The beginning point of fund-raising is always a campaign budget. For illustrative purposes, we will use Will Guzzardi's state legislative campaign expenditures in Illinois as a template for your budget making (see Tables 4.1 and 4.2).

Guzzardi's 2014 base budget of $144,100 provides a sense of the costs en-

Table 4.2. Budget after Major Endorsements Brought Large Campaign Contributions

Category	Description	Total
Campaign consulting firm	Progressive-agenda firm, mailers, professional ads	$ 35,000
Television ads	Targeted cable networks, production, Spanish and English	$100,000
Internet ads	Facebook boosting	$ 1,000
Hiring canvassers and full time data entry people	Best volunteers hired for last month	$ 18,000
Mailers	Additional mailers by more prominent company	$ 40,000
Election Day GOTV	Food and drink for volunteers	$ 3,500
Car	Rental of campaign car (candidate rode bicycle and borrowed cars for most of the campaign)	$ 2,500
Media services	Twitter, blogging, media consulting	$ 10,500
Printing	Miscellaneous banners and signs	$ 7,000
Bonuses	Win bonuses for staff; additional payroll	$ 10,000

countered at the state legislator level. His campaign was run with a strategy appropriate to a winning participatory campaign with a fairly large number of volunteers. To be successful, Guzzardi had to raise significant sums of money. Generally speaking, staff costs, office expenses, printing, advertising, and direct mail consume most of the budget of most local campaigns.

As we detail in Chapter 9, Guzzardi was fortunate to attract major funding late in the campaign, so he was able to add another $227,500 in spending to ensure his victory. Most campaigns cannot count on such a windfall.

The amount to allocate for each spending category differs according to the type of campaign, level of spending by opposing candidates, and the cost of media buys in your media market. Nonetheless, the items shown in the Guzzardi budget are usually the main categories of expenditures. Staff salaries, office expenses, printing and mailing costs, Internet services such as a voter database and donation capability, phone costs, fund-raising events, and supplies are always needed. The decisions whether to rely mostly on direct mail, volunteer-delivered campaign brochures, the Internet, social media, radio, newspaper, or television advertising will depend on the type of race, funds available, and the most effective methods of getting your message to the voters. In twenty-first-century elections, the cost of targeted direct mail and all forms of mass media advertising have increased campaign budgets most dramatically.

These higher campaign costs have caused some public officials and reform organizations to advocate public funding such as that institutionalized in New York City and the State of Maine. For now, most campaigns must raise sufficient funds on their own without what is called "small-donor democracy," in which small donations are matched with public funding.

A local election with a volunteer staff can be run for a few thousand dollars. A contested alderman election in a major city or a race for a state legislative seat will cost from $100,000 to $500,000. State legislative races are increasingly more costly. Herbert Alexander in *Reform and Reality* decried the skyrocketing costs of state and local campaigns back in the 1990s, noting that in California, state legislative races sometimes cost more than $500,000, and even in rural Vermont, the median cost of a state senate race jumped 50 percent from 1984 to 1988.[1]

Congressional races are even more expensive than local and state legislative campaigns because congressional districts are larger. Furthermore, most congressional campaigns must rely upon mass media ads and expensive high-tech methods to reach the voters. The average incumbent member of Congress spent $595,000 defending his seat in 1992 because the cost of congressional elections continues to go up from 20 to 40 percent each election cycle.[2] In Illinois in contested congressional races in 2014, the cost had jumped to $2 million–$4 million per candidate in the general election.

Just as a campaign is begun by determining the target number of votes needed to win the election, fund-raising begins by setting a realistic campaign budget. In Chapter 3, the clear division of labor in campaign finance is outlined. The campaign manager and campaign chair help the candidate determine a realistic budget. The campaign manager then spends whatever money is raised as effectively as possible. The campaign treasurer keeps the books, making certain that every campaign contribution and expenditure is legal. The campaign staff fund-raiser, volunteer finance chair, and event committee chairs help the candidate raise the necessary money.

Unfortunately, votes cost money. There are high financial costs to getting a campaign's message to voters. The first thousand votes are cheap—almost free—because as much as 5 percent of the vote is obtained just by getting your candidate's name on the ballot. A hardworking candidate can gather from 500 to 1,000 more votes by himself, meeting voters at public transportation spots, grocery stores, events, and door to door. Then voters get progressively harder to reach. The next few thousand votes require a headquarters, staff, and publicity. When you get within a few thousand votes of victory, advertising extras such as bumper stickers, radio or television ads, and direct mail must be bought. The systems and data to do analytics have to be purchased along with various social media and Internet platforms and ads. All these expenditures cost much more money than the costs of printing petitions to get on the ballot. Thus they all should be carefully budgeted in advance and then adjusted as the real costs become known.

Lawrence Grey in *How to Win a Local Election* describes the process of making a campaign budget as one of setting priorities.[3] First, a campaign's necessary expenses such as the rental of the headquarters, phones, postage, and equipment such as computers and a printer must be determined along with salaries for staff. It may be that some of these can be supplied as in-kind gifts to the campaign. If so, a campaign will not have to raise as much money as without in-kind contributions.

After basic campaign expenses have been calculated, discretionary costs that depend on a campaign's strategy for getting the message to the voters—the cost of campaign brochures, direct mail, telemarketing, and radio and TV ads, for instance—can be estimated. Optional expenses can then be determined and prioritized. If you raise $10,000 more than your basic expenses, you can execute your first priority—if you raise still more, the second priority, and so forth. It is important to execute each priority that can be afforded as completely as possible to win. As Grey emphasizes:

> The important thing to remember is the priority given to each procedure. You may want to do a bulk mailing and radio, but what happens if you do not raise enough money to pay for both? You could do a little of each, but we do not recommend that. If your first priority is to do a mailing, do that and do it well. Spend all the money you get on the first-priority item, and when you have completed that, then spend whatever is left on doing as much of the second as you can.[4]

In Dick Simpson's first congressional campaign, he ran out of money for media advertising at the critical period of the last few weeks of the campaign. He began by spending money on cable television ad buys. Although he got some free publicity on the TV ads, he was not able to buy enough time on the major stations to have the impact he wanted, so the campaign switched to radio ads, which cost less. Altogether the campaign spent $19,000 on media buys, but because the ads were split between radio and television, they did not have as big an impact as needed to win the election. In Simpson's second congressional campaign, he spent all $11,000 of the media advertising money on radio, and the campaign did not attempt to buy the more expensive television ads. It was strategically a better choice. However, the campaign still could not raise enough money to buy saturation media advertising, and both of his principal opponents were able to buy substantial television advertising. He lost both campaigns in large part because he could not raise enough money to carry out the plans in the original campaign budget.

Therefore, a winning campaign must create a realistic budget and raise the necessary funds to pay for at least the top spending priorities.

Developing a Fund-Raising Strategy

After having established a realistic budget for a campaign, raising the necessary funds begins. Hank Parkinson in *Winning Your Campaign* quotes Iowa's Thomas Murphy: "The best way to get money is to ask for it—the more people you ask, the more money you're going to get."[5] Or as Donald Page Moore, campaign chair for Illinois Constitutional Convention delegate Bernard Weisberg put it, "If you're not afraid of losing friends, go to everybody you know—tackle them in the hall, phone them, write them a letter, and then call them and simply say 'Give me money.' They will because it is right."[6]

Each candidate who runs for office starts with certain advantages. Some candidates are personally wealthy and can afford to buy the best staff and full media access out of their own pockets. Others have the endorsement of a political party or a powerful interest group that will supply the necessary funds. However, most candidates have to raise money by asking for it. Thus, a key prerequisite of running for office is the willingness to ask people for campaign contributions, especially because the most effective way for a local candidate to raise money is to personally request a donation.[7]

The bias of participatory campaigns is to get as many contributions as possible from small contributors. Everyone who volunteers time to the campaign is encouraged to contribute as much money as he or she can. Every piece of campaign and direct mail literature should have a coupon asking people to contribute their time and money. Everyone for whom the campaign has an e-mail address should be solicited. The donation button on the campaign website should be prominent, and social media should also be used to solicit donations. Then, if your candidate is elected, he will be beholden to hundreds or thousands of constituents, not just a few "fat cats" or wealthy PACs.

No matter how broad your contributor base may be, there are still some basic truths about fund-raising. David Himes in "Strategy and Tactics for Campaign Fund-Raising" lists these:

1. No campaign ever lost because the candidate spent too much time raising money.
2. Many campaigns have lost because they failed to raise enough money to implement a winning campaign plan.
3. No one can raise money more effectively than the candidate.
4. Do not rely on political action committees (PACs), direct mail, telemarketing, or special events with important personalities to raise money. Rely on personal solicitation.
5. Everyone loves to sit around and talk politics. But the real measure of your commitment to winning an election is the willingness to personally ask another person for a contribution.[8]

In this process, a candidate must be personally committed to spend more time and effort than he wants on this aspect of the campaign. To begin, a campaign must have a specific fund-raising plan. After the campaign budget is devised, the fund-raising plan is created. There are five principal sources of campaign funds:

1. The candidate and his family
2. Individuals in the district
3. Individuals outside the district
4. Political action committees (PACs)
5. Political party committees[9]

To begin the process, the candidate must decide how much he can contribute. If this race is expected to cost from $50,000 to $500,000, he might be expected to provide as much as 10 percent of the total. About half of that amount will probably be needed as startup or seed money to launch the campaign. The other half will probably be needed at the end of the campaign to help purchase the expensive media advertising. Often candidate contributions partially take the form of "loans" to the campaign, which can be paid back if the campaign raises enough money. However, no one should lend money to his own campaign that he and his family cannot afford to contribute outright. Some candidates make the mistake of mortgaging their home or going so far into debt that they end up bankrupt. No candidate should gamble more than he can afford to lose.

The second resource is family members, especially parents and wealthy relatives. In a federal election, each family member is limited to a maximum of

$2,700 per election as of 2016. Hopefully within these limits, several thousand dollars can be raised from family members *if the candidate personally asks them*. Here is the rub. Although it is emotionally hard for most candidates to ask their families for money, it must be done. A candidate's personal funds and contributions from his family are critical to providing the financial base of the fund-raising effort. If he and his family will not contribute, getting anybody else to make a commitment will be next to impossible.

A candidate must overcome his inhibitions and "put the strong-arm" on family, friends, and complete strangers for the money he must have to run a winning campaign. He must change his mind-set about fund-raising. If he has committed himself, months of his life, his own money, and his reputation, then he must be convinced that more is at stake than his own ego gratification. Asking people for money is *not* begging for a handout. Rather, the candidate offers everyone—family, friends, and strangers—an opportunity to contribute to a campaign that will end some inequity, right some injustice, overthrow a tyranny, reestablish democracy, pass an important law, or end corruption and government waste. The reasons have been persuasive enough to get the commitment of the candidate, his campaign staff, and volunteers. Now is the time to convince people to give the necessary funds. The chief job of a candidate is to ask for money, understanding that he is offering others a chance to contribute to political change and to exercise their citizenship by contributing their money as well as their vote.

After a candidate has contributed his own money and received contributions from his family, the next step is to put together a list of other potential major contributors. In a suburban, rural, or town election with a campaign budget of $25,000 or less, such a contributor might be anyone who contributes $100 or more. In a larger city, county, or national race, major contributors will be those who donate $1,000 or more. For most of us who run for office, there are never enough people willing or able to be major financial contributors.

The candidate, campaign staff, and key volunteer campaign leaders go through their personal address books. From these names a list of every potential contributor is constructed. Those who might be major contributors are earmarked. If the candidate has run for office before, a list of previous contributors, especially those who might contribute even more this time, is created from previous financial report forms.

Another important source of potential contributors is people who have contributed to previous campaigns of other candidates or to the campaigns of elected officials who have endorsed your candidate. Although it is illegal in some jurisdictions to use the official reports of major contributors published by the board of election commissioners website, studying these reports will highlight contributors who have given to similar candidates or causes in the past. If the candidate or others in the campaign know these individuals, they can be added to the list of potential contributors to be solicited.

The names from all these sources are then organized and prioritized as prospective donors in whichever computer database the campaign is using. The resulting list of prospective major donors gets the campaign started.

If there is a fund-raising staff member (or in more local campaigns, a finance volunteer), he and the candidate religiously set aside at least two days a week to make finance calls. More commonly, a candidate and his fund-raising volunteer or staff member schedule several hours *every day* to "dial for dollars." After the prospect is on the phone, the candidate himself must then ask for the contributions necessary to fuel his campaign.

The fund-raising staff member or office manager has previously seen that a personalized letter with an individual salutation, candidate signature, and personal note has been mailed to the prospects before they are called. The prospect will then have some basic information about the campaign. A phone call or a personal meeting will still be necessary to get a contribution of $100 or more. These calls are slow, hard work. All candidates avoid them if they are allowed to do so, but the price of a candidate avoiding personal solicitations is nearly always defeat.

Suppose you start with 100 prospects. After two weeks of phone calls and personal meetings with a few potential donors who agree to meet personally with a candidate, only five people agree to contribute $1,000, another five give $250, and fifteen give $100. You may be disappointed that you made more than a hundred calls, and people who could afford large contributions gave only small ones or none at all. However, this is a terrific result. Your campaign has just raised $7,750! If your candidate keeps calling each week at this level, you will probably raise enough money to win the election. By phone calls and a couple of personal visits, the candidate probably raised more money with less cost than most campaign benefits.

Going after individual contributions systematically and consistently is crucial. Can anyone but the candidate do this? In some cases a campaign chair, finance chair, campaign fund-raising staff member, and a handful of committed fund-raisers who have already made a major financial contribution themselves can make calls. Often, however, although they can make initial contacts, the candidate will have to "close the sale."

In larger campaigns for Congress, statewide office, or president, fund-raising staff members make phone calls for political candidates. Campaigns

also recruit "bundlers." These are wealthy businesspeople or lawyers who solicit large donations from their business associates and deliver contributions
as a group. PACs often bundle multiple contributions at the legal limit in the
same way. Sometimes private citizens "bundle" for a candidate on their own.
In the 2008 Obama campaign, volunteer bundlers often raised thousands of
dollars through contacting their own friends and associates.

Most local, participatory campaigns do not have bundlers working on their
behalf. However, some members of their finance committee can solicit a few
larger donations on the candidate's behalf. The campaign gives major contributors VIP tickets to campaign events and encourages them to mingle with the
candidate and other public officials at small cocktail parties just for such donors.
No matter how they were originally solicited, major contributors need to feel
they have a personal connection to the candidate. Sometimes these donors are
also given special titles by level of contribution such as *donor, sponsor,* or *captain.*

CONTACTING INDIVIDUAL CONTRIBUTORS

What about all the people who can make a significant, but not major, financial
contribution? They, too, have to be asked. Who are they, and how do you reach
them?

Once again, assemble a list of prospects. Get a list of all the candidate's
friends and the friends of staff members and campaign volunteers. Then have
the candidate ask for a membership or contributor list of any organization that
has endorsed him. Next, assemble lists of board members or contributors of
any organizations to which a candidate belongs, even though the organization
has not formally endorsed him. You may be prevented from doing so by tax
laws. If a candidate has run before, obtain the list of all the financial contributors and volunteers from those campaigns. The resulting prospect list will
consist of several hundred or even several thousand names, addresses, phone
numbers, and e-mail addresses. Each family on the list is sent a letter announcing the launch of the campaign, with a volunteer pledge card and a return envelope. They are asked to "like" the campaign on Facebook. They are also given
the opportunity to donate on the campaign website using their credit cards.

Those who agree to contribute either time or money are entered into the
campaign comprehensive database with all the appropriate information about
their gifts or pledges. This first campaign mailing will net a profit of a couple
thousand dollars even if the average gift is $25–$50. Some e-mail solicitations
ask for contributions as low as $5, although they always provide an opportu-
nity for larger contributions.

A campaign can double or triple the response to almost any solicitation by having volunteers call each prospect. They will either reach the potential supporters directly or be able to make a pitch on a phone answering service. These calls will encourage many more people to return their volunteer pledge cards along with their financial contributions to launch the campaign. Those reached can be invited to a press conference or another campaign event where they can meet the candidate. After they provide the campaign their e-mail addresses, they can be solicited frequently by e-mails to all supporters that can be personalized by addressing them by their first names.

Fund-raising in the district is mostly a mail and phone effort by campaign volunteers and then follow-up e-mail solicitations. These contacts with prospects can be specifically coupled with benefits, house parties, and receptions throughout the campaign to increase both the number of volunteers and the financial support. The idea is to get as many people as possible to make a commitment to the campaign even if their initial commitment is small—such as contributing $5–$25, attending an event, or working a few hours one evening at the campaign headquarters. After they are on the campaign contributor mailing and e-mail list, they can be solicited to contribute again. Often, later donations will be more generous because the contributors now feel a part of the campaign. Some may contribute as often as every month or more frequently *if they are asked*. Therefore, developing as large a list as possible of supporters is critical to raising enough money. Sometimes it is tempting not to contact someone who is abrasive or asks troublesome questions, but someone's pest may be someone else's donor.

CONTACT EVERYBODY

Only a small percentage of Americans contributes to political campaigns, and only a small percentage of those consists of major donors. For instance, in the 2008 campaigns less than 0.5 percent of the population contributed 82 percent of the funds to federal candidates. Only 4 percent made contributions in any amount in to campaigns.[10] In the 2010, 2012, and 2014 elections, these numbers remained basically unchanged. The Sunlight Foundation reports that in the 2014 elections, approximately 32,000 donors, or about 1 percent of 1 percent of the US population—donated $1.18 billion in disclosed political contributions at the federal level.[11]

Those who have contributed to previous political campaigns are much more likely to contribute to a new campaign *if they are asked to do so by a candidate or someone they know personally*. So, if other candidates have run before with the same general political philosophy or against the same incumbent or political faction, a candidate certainly wants their endorsement. They can be listed on campaign literature and on the campaign website as campaign chairs, honorary chairs, or citizens' committee members. More importantly, the campaign can ask them for their lists of contributors and volunteers. A candidate should contact their major donors directly, and their other supporters can be added to the campaign prospect list and solicited by mail, e-mail, and phone. Endorsements by currently elected officials are also valuable in helping persuade voters to vote for the candidate and in sharing volunteers and contributors. These endorsements should be listed on all campaign literature.

Based on the principle that prior political contributors are more likely to contribute to a campaign, volunteers should check the financial disclosure forms of other candidates who have recently run for office. As mentioned before, although it may be impractical or illegal to use the entire list of contributors, if a candidate knows even slightly some of the individual campaign contributors on these forms, they should be called personally because they are hot prospects. Thousand-dollar contributors to another candidate may only donate $100 to your campaign in the beginning. However, they are better prospects than someone who has never contributed to a political campaign, and these past contributors may well contribute more to a campaign later. Professional fund-raisers carefully develop lists of generous contributors to past campaigns and major contributors to charities. Each campaign has to develop its own lists the same way.

It is important to compile new lists of prospects every week. The candidate, staff members, and volunteers then continue to systematically call these lists. This is how large campaign contributions and many of the smaller ones are obtained. There is no other way.

After a campaign has its own lists of campaign contributors, they can be solicited at least once a month to contribute again. A number of them will do so. This is made particularly easy and efficient by e-mail solicitations, so campaign leaders should carefully collect e-mail addresses of each contributor and potential contributor. They will need to change the pitch or reason to contribute with each solicitation. They must always send a new thank-you note for each new contribution received.

INDIVIDUAL CONTRIBUTORS OUTSIDE THE DISTRICT

Raising money from outside the district, other than from your candidate's family members, is difficult. As Himes writes, "If a campaign plans to raise a significant amount of cash from outsiders, it will probably have to focus on the very wealthy or the very political."[12] If prospects live in your city or state, you have a better chance of getting contributions. People from other states have much less interest in what a local candidate may do as a state legislator, alderman, judge, mayor, or even a member of Congress.

Nonetheless, potential contributors who live outside the district are contacted by direct mail and phone. Simple receptions held away from the district can also bring in needed funds. In each of Simpson's races against US Representative Dan Rostenkowski, he raised more than $50,000 from contributors outside his congressional district, but most of these contributions were from contributors who lived within Cook County or from family members who lived out of state. Although a few thousand dollars raised outside the district can help reach the financial goals of a campaign, few campaigns can win with individual outside contributions unless they are generated by PACs such as Emily's List. An exception would be Rahm Emmanuel's campaign for mayor of Chicago, in which an estimated 30 percent of his $15 million raised in 2011 came from contributors outside the state.[13] However, few candidates have the contacts with distant wealthy donors to make that happen.

Obtaining lists and contributions from specific organizations that want to defeat an opponent or elect your candidate because of his stand on key issues may be possible. For instance, because Simpson was a political science professor, a direct mail and telephone campaign to college professors in Cook County who did not live in the district allowed him to raise an additional $4,000.

Similarly, a senior citizen national organization concerned about inequities in Social Security payments to "notch babies" (those seniors born between 1918 and 1926) sent a mailing for Simpson to their membership. This was financially less helpful, but it allowed them to urge seniors in the district to vote for him because of his position on this one issue. If an organization will provide a list, and particularly if it will pay for the mailing, a direct mail effort inside and outside the district builds support for a campaign.

A campaign can also hold fund-raising benefits attended by major donors in big cities. For these to be successful, contacts in those cities must organize the event to make it worth a candidate's time and expense to attend. Usually, such external fund-raising events are targeted to raise the last of the big bucks for radio or television ads.

Campaign Benefits

Depending on the level of a campaign, fund-raising benefits can raise up to 25 percent or more of your budget. Also these days, it is not surprising to have people write out $100 checks at house parties where a candidate has been particularly persuasive. At one coffee in Simpson's congressional campaign, a neighbor of the hostess gave $1,000. In Simpson's second campaign, that neighbor and his wife gave $2,000, served on the finance committee, and hosted a successful modern art benefit at their home. One never knows how small campaign events such as a neighborhood coffee can lead to greater fund-raising successes.

Most campaign benefits are larger and more formal efforts than house parties. Successful benefits must be imaginative, enticing for people to attend, carefully organized, and hosted by a benefit committee that agrees to help sell tickets to the event especially to their friends, families, and associates.

A successful benefit should be "different"; ideally, it should be something other than the usual politician's dinner. One of the most successful benefits of the Weisberg campaign was held at an architectural landmark in the district and featured a harp and piano concert at which the candidate himself played. A benefit that helped pay off the debt from Simpson's congressional campaign was an Independence Day outing for major donors and their families featuring fireworks viewed from a suburban mansion on Lake Michigan. A larger, much less expensive benefit was a salsa party at a jazz bar in the district, complete with dance instructor and band. All of these events are much more appealing than a rubber-chicken dinner with boring speeches in a downtown hotel.

Almost any event can be made financially successful if it is carefully planned. Here are some rules to consider in planning a benefit:

1. It should be different from any previous benefit.
2. It should only be attempted if there are at least six weeks in which to make preparations and sell tickets.
3. The main event or entertainment must be donated or inexpensive. When you pay actors or performers, the event costs so much that you make no profit. With donated talent, or with a big reduction in ticket prices at a theater, you can make close to 100 percent profit.
4. The rental of facilities should be relatively inexpensive.
5. Unique invitations, flyers, and tickets should be printed for the benefit to make it seem special and worth the price (see the sample invitation in Figure 4.1).
6. The price per person must either be relatively high ($100, $500, or more) or relatively low ($25 or less). With the higher price, you shoot for an audience of at least a hundred. With the lower price you seek an audience of several hundred. By using special sponsor tickets at a higher price or by selling advertisements in a program, more money can be raised at lower-priced events.

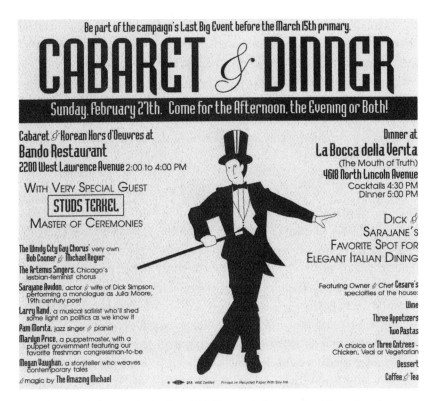

Be part of the campaign's Last Big Event before the March 15th primary.

CABARET & DINNER

Sunday, February 27th. Come for the Afternoon, the Evening or Both!

Cabaret & Korean Hors d'Oeuvres at
Bando Restaurant
2200 West Lawrence Avenue 2:00 to 4:00 PM

WITH VERY SPECIAL GUEST

STUDS TERKEL

MASTER OF CEREMONIES

The Windy City Gay Chorus' very own
Bob Cooner & Michael Regier

The Artemis Singers, Chicago's
lesbian-feminist chorus

Sarajane Avidon, actor & wife of Dick Simpson,
performing a monologue as Julia Moore,
19th century poet

Larry Rand, a musical satirist who'll shed
some light on politics as we know it

Pam Morita, jazz singer & pianist

Marilyn Price, a puppetmaster, with a
puppet government featuring our
favorite freshman congressman-to-be

Megan Vaughan, a storyteller who weaves
contemporary tales

& magic by The Amazing Michael

Dinner at
La Bocca della Verita
(The Mouth of Truth)
4618 North Lincoln Avenue
Cocktails 4:30 PM
Dinner 5:00 PM

DICK &
SARAJANE'S
FAVORITE SPOT FOR
ELEGANT ITALIAN DINING

Featuring Owner & Chef Cesare's
specialties of the house:

Wine

Three Appetizers

Two Pastas

A choice of Three Entrees -
Chicken, Veal or Vegetarian

Dessert

Coffee & Tea

4.1. Cabaret and Dinner Invitation from Dick Simpson's Congressional Campaign. Courtesy of Dick Simpson.

Every campaign will have fund-raising benefits. If a campaign keeps the number of them low, really concentrates on making them successful, leaves plenty of time for preparations, and keeps the overhead costs at a minimum, it can raise the money it needs.

Much of the money in local participatory campaigns is raised from small contributions of less than $100. Each person who contributes even $1 is likely to vote for the candidate and actively encourage other citizens to do so. Therefore, even in campaigns in which more money is raised in larger contributions, small contributions and benefits are vital. Many contributors will also become house party hosts or chairs, office volunteers, or precinct workers.

Increasing the level of contributions should be a continuous process. In Simpson's first alderman campaign, he worked hard to increase the number of $50 and $100 contributions through a series of luncheons. Many people who were far from wealthy were convinced at these events to make a larger contribution than they had previously given to political campaigns. During the lunch, they discussed the campaign and what it meant to Chicago political reform. The host or luncheon chair told of Simpson's plan to get one hundred $100 and one hundred $50 sponsors. The host then asked those present to become sponsors at these levels. At no luncheon did the Simpson campaign raise less than $250 and, through a series of luncheons, it raised $3,500. Today, the amount asked for might be greater, but personal contact with potential contributors in a social situation is still an excellent way to raise money.

Political Action Committees

PACs are providing an even greater amount of money for campaigns. Super-PACs now fund millions of dollars to pay for television ads. PACs dominate congressional and expensive state legislative campaigns. Normally, PACs have not funded local elections, but they are beginning to do so because local laws have begun to have a greater impact on businesses and interest groups.

Surprisingly, PACs provide an even greater percentage of donations for state legislative races than they do for congressional races. Alexander in *Reform and Reality* stated that even in the 1980s interest groups generally funded about 31 percent of the federal campaigns but as high as 74 percent of state elections. The Wisconsin Democracy Campaign reported that total spending by legislative candidates, their fund-raising committees, and outside interest groups was almost $17 million on Wisconsin state legislative races alone in 2014.[14]

It must be decided up front whether a campaign will accept PAC contributions. In Simpson's first campaign to defeat the congressional incumbent Rostenkowski, he pledged not to accept PAC contributions and used this stand to distinguish himself from Rostenkowski, known as the "Congressional King of PACs." In Simpson's second campaign, he dropped this absolute position and sought contributions from PACs promoting women's rights, gay rights, and other liberal agendas. However, he did not seek support from PACs wanting tax breaks or regulatory changes for corporations.

Many candidates take a similar position, although their definitions of good and bad PACs may differ radically. From their side of the fence, PACs inevitably look for "winners," and they fund incumbents at much higher rates than challengers. Himes provides the following useful advice about PAC funding:

> It is easier for incumbents to raise money from PACs than it is for challengers and openseat candidates. . . . Nonincumbents need to plan to work very hard to get PAC money, *but they should plan on getting none*. . . . PACs will usually ask for some evidence that a candidate can or is likely to win.

PACs will want information about a candidate and a campaign including committee name and address, the treasurer's name, distinct profile, voting history, primary date, opposition research, special interest group ratings, key personnel, budget, and endorsements. The campaign must give it to them.[15]

Soliciting PAC contributions is not so different from courting individual donors. A campaign begins with a list of potential PAC contributors. At the top of the list go any PAC contributors with whom the candidate or other campaign leaders have personal contact. If the national PAC has a local organization or affiliate, a candidate needs the endorsement of the local organization or its leaders to get a contribution from the national group. Thus a candidate should seek the local endorsement first, and the group will provide the campaign the name of the individual to contact at the national office. If a professional fund-raiser is hired, he should have a list of all PACs that might provide support.

A campaign assembles a special packet of materials for each PAC. (Some PACs have their own questionnaires to fill out.) The packet will include a personal letter on campaign stationary selling a candidacy from the PAC's point of view; appropriate campaign position papers and campaign literature; evidence that the candidate can win, such as positive public opinion polls or returns from earlier elections; and a list of similar organizations that have endorsed the candidate. Then the campaign follows up with a personal phone call or meeting with the PAC staff member(s) responsible for recommending what the PAC should do in this race.

Staff members from like-minded PACs meet with each other and frequently coordinate their contributions. Therefore, a key to success is to find at least one PAC staff member to endorse the candidate and sell his candidacy to the PACs solicited by the campaign. After a campaign has the endorsement from one or two PACs, getting endorsements and contributions from like-minded PACs will be much easier.

Our political system should be reformed to provide public campaign financing, set stricter limits on PAC contributions, and prevent incumbents from being automatically reelected because of campaign finance inequities. In the meantime, many candidates must turn to PACs for critical contributions needed to run viable campaigns. However, if candidates seek PAC contributions and are not incumbents, they should not plan on receiving any PAC funds until the checks are received. Plan to use these funds only for discretionary spending, such as buying extra radio or television ads. Do not depend on PACs for basic or necessary expenses. In short, court PACs if your campaign decides it needs their support, but do not count on them to save your campaign.

Political Party Committees

Himes also has useful advice regarding the role of political party committees in a fund-raising strategy:

> Before any party money is included in a finance plan, all of the appropriate party committees should be contacted and asked for their criteria for making contributions to a campaign and for participating in coordinated expenditures. Typically the primary factors considered in these decisions are potential for winning, quality of the campaign, the campaign plan, extent of local party support, and extent of other local support. *Most campaigns overestimate the support the party committees can give them.*[16]

You will not get party funds until you have won the party primary or party nomination. Most local candidates find that even then they are expected to contribute to pay for party literature and joint advertising campaigns. Party committee funds usually become available only to candidates running in districts critical to their party winning control of a house in the state legislature or Congress. Other campaigns most often go unfunded, although the general party effort to elect candidates to higher offices such as president, governor, and senator and to get party supporters to the polls might also serve in electing a candidate.

Receiving party contributions in cash or in-kind donations, such as paid staff members sent to your campaign, is great. However, most candidates find they have to raise the needed funds without much help from political party committees. Unless a firm commitment from the party is forthcoming, those funds cannot be factored into a campaign budget.

Some local organizations are hybrids of grassroots organizations and political parties. These groups, such as the Illinois 10th Congressional District Democrats from Chicago's northern suburbs or Democracy for America's local groups will generally donate money to a candidate who supports positions held by most of their members.

Financial Reports

It is no longer enough to raise the funds necessary to run a winning campaign. A campaign must also file detailed financial reports—often every few months or even daily for large contributions in the last days of the campaign. A campaign is responsible to guarantee that all contributions and expenditures are completely legal. In addition to all the ethical reasons for this reporting, there are practical reasons. Opponents will carefully scrutinize all financial reports. They can defeat a campaign if they are able to discredit it for failing to file a report on time or for accepting illegal or questionable contributions. In addition, there are heavy financial penalties, jail sentences, or forfeitures of election for violation of financial disclosure laws.

An entire section of the campaign must be established to produce these reports. The office manager or assistant office manager records every contribution and expenditure by using a special computer program geared to producing financial reports.[17] This makes printing and filing the final report forms relatively easy. Day-to-day accounts are kept in another computer program such as Quicken and then merged into the official reports. However, the computer programs do not determine if the contribution or expenditure is legal. That job rests with the office manager, the candidate, and the campaign treasurer, who signs the reports. This is another reason for recruiting a CPA as the campaign treasurer whose sole duty is ensuring that the laws are carefully obeyed and the reports are filed on time.

Candidates who have not run for office before often wait until they have raised and spent a lot of money before setting up the legal reporting system. This is a mistake. The reporting system should be in place as soon as a decision to run is made. The government provides plenty of forms and copies of the regulations for campaign financial disclosure on its website, but the campaign management must act to comply. Errors in raising or spending money (unlike some other areas of the campaign where mistakes are normal and expected) can cost the election.

Following Up

When people contribute money to a campaign, they must receive immediately (within the week) a personally signed thank-you letter from the candidate. For all but the largest contributions, a neatly printed letter is sufficient as long as the contributor's name is individually typed in the salutation. This letter should be carefully composed, updated every few weeks as new developments occur, and signed by the candidate individually, often adding a handwritten note to the donor. People thanked early in the campaign can be called upon to contribute again later. Fail to thank them, and they will not contribute to the campaign again or even to future participatory campaigns.

Supporters will want to know how the campaign is going after having been sent the original thank-you letter. It is best to write them at least once a month with a formal newsletter or solicitation letter. (A campaign newsletter can also be used in press packets, at news conferences as background material, at house parties, in letters to prospective financial contributors, and at other campaign events such as benefits.)

Of course, with blast e-mails, Facebook posts, and tweets, it is possible to send immediate notification of breaking news from the campaign. You can notify supporters that your candidate will be interviewed on television news or post a YouTube video produced by the campaign. You can let your supporters know that the campaign met important benchmarks such as the number of petition signatures filed to get on the ballot, the first $100,000 raised, registering hundreds of new voters in the district, and important endorsements from famous political figures or powerful organizations. A campaign can add to these posts that if supporters contribute more time and money, your candidate will be elected.

It is important, however, to send some special Internet communications just to financial contributors. They need to feel that they are insiders, that they have a special relationship with the candidate, and that their financial investment in the campaign is paying off. A campaign cannot expect a contribution of either time or money every time it contacts past contributors, but if they feel they are part of the campaign, they will help it win.

Big Money and Politics

The *Citizens United* and *McCutcheon* US Supreme Court decisions have opened the floodgates on big money in political campaigns. *McCutcheon* overturned the limits on the total amount individuals can contribute to campaigns. *Citizens United* overturned limitations on independent communications by corporations, associations, and unions such that corporations and labor unions may spend unlimited amounts to support or oppose political candidates through independent communications such as television advertisements. This is credited with the creation of superPACs. In the 2012 presidential election for example, gambling entrepreneur Sheldon Adelson gave approximately $15 million to support Newt Gingrich, and Forster Friess, a Wyoming financier, donated almost $2 million to Rick Santorum's superPAC. Karl Rove organized super-PACs that spent more than $300 million in support of Republicans during the 2012 elections.[18] On the Democratic side, George Soros donated $5.1 million to superPACs supporting Democratic candidates.[19] According to the Center for

Responsive Politics, at least $86 million in that election was attributed to donor groups in the networks of Charles and David Koch.[20]

These decisions have drastically affected twenty-first-century political campaigns. In the 2010 elections, after the *Citizens United* decision, superPACs spent more than $65 million to influence election outcomes.[21] Not only have the limits on spending by interest groups been eliminated but also PAC donors remain secret.

Similar trends are seen in more local races. In its study of fund-raising in six midwestern states in 2010, the Campaign Finance Institute found:

1. Big money dominated and small donors were small factors in most states. (In many states, large contributors dominated and small donors accounted for only 3 to 12 percent of the total raised.)
2. Public matching funds for small donors would radically change the source of campaign funds. (A matching fund system in which public funds matched the first $50 from every contributor on a five-to-one basis would bring all of the midwestern states up to Minnesota's 57 percent funding from small donors of $250 or less.)[22]

Clearly participatory campaigns depend primarily on many smaller contributors rather than a few wealthy donors or interest groups. Therefore, public funding of campaigns is a goal to be desired. However, for the time being, campaigns are going to be fought in the political and legal environment that exists. Campaigns will have to raise money from both major and small donors.

Big money in campaigns is a real threat to our democracy, but the only way to overcome that is to elect public officials who favor public funding, full disclosure of all campaign contributions, and reasonable limits on large contributions to the extent possible under the law. President Obama's campaigns and many more local ones have shown that it is possible to raise a lot of money from small contributors, but it requires that candidates and their campaigns properly and creatively prioritize fund-raising from both major and small donors.

Chapter Five

Sending Your Message

....

A campaign could craft an outstanding image for your candidate, develop a great contrast to opponents, define campaign issues brilliantly, and still lose. Conversely, a campaign could have a mediocre image, blurred distinctions, a poor definition of the issues, and win. The determining factor is often the ability to project a candidate's image, campaign theme, and issues to the voter. Your campaign message means nothing if the voters never get it.

The most obvious way to get your message to voters is to have your candidate go out and meet them. A memorable scene from the film *Blaze*, in which Paul Newman portrays Earl Long of Louisiana, focuses on handshaking campaign stops. Governor Long, with a police motorcade leading the way, stops at every country store along highways in Louisiana greeting the voters and reminding them to vote for him. Other books and films such as *The Last Hurrah* also portray old party bosses making the rounds of wakes and marching in torchlight parades.

The film *Game Change* shows a different kind of campaign in which Sarah Palin, the new Republican vice-presidential candidate, struggles to cope with "handlers" who make all the campaign stops, television appearances, and interviews possible. Although she is good at shaking hands and firing up the crowds, she falls apart under tough questioning by good interviewers on television.

Today's campaigns require candidates to do both individual voter contact and television interviews. The television footage we see during presidential campaigns shows candidates also addressing campaign rallies. Although candidates do not do whistle-stop train tours anymore, they take bus caravans across the country. We see mayors and members of Congress leading St. Patrick's Day parades or speaking at the annual conventions of organizations. Our common perception is partially true, that campaigning is about meeting the voters, shaking their hands, being seen in parades, and speaking at large rallies.

The public expects this part of a campaign, so campaigns have to plan for it. Even if average voters never meet a candidate in person, they need to see through the mass media and YouTube clips that she is out asking for the votes of people like them.

Personal Appearances by the Candidate

In this modern era of mass and social media as well as targeted direct mail and automated phone calling (or robo-calling), a candidate still has to make personal appearances to be elected. A candidate running for the first time or as an underdog will definitely need to make many such appearances. She not only needs to be seen by as many of the voters as possible but also needs to meet and talk directly with them to learn more about the people she seeks to represent. Any candidate needs to learn about voters in ways that public opinion polls and statistical analyses of voter registration data cannot teach her. Voter contact will provide information about particular local problems that matter to voters in different sections of her district. These issues may differ from those the office she seeks has the authority to resolve, but this direct knowledge will make her a much better representative of the voters.

As in the movies, it is important that voters see the candidate in a positive light throughout the campaign. They *and the press* have expectations as to how successful candidates look and act. Any successful candidate must meet those expectations.

What a candidate wears is nearly always important. Unless there is a special reason for casual dress, a male candidate in public will always be dressed in a suit and tie. Women's attire is similarly formal. A male candidate may take off his coat, throw it over his shoulder, roll up his sleeves, or loosen his tie, but he will still be formally dressed. Successful male candidates are usually clean shaven, although some wear a mustache if that is their style. Candidates with beards should shave them off before running for office.

Except in the dead of winter, candidates generally do not wear hats because hats always convey strong impressions to voters, often the wrong ones. They can easily make a candidate look foolish, and news photographers and television camera people love to capture colorful pictures that can convey unwanted images. Candidates are wise to avoid hats.

For female candidates the style challenges are more formidable. "The importance of clothes cannot be underestimated. For women in power, finding the right balance in the wardrobe is difficult but imperative. . . . Whether one chooses a conservative-looking dress, suit, or pantsuit, one can still look feminine with the choice of color and accessories."[1] In addition to a suitable conservative wardrobe, a woman candidate has to consider hair, makeup, jewelry, and shoes.[2]

Unless a candidate is a businessperson or lawyer who has to be formally dressed in her work life, running for office will usually require a shopping trip to buy a more appropriate wardrobe. A candidate running for a higher office may need to obtain the advice of a style consultant on exactly what to purchase. The consultant will usually cost less than $1,000 and will have useful and surprising suggestions on how to improve a candidate's image. For lower offices, the clean, formal look, carefully scrutinized by your campaign manager and public relations coordinator, will be sufficient. A speech coach may also be necessary to improve public presentations and to prepare for television interviews or debates. A candidate seeing herself on a videotape during a practice speech or mock debate can correct image problems she did not know existed.

Dress is one of the least difficult problems regarding candidate appearances. Potentially more problematic is the candidate's entourage. A candidate *never* appears alone at a public function—whether gathering petition signatures at a grocery store, shaking hands at a public transportation stop, attending a community meeting, or speaking at a political event. To project the image of a successful candidate, there must be accompanying supporters, even if this entourage consists of only one other person. In most campaigns volunteer drivers also appear as supporters at campaign stops. To draw even more attention to a candidate, a news crew with a television camera will do the trick. If this is not a press event, a campaign volunteer with a video camera that looks professional will also attract attention and can record footage the campaign can post on YouTube and its website.

Drivers are among the easiest campaign volunteers to recruit. The job seems glamorous. They get to go with the candidate everywhere: press conferences, television stations, and major political rallies. However, few people can serve as the candidate's full-time driver. Usually, campaigns recruit a different driver for every evening and for weekend days when there are campaign events. Other drivers are recruited for specific functions such as early morning appearances at public transportation stops. Frequently, two or more drivers will be needed to cover all the stops on a busy campaign day.

If your candidate has a driver, it is easy to add supporters as needed. If she is going to an editorial interview, her public relations coordinator or press secretary goes with her. If she is going to a debate at a community organization, her supporters from that community are in the audience as well as the driver and staff members who accompany her. If she is attending a coffee, she is taken by the driver and met by the chair and hosts. When she marches in a parade, she joins a particular float or group that has agreed to let her campaign signs be carried in its section of the parade. At other events, her family will join her. A candidate in public is never alone but always accompanied by supporters who, by their presence, guarantee that this is a genuine campaign.

For instance, if a candidate is gathering petition signatures at a grocery store, she should have three or four supporters with her. Usually, there are at least two separate doors to the store to be covered. The candidate can stand with a volunteer at one door, and the other two volunteers can go to the second door. As each potential voter comes by, the candidate shakes his or her hand, introduces herself, offers the voter a piece of campaign literature, and asks him or her to sign the petition her volunteer has on a clipboard. Volunteers at the second door point to the candidate and ask the voters if they would like to meet her as well as sign the petition. The image created by having several campaign volunteers with your candidate is that this is a strong campaign for an accessible candidate out meeting the voters. By the way, political lore holds that anyone who shakes a candidate's hand will vote for her unless he or she is dissuaded by later information from the other side. Handshakes add up to names on your petition and votes for your candidate on Election Day.

Buying Voter Access

Candidates with lots of money have an advantage in sending their messages. They buy their way into the voters' living rooms. They can afford radio and television commercials along with fancy Internet ads and a fully developed social media campaign. For a few hundred thousand dollars, any campaign can buy enough airtime to guarantee voters will know the candidate's name, have a positive image, and be given strong reasons to vote for her. If money is spent to hire professionals to conduct polls, run focus groups, and then to write and produce media ads and develop a professional website, direct mail campaign, and social media effort, a powerful message can be sent to voters. These paid media efforts do not guarantee that wealthy candidates always win, but money makes sending their messages much easier.

Dozens of books and documentaries have warned of the dangers of Madison Avenue, "synthetic" campaigns.[3] The dangers of selling the false persona of a candidate are well known and understood. There is, however, another way in which money spent on high-tech campaigns can buy access to voters.[4]

Targeted, "narrowcast" campaign messages by direct mail, cable TV, or the Internet to selected groups of voters can be just as effective and just as dangerous to democracy as mass media campaigns.

We will explore these "high-tech" campaigns in greater depth for three reasons: (1) many of these techniques can be adapted to modern participatory campaigns, especially because the technologies have become much cheaper; (2) an opponent may use these techniques against your candidate, so they must be countered; and (3) there are new potentials and threats to our democracy in these techniques.

What are these targeted strategies of persuasion? Gary Selnow in *High-Tech Campaigns* explains: "Targeting begins with the assembly of audience information—through polls and databases—and continues with data analyses that determine targetable clusters—those groups of people sufficiently like-minded that they will respond similarly to the same message."[5]

In other words, targeted communications assemble information about the voters in ways we discuss in Chapter 7 such as analytics, microtargeting, and nanotargeting. Available information has only increased as software companies package more information on each voter and merge that information with demographic data and data on consumer purchases. Campaign strategists use this detailed information to target subgroups of the electorate such as women, senior citizens, the wealthy, or Hispanics. They select voters with specific characteristics, add polling data or voter contact data to what is known about such voters, and then tailor a special campaign message with appeal to members of that subgroup. They then send a selected message to these specific voters directly through mail appeals, phone calls, e-mails, or narrowcast media directed at selected audiences. With analytics or the analysis of large datasets of information about voters, it is possible to "personalize" the communications to groups of voters with common interests within the district such as gun owners, senior citizens on Medicare, or unemployed voters.

These narrowcast (as opposed to broadcast) media include cable television, radio talk shows, Internet discussion groups, targeted e-mails, Facebook posts, and tweets.

> [Public opinion] surveys tell you about population subgroups: how they think, how they behave, how they can be moved. Database analyses give you the members of these subgroups, separating them one from the other, allowing you to reach them one at a time or in small clusters. . . . This is the heart of communication targeting: the identification of audience segments and the exposition of the issues that relate to each.[6]

These techniques are even worse than party precinct captains in the old days who promised Mr. Smith a government job, Mrs. Jones a government favor, and Mr. Sullivan Irish candidates. The new technologies allow campaigns to divide voters more efficiently into small groups, promise them limited actions on specific issues, and play to their prejudices rather than fashion a common agenda that a majority of citizens supports. Voters may be deceived into believing that the campaign letter, e-mail, or phone call addressing them individually is a personal communication they can trust.

These targeted communications produce what Selnow calls *displacement*, which "occurs when the use of narrow channels, with special messages to special audiences, displaces communications on mass channels, with general messages to general audiences. People expect public officials to communicate with them. They once anticipated face-to-face contact, as in the ward-and-precinct system . . . people still expect some contact with the leaders who represent them, spend their money, and run their government."[7] Targeted communications give the illusion of meaningful contact between voters and candidates. It is easy to use this form of communication to deceive voters into believing that their concerns have been responded to when, in fact, critical issues of government, candidate qualifications, and democratic discussion have been skillfully avoided.

Direct Mail and Phone Campaigns

A campaign can now purchase a relatively inexpensive mailing list of all registered voters in a district, their addresses, and their voting histories. Enriching this computer listing with voters' phone numbers and demographic data is a straightforward process with a variety of data management packages such as VoteBuilder. With these lists a campaign is ready to mail material to voters, call them on the phone, and prepare walk sheets for volunteers to go to their doors. If a campaign has sufficient funds, it can hire a public relations firm to write its message and direct mail companies to print, sort, and mail its communications. Telemarketing firms can call voters. If a campaign has even more money, it can use public opinion polls to make its message more effective. Various campaign themes and images can be tested with a sample of the voters or focus groups until just the right image or issue has been found to convince voters to vote for a candidate.

Most modern participatory campaigns do not have the money to undertake a completely high-tech campaign of this sort. For instance, the most expensive and effective direct mail campaigns, which ensure a message moves voters, often include from seven to nine different letters or oversized postcards sent to every voter in the district. These mailings are also targeted to subgroups with special issues. In direct mail campaigns, the first three or so pieces introduce the candidate, her family and background, and her qualifications in order to establish name recognition and a positive candidate image.

The next mailings often vilify an opponent and are not identified as coming from the campaign other than the minimal disclosure required by law. Direct mail can produce particularly virulent and hard-to-answer negative allegations in the weeks just before the election. The last several pieces of mail let a candidate push a single issue, list key endorsements such as newspaper endorsements, and give voters a final reason to elect her.

Like costly mass media campaigns, multiple mailings to a large district cost as much as several hundred thousand dollars. They are often reinforced with phone calls reiterating the campaign's message to voters.

AUTOMATED PHONE CAMPAIGNS

According to Mac Hansbrough of the political consulting firm NTS, in the new millennium, the number of phone calls made in state and local campaigns by professional telephone (phone bank) firms has increased exponentially.[8] Both the number of calls made professionally and the number of campaigns doing such calls have increased. The cost of making the calls has steadily decreased because of competition among phone companies, while simultaneously computer-assisted dialing has become available to local and regional political phoning firms. Finally, the increasing availability of personal computers allows electronic voter files, scripts, and instructions to be moved with ease among campaigns, political phone vendors, and call centers. Most of all, updated voter files from political data firms targeting voters in specific districts make this easier and cheaper. Thus, there has been a dramatic increase in the number of phoning vendors and in the number of campaign-related phone calls each voter receives.

It is now commonplace for a phone vendor to get an order from a campaign in the morning, have the necessary voter file by the afternoon, and be calling voters from that file in the evening. Computers and the Internet have made all this possible.

Automated calling, also known as robo-calling, began in earnest in the mid-2000s. Candidates and their supporters can now make and distribute brief recordings cheaply, quickly, and easily because of the advent of computer dialing. Messages are recorded on lines provided by the political phoning firms. The phone vendor then sends out the recorded message to the target database of phone numbers. Using this technology, it is easy for a campaign to reach from 10,000 to 1 million voters in a single day.

New problems have developed with both public opinion polling and robocalling, making public opinion polls much less reliable and automated calling less effective. This is part of a larger problem facing pollsters today; public opinion may be harder to measure in the digital age.[9] Both technological and social shifts have made it more difficult to reach potential voters to get their opinions, convince them to vote for particular candidates, and deliver campaign messages: "The problem stems from a number of causes but begins with a fundamental shift in the public's relationship with the telephone. For decades the vast majority had landlines that they answered faithfully, and when asked to take part in surveys, mostly did so."[10]

More people now have mobile phones, and automated calling for either public opinion surveys or political persuasion on mobile phones is illegal. Moreover, those called on mobile phones are less willing to answer questions for either pollsters or campaigns.

The situation has deteriorated so much that many of the polls of the 2012 election were inaccurate, and many incorrectly predicted Romney as the winner. Because of this, one of the oldest and most respected polling firms, Gallup, decided not to do public opinion polling to attempt to predict primary winners in the 2016 election.[11] Despite these additional problems, public opinion polling and phone canvassing will still be used by campaigns until better alternatives are perfected.

ADAPTING MAIL AND PHONE TECHNIQUES

Modern participatory campaigns also make use of direct mail and phone campaigns. However, in contrast to synthetic campaigns, they make much greater use of volunteers and avoid the worst forms of negative campaigning. For instance, a more participatory campaign might decide to concentrate on only three literature blitzes and direct mail pieces. The literature drop is done by volunteers going door to door dropping campaign pieces at homes throughout the district. The first piece might be a general campaign brochure introducing the candidate or even a campaign newsletter on newsprint. The second piece is usually mailed before the voter registration deadline, and the third is timed to arrive during the last weeks of the campaign but before early voting begins. More often, rather than simply having volunteers deliver these campaign materials door to door, volunteers will do mailings. If a professional mailing firm does the mailing instead, voter lists provided by the campaign's computer operation significantly lessen the costs involved.

5.1. CAMPAIGN TELEPHONE SCRIPT

A particularly effective approach is to use a part of the script for several alternative issues. Since you should know precisely where you are calling, you can use this part of the script to cover your candidate's activities or positions of particular interest to people in that area. If you are not aware of such issues, you may hear about them from the voters themselves. You should find out your candidate's position on such issues and use that in future phone calls. Most importantly, you should let the phone bank coordinator know about the issues so that they can be addressed generally in the campaign.

Hello, I'm_____ a (neighbor, friend of _____) and/or a volunteer for_____ who is running for _____ in your (political district). I'm supporting him/her because his/her stands on (issues) are important for our area and the (city, state, country). (CANDIDATE'S NAME)'s background in _____ and educational credentials (state here) make him/her uniquely qualified for this office. Have you heard of (CANDIDATE'S NAME)'s campaign? Do you have any questions about the candidate or the campaign?

If the voter has heard of the campaign and has no questions, you should ask "May we count on your support on [_____(Election Day)]?" If the voter has not heard of the campaign or is un-

Phone canvasses and get-out-the-vote (GOTV) efforts can also be accomplished from campaign headquarters by volunteers but only if the campaign has purchased the right voter data and added to it their own door-to-door efforts. Figure 5.1 gives an example of the type of simple telephone script volunteers can use to supplement the canvass by calling from the campaign headquarters, call center, or on their own cell phones coordinated by e-mail. A similar script can be developed to encourage "plus" voters who favor the candidate to get to the polls to vote early or on Election Day. A telephone canvass is not as effective as a volunteer on the doorstep, but it is the next best thing.

Participatory campaigns that successfully recruit volunteers and get good coverage in the mass media can match the paid targeted communications of wealthier opponents, especially if a candidate has charisma, the issues are strong enough to recruit both volunteers and voters, and the race is important enough to matter to the press, potential volunteers, and voters. The strategic tasks of the campaign staff are to decide on the proper mix of paid and volunteer efforts to get out a campaign's message and make sure that sufficient funds are raised to pay for these efforts.

COMMUNICATIONS FROM NEIGHBORS

A personal letter from neighbors can be as effective with voters as supporters wearing buttons or putting campaign posters in their windows or yards (see Figure 5.2). If supporters in a particular neighborhood or important community leaders have endorsed a candidate, they can be encouraged to send "friend of a friend" letters, Facebook posts, e-mails, tweets, or postcards. However, to have any real impact this must be a systematic, well-organized campaign project. A campaign designs a model letter and provides a list, e-mail addresses, or computer labels of several hundred neighbors who are voters. Supporters then sign them, put on a stamp, and mail them, or they send an e-mail with the message the campaign has designed. They can also "like" the campaign on Facebook or retweet campaign messages. These various "friend of a friend" communications can be sent early in the campaign to build support or sent later to arrive during the last few weeks before the election as a final argument presented to voters before Election Day.

The Precinct Work Alternative

Staffing a field operation with leaders and trained workers able to carry out a petition drive, registration campaign, mail and early voting effort, and door-to-door voter canvassing is still the secret of winning most elections. As detailed in Chapter 7, social media is playing an ever more important role in campaigning. However, precinct work still provides a personal and relatively inexpensive way to reach voters, register them, and get them to the polls on Election Day. It must not be overlooked. Success with this form of campaigning requires volunteers, good leaders, and a clear structure for the field operation.

After a precinct structure for your field operation has been established, the petition drive allows its efficiency to be tested. Then the registration drive allows a campaign to enlarge the constituency of voters likely to be favorably disposed toward a candidate. A final canvass allows favorable voters to be found and brought to the polls on Election Day. This canvass is now being done earlier than in the past because of the easier absentee voting in many states and more early voting opportunities.

sure about supporting your candidate, ask if you may send information about the candidate. If the voter agrees, be sure to indicate this on your worksheet.

Rate the voter "+," "–," or "0" just as you would in a face-to-face situation, and enter this on the form or poll sheet from which you are working. If you find an enthusiastic "plus" voter, ask if someone from the campaign may contact him/her about participating in the campaign. If the voter agrees, be sure to tell the phone bank coordinator.

Source: Independent Voters of Illinois, "IVI-IPO 2010 A–Z Campaign Training Manual," 13.

5.2. LETTER TO RECRUIT CAMPAIGN SUPPORT

Dear_____,

Hello. I'm your neighbor, Barbara Jones, from down the street. I'm writing everyone on the block to ask them to vote for Dick Simpson in the March 15 primary. Dick is running for Congress against Dan Rostenkowski.

First, let me say what a joy it is to live here, in one of Chicago's great neighborhoods. Chicago is built around neighborhoods, and, unlike a lot of big cities, Chicago manages to have a "small town" feel to it.

Of course, we still have big city problems. I'm more than a little anxious about crime, schools, and the loss of jobs in Chicago. What angers me is that while our city is exploding with crime and poverty some Congress members are devoting their efforts to lining their own pockets. Dan Rostenkowski ought to start a Scandal-of-the-Month Club.

A lot of people think Rosty brings tax dollars into the state. It's a myth, though. Illinois ranks forty-sixth out of the fifty states in federal dollars returned to the state. They say our Congressman is one of the most powerful men in Washington. Powerful for whom? Insurance companies? Sure. Rich developers? You bet. Drug companies? Absolutely. You and me? No. If he was looking out for us, he would have saved the Stewart Warner Plant. If he cared about the district, we wouldn't

In 2006, 24,811 Chicago voters cast early, in-person ballots. That number tripled to 85,604 in 2010, and the suburban Cook County, Illinois, voting by mail early voting in 2014 accounted for more than 26 percent of the votes cast.

Fairly soon, more states may allow mail-in ballots, same-day registration at the polls, and e-mail voting, which means that canvassing has to begin at least a month before Election Day rather than in the last two weeks as had been the practice in many previous elections. As the election rules and practices change, the campaign timetable will have to be adjusted, but the four steps of petition drive, registration drive, canvass, and GOTV on Election Day are likely to remain the building blocks of successful door-to-door campaigns that win elections voter by voter.

Precinct work wins or loses participatory campaigns. You can have the best candidate, good publicity, lots of money, and successful campaign events, but if you lack the workers to go door to door informing and convincing voters, a campaign is doomed from the beginning. A strong precinct effort can overcome campaign problems such as having less money than an opponent or limited coverage in the mass media.

Precinct work provides the most direct and effective contact with voters. It gives neighbors a chance to talk with each other about the kind of men and women who should represent them. Translating campaign issues so that each voter can understand what the election really means to her and her community forces precinct workers to bridge the gap between rhetoric and reality and wins elections by reestablishing trust and human communication. Precinct work not only allows campaign volunteers to participate effectively but also prepares voters for meaningful participation on Election Day.

Precinct work is so essential and the task so mammoth that it can be accomplished only by a highly structured organization in which each worker knows her tasks, does them well, and accurately reports her results. The success of the entire effort depends on the precinct coordinator who heads it. A precinct coordinator, like the candidate, must give hundreds of hours to the campaign, including most evenings and weekends for three or four months. A good precinct coordinator also should be smart, efficient, and aggressive enough to get volunteers to do the hard door-to-door canvassing as well as hard working enough to set an example for other campaign workers. She must also be open enough to communicate effectively with workers and to encourage constructive responses and suggestions. Last of all, a precinct coordinator must have prior campaign experience, at least as a precinct worker. Locating favorable voters and getting them to the polls is the secret of success, and a good coordinator understands this.

Because the precinct coordinator cannot supervise hundreds of precinct workers personally, ward coordinators and area chairs are also needed. The responsibility for recruiting and coordinating precinct workers rests directly with these campaign leaders. Ward coordinators and area chairs must possess many of the same qualities as the precinct coordinator. Finding enough good leaders to staff these critical middle levels of the campaign is not easy. Sometimes precinct workers from prior campaigns can be promoted, but some outstanding precinct captains make bad area chairs because the two jobs require considerably different skills. A precinct worker goes personally to each voter. Campaign coordinators, such as area chairs and ward coordinators,

have lost 25,000 jobs in the past decade. If he was concerned at all, he would appear in public and listen to our concerns.

Dick Simpson is both a neighbor and a friend. He is running for Congress in the March 15 primary. I have known Dick since he was an alderman, and I can tell you from personal experience that Dick Simpson is a man of great integrity, intelligence, and compassion. His political involvement is long and distinguished.

I know you're busy, and I won't take time to list all the things Dick Simpson has done and all he plans to do. I'll let his campaign people send along that information. But I do want to personally urge you to take this letter along when you vote in the primary on March 15. Remember the name Dick Simpson. We have a neighbor who cares about our future. Help send him to Washington in the next election.

With warm regards,

spend their time on the phone or e-mail convincing other people to work, giving instructions, and receiving reports.

If experienced campaigners are not available or would be better as precinct workers, then inexperienced volunteers will have to be appointed as ward coordinators and area chairs. Some people are natural organizers or have professions such as that of salesperson or business executive that may suit them to the task. However, there is always a risk in making someone a leader. Campaign staff must constantly check coordinator reports and check with the people they coordinate to make sure ward coordinators and area chairs do their jobs properly.

After volunteers have been found to serve in these critical middle management positions, they become part of the decisionmaking process. Weekly leadership meetings focus on the precinct progress reports of area chairs, their suggestions for changes in strategy, and their reactions to proposals by other campaign leaders. The candidate should personally attend the weekly leadership meetings for at least half an hour. Staying for the entire meeting would inhibit discussion and keep her from meeting with potential voters and workers. However, the candidate should report on the state of the campaign to the campaign leadership and receive suggestions from them every week. In addition to leadership meetings (unmatched for developing loyalty, enthusiasm, and full discussion of the campaign), frequent e-mails should be sent to all campaign leaders detailing accomplishments, the goals of the next leadership meeting, and instructions on the next phase of the campaign. Frequent communications should also be sent to all campaign workers, particularly precinct workers. Many campaigns post updated information on their campaign website frequently but send targeted e-mails just to precinct workers and other campaign volunteers.

A good precinct structure for your field operations is much more than a chart at campaign headquarters. A large group of people must work together and constantly talk about their work. The personalities, personal concerns, enthusiasm, and loyalty of the leaders and workers can be more critically important to election results than abstract descriptions of roles they are supposed to play. Any successful structure must be flexible enough to take advantage of the unique abilities of its members, and their involvement must be fostered at every opportunity.

Locating hundreds of precinct workers to fill out the precinct structure might be difficult. The existence of permanent independent organizations, political parties, interest groups such as labor unions, and a history of prior participatory campaigns in a district makes a significant difference. These organizations and prior campaigns can be a major source of experienced precinct workers.

New volunteers must also be recruited, but beginning with many of your precincts already covered makes it possible to concentrate on weak spots. To recruit enough workers, meetings must be held, hundreds of house parties scheduled, and every potential worker whose name is given to the campaign must be called. No campaign begins and few campaigns end with enough volunteers. Ideally, three or more workers should cover every precinct in the district. (Precincts differ in size in different states. In Chicago they consist of about 350 voters and range from a single high-rise building to three or four blocks of single-family homes. Rural precincts cover a much larger area and include fewer voters.) Whatever the size of precincts, not even the best-run campaigns achieve perfect precinct coverage, but the more precincts worked, the more votes obtained by the campaign.

Political campaigns always face the reality of scarce resources: too few volunteers, too little money, and not enough time. Recruiting campaign volunteers has become much more difficult in recent years. Everyone now has a full-time job or a couple of part-time jobs, and those jobs are much more competitive and demanding. Many people also take on extra work to earn enough income to support their families. The Great Recession that began in 2008 only made people more anxious about keeping their jobs.

In addition, the public has become more alienated from the political process and less certain of the benefits of working for political candidates. Peoples' lives have become more fast-paced, social media has become more consuming, and information overload turns people off. Because of these and other trends, recruiting enough volunteers requires time and effort.

Because there are never enough precinct workers to cover all precincts completely, decisions must be made about the most effective apportionment of all campaign resources. One choice is to depend on direct mail, mass media ads, social media campaigns, and phone canvassing that can be purchased from campaign consulting firms. However, most campaigns will also do fieldwork.

There are three competing principles in mounting a precinct effort:

1. Cover the maximum number of precincts possible.
2. Completely cover the precincts with the greatest potential vote for a candidate. (It is best to go hunting where the ducks are.)
3. Based on analytics, use voting data to select the voters to be contacted in the precincts and the pitches to be made to them.

None of these three principles can be ignored without jeopardizing victory, but there are almost never enough volunteers to reach all the potential voters who would vote for a candidate. Never is there perfect information to predict exactly which voters would support a candidate, so precinct coordinators do the best they can to balance all three imperatives.

Usually, covering every precinct is not possible because you do not have the volunteers to do the job. However, the other strategic choice can backfire as well. Robert Friedlander, a white, Republican candidate for state senate in Illinois, wrote off thirty-eight precincts in a poor African American neighborhood. The Friedlander campaign concentrated instead on Republican and potentially independent precincts. His opponent won by 30,000 to 27,000 votes. Some of the precincts he failed to work voted against him by ratios as great as 400 to 10. Although many Republicans and independents in other parts of the district voted for him, they did not turn out in the hoped-for numbers, and the racial and ethnic Democratic vote killed his chances of victory. If he had not given away all the votes in those thirty-eight precincts, he might have won.

Precinct worker placement must strike a balance between the principles of covering all voters versus targeting the most likely precincts and voters for contact. Every precinct in the district should be covered in some way to win at least some of the votes and to reverse the proportion by which the weakest precincts are lost. In addition, a campaign's strongest precincts have to be worked well to obtain as many votes as possible from them. That means in practice covering weak precincts thinly and concentrating volunteers on the campaign's best precincts. As an added complication, people will often only volunteer to work the precinct where they live, so most volunteers must be left in their own precincts, and only the best workers will "carpetbag" in precincts where they are most needed.

As we discuss in Chapter 7, using sophisticated data management systems can help target the individuals most likely to be persuaded to vote for a candidate. Analytics can help locate possible supporters in precincts that overwhelming favor an opponent, and avoiding them can let volunteers skip contacting voters in the strongest precincts likely to vote for other candidates and concentrate on precincts most likely to have supportive voters. However, even with the most sophisticated targeting, there are thousands of potential supporters who must still be contacted and actually vote. There are also undecided voters who must be persuaded to support a candidate.

An important pool of volunteer workers is college and high school students. Sometimes students may serve as interns receiving course credit for their work; other times they simply become campaign volunteers. In well-financed campaigns, they are often paid, but in most campaigns they are not. In Simpson's congressional campaign, he recruited about thirty college students and a dozen high school students invaluable in helping staff his campaign and in getting his message to the voters.

It is important that high school students, and even young college students, are trained properly. In the bad old days, often party workers (untrained themselves) would send teenagers out to pull up the opponents' yard signs or commit other acts of vandalism. This is illegal and not to be tolerated. It is vital that young volunteers are given the same training as the adult volunteers. In addition, the campaign should remind them to dress neatly and act professionally. They are representing the candidate. It is a good idea to send them door to door with a community volunteer to show them the ropes and have no more than two high school students go together. If they are not properly trained, it is possible they can give the campaign a bad name. If they are trained well, they will impress the people with whom they interact, benefiting the candidate.

In the Will Guzzardi campaign for state legislature in 2014, his staff was able to recruit many students to help canvass the precincts. Several student interns worked more than ten hours a week coordinating different campaign efforts. The hard work of these students helped to make his victory possible.

Students often work more hours with more energy and enthusiasm than other volunteers. The best use of these student volunteers is to (1) make them assistant staff members with major campaign responsibilities, (2) supplement an existing precinct organization with individual students assigned to beef up precincts short on volunteers, (3) send teams of students to marginal precincts where the vote potential is strongest but organization is the weakest, and (4) assign them to critical operations such as phone bank coordinators and callers.[12] If students canvass for votes in weaker precincts, they can, while they are canvassing, search for potential workers who can build up an indigenous leadership in each precinct to take over the task of campaigning. Then they can move on to help develop new precincts.

A field operation requires careful records. Even though computerization can help, organization is still labor intensive. At the beginning of the campaign, lists of potential workers are obtained from political organizations and from previous political campaigns in the district. These lists are transferred to a "potential worker" computer file with names, addresses, phone numbers, ward numbers, area letters (areas are lettered A–Z to avoid confusion with wards and precincts), and precinct numbers. This information provides the beginning of a comprehensive campaign volunteer file kept at the headquarters. A printed list of potential precinct workers by area is given to area chairs. Each

5.3. THIRTEEN STEPS IN A PARTICIPATORY CAMPAIGN

1. Bringing together a citizens' search committee and locating a good candidate
2. Preparing a voter profile based on census data, prior election figures, and public opinion polls; choosing the "target number" of votes needed to win the election, on which all future strategies will be based
3. Deciding upon a campaign theme and candidate image, creating the campaign structure, and selecting key campaign staff members and volunteer leaders; doing opposition research on both your candidate and his opponent
4. Announcing candidacy and releasing first publicity; preparing press packets and holding the announcement news conference
5. Beginning events and direct contact with potential donors by the candidate to raise funds and recruit volunteers; beginning issue petition drives or other activities if this is to be a long campaign
6. Opening headquarters, hiring fulltime staff, selecting and purchasing the necessary software packages and voter data management systems such as VoteBuilder or rVotes, printing buttons and first campaign literature, creating the campaign website
7. Collecting petition signatures to put candidate on

area chair gives the appropriate list of potential workers to each precinct captain. When potential workers officially become precinct workers, their information is entered into the comprehensive campaign volunteer file so that other campaign workers do not call them in search of volunteers to help with their projects.

After the initial precinct workers are recruited, additional volunteers sign up at events or send in pledge cards from mailings, e-mails, and the campaign website. The pool of potential workers is also enlarged by the recruiting efforts of area chairs and precinct workers. By the end of the campaign, the comprehensive file may number several thousand workers, potential workers, contributors, and supporters.

In addition to the volunteer file, the precinct coordinator, ward coordinators, and area chairs keep their own records and computerized spreadsheets, including names of precinct workers and reports for each precinct showing the results at each stage of the campaign, from the petition drive to the vote count.

In better-funded campaigns a software package such as VoteBuilder, rVotes, or Data Vault is used to keep track of all of the information. However, it does not solve the problem of carefully inputting all the necessary information and keeping the files up to date.

It is important to remember that precinct workers are the front-line warriors of a campaign. They go door to door convincing neighbors to support a candidate by signing her nominating petitions, registering to vote, and electing her on Election Day. Ideally, they should be personable and well dressed as the personal representatives of the candidate. They should be absolutely reliable and willing to work hard. Although a participatory campaign inevitably finds a use for nearly everyone who volunteers, potential precinct workers are carefully screened to ensure that they will represent the campaign well in the precincts.

THE PETITION DRIVE

As Figure 5.3 shows, there are many steps to a campaign, but the petition drive begins the precinct effort. The nominating petition drive necessary to meet the _legal requirements_ to get a candidate on the ballot is not difficult. Nonetheless, many candidates fail to get on the ballot or waste this opportunity to gain other benefits from the petition effort. Candidates are frequently thrown off the ballot for failing to meet a residency requirement, failing to have a change of voting address properly recorded, technical errors on their petitions and statement of candidacy, and, most often, failing to get enough legal signatures. No errors can be allowed if a candidate is to get on the ballot successfully. However, the petition drive does more than meet legal requirements. It builds the necessary support to mobilize at this early stage in order to build a winning campaign.

After a citizens' search committee or political organization has decided on the best candidate, petitions must be printed. If 500 signatures are needed to get on the ballot, at least 1,000–2,000 signatures should be collected. Not every worker who takes a petition gets it signed. Many workers get only ten signatures. Some petitions get lost, so a good supply of petitions should be printed to begin, and more should be printed whenever necessary.

The petition drive is important. You need the _maximum_ number of signatures that can be filed, because signatures gathered by volunteers can always be challenged on technicalities such

ballot and influencing other groups' (including political parties') endorsements; putting out campaign literature through literature drops, direct mail, leafleting, campaign website, email, and social media; collecting email lists of supporters and potential supporters

8. Planning and holding rallies, benefits, special events, and training sessions for workers, sending final campaign literature to the printer, developing registration and early voting campaigns

9. Canvassing to register voters, sending at least three direct mail letters/brochures (as many as nine or more mailings are used in some hotly contested larger races), using micro- and nanotargeting and email communications to voters not canvassed in person

10. Increasing number of events, candidate appearances; intensifying mass media and social media exposure

11. Canvassing to locate voters favorable to the candidate, stuffing mailboxes, and leafleting at supermarkets and bus stops; sending final direct mail and supplementing precinct work with phone canvassing; intensifying social media campaign

12. Scheduling and training Election Day workers

13. Election Day: leafleting voters on the way to the polls, ensuring that voters favorable to your candidate remember to vote, and poll watching

as voters who did not sign their names the same way they registered or who did not fully spell out their street addresses.

More importantly, *signatures provide names of potential supporters.* The degree of success in obtaining petition signatures is also an excellent test of the fitness of a field organization. A precinct worker who turns in twenty-five to a hundred signatures on her petition is obviously doing the job of contacting neighbors. A precinct worker who gives only excuses should be replaced. An area with few petition signatures needs special attention, such as appearances by the candidate, events in the area, direct mail, or a phone canvass to find precinct volunteers and build voter support. There is no such thing as too many signatures, although if there is a maximum legal limit not all the signatures will be filed officially. They still provide a list of supportive voters, potential contributors, and volunteers from which to build a strong, winning campaign.

The materials provided for a petition drive are minimal. Each worker should have instructions telling her who can pass petitions, who can sign petitions, when and where the petitions must be turned in, and when reports are expected. A worker will also need simple campaign brochures with basic information about the candidate to distribute to the voters. The worker should also have a poll list or a computer-generated walk sheet provided by the campaign with the names of every registered voter in the precinct.

In many places poll lists of all registered voters may be obtained free at the board of election commissioners or at city hall. Many campaigns choose instead to purchase a computerized list of all voters from any number of commercial providers or data management systems. Campaigns can then print out walk sheets for each precinct as needed. Because the petition drive will take at least four weeks to complete, lists of registered voters must be prepared at least a month before the petition filing deadline.

Because most voters who sign a candidate's petition will vote for her, this is an excellent way to begin to reach the "target number" of voters needed to win. If precinct volunteers collect 2,000 petition signatures, at least 1,200 votes are guaranteed on Election Day. About 60 percent of those who signed will vote for the candidate, assuming they go to vote. The support of the rest of the needed voters can then be obtained incrementally and systematically. Obviously, the more valid nominating petition signatures obtained, especially from door-to-door precinct work, the closer the candidate is to the target number needed to win.

VOTER REGISTRATION

There are often up to 100,000 eligible voters unregistered in every congressional district.[13] In every large city ward or state assembly district there are likely to be at least 10,000 voters who could be registered. There are enough unregistered voters to change the outcome of almost every election. A campaign should establish a registration goal and work to meet it by focusing on special registration efforts such as registering high school or college students, low-income people, or new citizens. A campaign may even attempt to register all potential voters in the district. Now that potential voters in more jurisdictions can register online, registering new voters or changing their registration to their new addresses has become easier as long as precinct workers are trained to do so and have the correct equipment, such as a laptop or tablet with an Internet connection.

The warm-up effort with petitions sets the stage for the registration drive. This stage of the campaign is particularly useful because:

- Workers are introduced to citizens on a nonpartisan basis. People contacted during this nonpartisan effort will be more receptive when volunteers return to solicit their vote.
- It is an opportunity to help eligible voters to register for the first time. The vast majority of the people registered will vote for the candidate on Election Day.
- It is an opportunity to locate supporters and recruit them to help with the precinct work. Every worker recruited multiplies the votes for a candidate.
- It allows a campaign to locate weak spots in the field operation and correct them. Just as with the petition drive, reports of voters registered by precinct and area will determine which workers are producing results and which must be replaced.

Remember that voter registration is not just a good government goal. *As many as three-quarters of the voters a campaign registers will vote for its candidate on Election Day* (if you get them to the polls). Some will do so out of gratitude for the service rendered and some because they specifically registered to be able to vote for a particular candidate.

In Harold Washington's campaign for mayor of Chicago in 1983, voter registration clearly made the difference between victory and defeat. Washington enjoyed his role as a member of Congress serving one of Chicago's inner-city districts. Before he agreed to be drafted as a candidate for mayor, he insisted that at least 100,000 new voters, principally from the African American community, be registered. A grassroots effort by community and political organizations supported by a major campaign on African American radio stations successfully met that goal. Washington was then able to motivate these newly registered voters, who provided his margin of victory in the mayoral campaign.

The arena of voter registration is changing rapidly. New "motor voter" laws have been implemented in most states. Citizens can register to vote or change their voter registration to new addresses when they obtain or renew their drivers' licenses. In the first three months after motor voter took effect nationally in January 1995, more than 2 million citizens registered to vote. In the nine states that implemented motor voter between 1988 and 1992, voter turnout increased from 9 to 12 percent by 1995.[14]

New laws restricting rights of immigrants to education, health, and welfare benefits have encouraged many legal immigrants not previously citizens to register and vote. This has greatly increased both Latino/a and Asian American voter registration. However, legal barriers obviously remain for undocumented immigrants, and a number of states have passed laws still being litigated in the courts to require photo IDs and other restrictions on voters.[15] At the same time, some states have begun to experiment with same-day voter registration and online registration, which make voter registration easier.[16]

Many communities and states also make it easier for volunteers and nonprofit group members to become deputy registrars and voters to register at libraries, grocery stores, or by mail. With all these changes, each campaign will have to determine its exact registration drive strategy based upon new rules of the game.

For registration drives in the precincts there are two general alternative strategies: (1) selective or (2) saturation registration. Registering voters is more than a civic good deed; it is a vital component of winning elections, so the choice between strategies must be based on the advantages of each method for a campaign.

The selective strategy is particularly appealing when a candidate is running on a party ticket in a general election, and candidates from only one party are being backed. The easiest method of selective registration is doing saturation registration in precincts that, based on past voting performance or poll data, are most likely to support a candidate. With more voter data now available, it is also possible to target potential voters of a certain race, ethnic group, or economic class for special registration efforts because members of those groups are most likely to support the candidate.

Most participatory campaigns employ a general strategy of saturation registration. Experience has demonstrated that in addition to expanding political participation, reform candidates have found that most newly registered voters are receptive to their campaigns. Existing political parties already have their game down pat, believing that as long as they can keep the players the same, they stand a good chance of winning any election. Therefore, they would prefer no one rock the boat. It is advantageous for existing groups such as the dominant political party to keep participation low. It is usually to the advantage of reformers to start a political battle and draw as many people as possible into the fight. If the fight stays small, one of the current party candidates will win. If the larger audience gets drawn in, then the outcome is in doubt. As political scientist E. E. Schattschneider has written, "It follows that conflicts are frequently won or lost by the success that the contestants have in getting the audience involved in the fight or in excluding it, as the case may be."[17] The very process of registering new voters changes the constituency of the district, and a new candidate is given more of a chance to win as Mayor Harold Washington did in Chicago.

There are two ways in which you can get voters to make the effort necessary to register:

- Lower the costs [in time and effort] of voting by making it as easy as possible to register and vote.
- Increase the perceived benefits of voting by convincing potential voters of the importance of the impending electoral contests.[18]

Providing potential voters correct information about registration helps the registration effort. Knowing the rules governing registration is essential. The following rules apply in Illinois but may differ in other states:

- To be eligible to register, a voter must be a US citizen, eighteen years old, (although seventeen-year-olds are eligible to vote in primary elections if they turn eighteen by the general election). Voters must also have lived in Illinois for thirty days and cannot be serving a sentence for commission of a crime.
- A voter must register twenty-seven days before an election, although there is a new experiment in same-day registration currently taking place in Illinois.
- A voter may register in person at city hall, by mail, with a deputy registrar, or at the local driver's license office when applying for a new driver's license.[19]

Volunteers undertake four jobs in a registration drive: (1) to delete the names of voters no longer living in the precinct; (2) to get previously registered voters to fill out change-of-address cards or to make registration corrections online; (3) to get new voters to register in person at city hall, at a branch of the public library, at a neighborhood polling place, or online; and (4) to get voters registered by a deputy registrar who may be a campaign volunteer in a nonpartisan role.

In none of these cases can you trust the voter. If she needs to reregister, most campaigns have her give her completed change-of-address card to their precinct volunteers to take to headquarters or fill out the information on the volunteer's computer or tablet. When change-of-address cards are used, the campaign staff will forward the change-of-address cards to city hall, whereas many voters would forget to mail them on time. Sometimes this process is too cumbersome, and voters are just instructed to mail their change-of-address cards to the board of election commissioners or to go online themselves directly. However, this approach risks the voters not following through.

If a voter has to register in person, volunteers will have to go back and remind her. Most voters will not remember on their own. *Even on Election Day, voters must be reminded to vote or as many as one-third will forget!*

The registration drive requires coordinating campaign volunteers to do exacting work. Many will not have worked on campaigns before. Therefore, a training session is held at which volunteers receive instructions, hear an oral explanation, ask questions, meet the campaign leadership including their own area and ward chairs, are encouraged by the number of other people working on the campaign, meet the candidate for whom they are working so hard, and pick up the necessary registration materials. This kind of formal training gives the workers motivation and a general understanding of their jobs. Similar training sessions will be repeated again before the precinct canvassing and Election Day. Each training session can thus be brief and focus on the job at hand at a particular stage in the campaign. Some campaigns choose to do their precinct worker training with smaller groups of volunteers each week at the campaign headquarters, whereas others plan mainly large precinct training sessions. The written instructions for a campaign registration drive explain the details of the drive more fully but do need to be adapted to different states and different campaigns.

Precinct work requires much more than an intellectual appreciation of the task to be done. It requires ringing doorbells and talking to people. Area chairs and precinct captains should supplement formal training sessions with direct help for their workers doing precinct work for the first time. Whenever possible, someone with campaign experience should accompany new workers on their visits to their first few voters either during the registration drive or the canvass. Working with an experienced campaigner will help the new worker to understand her job, to know what to say, and to get over the hurdle of the first doorbell. After this on-the-job training the new worker will have the confidence and experience to finish the task.

The real test of a successful registration drive is the number of change-of-address cards workers collect and the number of online registrations completed.[20] A registration drive informs voters when they need to register or change their registration. It is also used to drop voters from the official voting lists who have died or moved. Voters who only need to change their voting addresses to their new precincts are the easiest to add. Deleting names from the poll list of those who have died or moved is relatively simple and is often accomplished these days by mail to the board of election commissioners. However, getting new voters registered requires talking to people.

The number of change-of-address cards turned into the campaign headquarters, along with the number of new voters registered or who change their voter registration online, is proof that precinct workers are doing their job well. These indicators are important because new precinct workers are often shy about pushing the first doorbell. If they learn to contact voters during the registration drive, then they will do a good job on the canvass. If they do not overcome their timidity during registration, they will be of little help in the election. To ensure that the workers are doing their job, there are carefully timed report dates when the precinct workers tell their area chairs by phone or e-mail, area chairs tell ward coordinators, and ward coordinators tell the precinct coordinator specifically how many change-of-address cards have been collected, how many names on the poll sheets are to be challenged, how many people registered online, and how many voters must register in person. At least four report dates are set to allow for ample prodding of workers and to obtain complete information on the progress of the registration drive. In most campaigns, Thursday and Sunday evenings during the registration drive and the canvass are set as report-night deadlines.

As Figure 5.4 illustrates, reporting procedures for the precinct petition drive, voter registration effort, and canvassing are important in winning campaigns. This is true no matter whether the reports are given on paper, by phone, or via the Internet. Reports are critical to a winning campaign because they indicate the progress being made, campaign weaknesses that need to be fixed, and strategies that must be changed.

For instance, reports of changes of address and the number of voters registered online are hard data about the effectiveness of a precinct organization. The petition drive and voter registration effort are the best times to strengthen your structure, so results of the registration campaign must be carefully eval-

5.4. CAMPAIGN REPORTING PROCEDURES

After precinct chairs and precinct workers have been recruited (keeping in mind that the recruitment and assignment of volunteers is an ongoing task throughout the campaign), the area chairs' second job is to establish a reporting procedure to communicate regularly and efficiently with their precinct chairs and precinct workers.

Because critical campaign decisions depend heavily on information gathered in the precincts, the area chairs must impress upon the precinct chairs and then upon the precinct workers the importance of

- collecting the required data quickly and accurately
- adhering to the reporting so that information coming in from across the area has meaning and does not distort results, resulting in distorted campaign decisions
- reporting reliably on report nights

The campaign will establish one or two standard nights each week to gather information from the precinct operations. On those nights, information from precinct workers should be collected by telephone, email, or interview by the precinct chairs and transmitted similarly to area chairs, who in turn transmit their report to the precinct coordinator. Information collected on report nights is

uated. In those areas where a campaign gets no reports or only reports of deletions of voters from the voting roles, the area chair must be provided with the names of potential new workers. If the area chair has failed to recruit precinct workers or supervise their work, then she must be replaced. If few change-of-address cards or online registrations are reported, something has gone wrong. If an area chair cannot do the job, she can be made a precinct chair, or, if the "demotion" would be too embarrassing, she can be kept as assistant or area cochair. However, workers unable to produce good results during the registration drive cannot be counted on. They must be supplemented or replaced. Failure to do so means that area will be lost on Election Day, and possibly the entire campaign will go down in defeat.

The petition and registration drives are the opening shots fired in the battle of the precincts. They provide the opportunity to ensure that most voters will have heard about a candidate and her issues. These drives are only the prelude to the final battles that occur during the canvass and on Election Day. Registration drives provide an opportunity to recruit a volunteer army and to transform the electorate into one more receptive to a campaign. They set the stage for the final and decisive acts of the campaign.

Campaigns for Minority Candidates

So far we have treated all campaigns as if they were the same. Certain general principles apply in every case: workers must contact voters, record their preferences, and get their voters to the polls on Election Day. However, campaigns in poor, minority communities have special problems in accomplishing these tasks. They suffer from two liabilities: (1) lack of resources such as volunteer workers, trained staff, and money, and (2) special difficulties in ascertaining voter preferences.

Many minority candidates run campaigns in minority communities, which given the realities of the urban and suburban United States today, are often racial or ethnic ghettos. Ghetto campaigns are critical to efforts for political change because these communities are most likely to suffer from political oppression and would benefit most from new political leadership. These communities need the community control made possible by participatory politics. Too often, they are controlled by political party machines. Voters are forced to support candidates who do not serve them but control them through payoffs and fear. If participatory politics is to become a national political force, it must be practiced successfully in poor as well as middle-class and wealthy communities.

The problem of inadequate resources for campaigns in poor communities requires a dual solution. First, more resources, particularly skilled volunteers, must be raised within the community itself. A shortage of trained staff members can be remedied to some extent if participatory campaigns outside poor neighborhoods make it a point to employ minorities on their campaign staffs so that the skills of running winning campaigns are spread as broadly as possible. This obstacle can also be better overcome by running strong campaigns in poor communities themselves. It may take one campaign for a candidate to become known, for people to trust her, and for campaign workers and staff to gain the experience necessary to win the second time around.

Even with trained campaign leaders, money remains a scarce resource for most participatory campaigns in poor neighborhoods. Funds raised

- in the petition drive—number of signatures collected
- in the registration drive— number of new voters registered and number of voters deceased, moved, or otherwise removed from the rolls
- in the canvass—number of voters supporting your candidate, opposing, or unsure. This is called the plus count

Report nights provide an opportunity for area chairs, precinct captains, and precinct workers to trade names of prospective workers, discuss problems arising in a precinct and strategies for solving them, clarify issues raised by voters so workers can better address their questions, and arranging for the delivery of whatever materials the precinct captains or precinct workers feel they need to better cover their precincts.

Additionally, the area chairs keep the precinct captains abreast of overall or changing campaign strategy, recent positions taken by the candidate, new endorsements, dates when the candidate will be in or around the precinct captain's precinct and, in general, encourage the precinct captains to motivate the precinct workers to continue their efforts to reach every voter in their assigned precincts.

After the area chairs receive the required information from their precinct captains, they report area-wide results to the precinct coordinator. They will discuss the progress of the campaign as reflected in the precinct results. This vital feedback from the neighborhoods, if accurately drawn and reported, tells the campaign management if the strategy they have chosen is effective and, if not, how to modify it. Area chairs report not only the numbers of voters contacted, but the reaction of the voters when approached by workers, evidence of work by other candidates in the precinct, the morale of the precincts captains and precinct workers, and requests for special materials or special assistance—such as a meeting of the candidate with a neighborhood group or a phone call from the candidate or other member of the campaign committee.

Reciprocally, the precinct coordinator supplies each area chair with the dates, times, and locations of coffees scheduled for the area for transmission to the precinct captains and precinct workers. . . . Finally, the precinct coordinator assists each area chair with strategy on how to solve thorny problems such as ways to work high-rise buildings where security prohibits workers from going door to door. Together they may conclude that those buildings can best be penetrated by calling or mailing to residents. . . .

Another example of a common but touchy problem is the encounter with a recalcitrant voter. Perhaps the precinct coordinator, area chair, precinct captain, or precinct worker might consider

in minority communities must often be matched by outside funds from middle-class communities. Although most funds will have to be raised internally by the campaign, a few thousand dollars of outside support can mean a lot for campaign morale, especially if the money is used to hire adequate staff, open a campaign headquarters, and print campaign literature.

Fund-raising within poor communities differs considerably from fund-raising in middle-class and wealthy communities. For instance, facilities and services may be provided by institutions such as churches in poor communities, whereas they play a more neutral, nonpartisan role in wealthier neighborhoods. Even so, campaigns in poor communities still must raise funds from individual contributors. Small donations are raised from events such as dances and potluck dinners. The same creativity is needed as used to plan fund-raising in any campaign, however. Fund-raising in wealthier communities is also a necessary part of the financial plan for campaigns in poor neighborhoods, and it is often quite successful.

The other problem for campaigns in poor communities, obtaining honest responses from the residents, is not easily resolved. Because many ghetto dwellers live at a bare subsistence level and depend upon various forms of public assistance, they are often at the mercy of regular party precinct chairs. These party officials may threaten to terminate voters' welfare payments, have them thrown out of public housing, or get them fired from government jobs, so many poor folks are cautious about opposing the party in power.

For practical reasons, many residents of poor communities support regular party candidates. Even more problematic, many residents will not tell canvassers the truth about how they plan to vote. After all, why should they make an enemy when they can just say they will vote for your candidate?

Canvassers sometimes return with reports that *all* the voters on their poll lists or walk sheets will vote for their candidate. Their precincts therefore cannot be effectively worked on Election Day because the task of getting all voters to the polls is too large to accomplish in a single day and because too many of the voters who said they would support a candidate, in fact, will vote against her. The only remedy for the unwillingness of voters to tell precinct workers their true preferences is well-trained workers who carefully probe the voters' initial responses to be sure that most of those they record as supporters will really vote for their candidate on Election Day. At least volunteer precinct workers going door to door guarantee that campaign information reaches every voter, which will gain some support for your candidate.

Because of the shortage of precinct workers in most campaigns in poor communities, hiring people who say they have worked in previous campaigns is a great temptation. Usually these folks will take the campaign's money but bring no votes on Election Day. It is much safer to hire only members of the central campaign staff or pay workers only for the time taken from their regular job to work on Election Day. Participatory politics depends on voluntary participants. Highly paid, mercenary armies of workers are simply no substitute.

Despite these problems in canvassing in minority communities, supporters must be located and brought to the polls. Sound trucks, posters, campaign literature, public relations, and talking

persuading a person well known in the area to write a personal note to voters whose ambivalence he or she might sway. Whatever the problem, it is clear that the precinct coordinator, area chairs, precinct captains, and precinct workers are dependent upon one another—up and down the line— for problem solving and supportive relationships throughout the course of the campaign.

Source: Independent Voters of Illinois, "IVI-IPO 2010 A–Z Campaign Training Manual," 11–12.

to random voters will not win elections. An effective voter canvass will—even in the most difficult political situations.

More and more frequently these days, minority candidates run in races beyond the boundaries of racial and ethnic ghettoes. They must appeal to voters from other ethnic groups. Similarly, white candidates often need blacks, Latino/as, Asian Americans, and American Indians to vote for them. The task for such candidates is to mobilize a solid vote of their own racial or ethnic group without alienating voters from other ethnic and racial blocs.

ELECTING AN AFRICAN AMERICAN MAYOR

In his 1983 and 1987 races for mayor of Chicago, Harold Washington used these techniques effectively. In the 1983 primary campaign he ran against the incumbent, Mayor Jane Byrne, and the son of Chicago's most famous mayor, then states attorney Richard M. Daley. The two white candidates split the white vote, and Washington won with unified African American votes and the support of progressive whites and Latino/as.

Washington was drafted primarily by political activists and community organizers in the African American community. Because of his years in public office, independence from the political party machine, wit, and charisma, US Representative Washington was the most popular possible black candidate as demonstrated by a series of informal polls taken in the community. He agreed to run on the condition that at least 100,000 new voters be registered. A broad-based alliance was put together under the rubric of People Organized for Welfare and Employment Rights (POWER), and its voter registration drive was funded by the president of Soft Sheen Products. The money allowed "radio commercials, eye-catching posters, and bumper stickers that spread the registration message—'Come Alive October 5' [voter registration day in the precincts]—across the black community."[21]

This massive drive registered an additional 125,000 black voters.[22] The Washington campaign thus began with the most successful voter registration drive in the city's history. Fueled by anger at Reaganomics nationally and by racially insensitive mistakes of Mayor Byrne in failing to appoint blacks to high-level city government positions, an entirely new voter support base was created even before Washington formally became a candidate.

Early in his campaign Washington met with some progressive leaders of the Mexican and Puerto Rican communities who pledged to endorse his candidacy and to work for him. These Latino/a leaders saw in the Washington campaign an opportunity to build their own political base and power as a third force in city politics. When Washington was elected, his administration vastly increased the number of Latino/as appointed to top jobs and positions of authority in city government. Liberal whites and their political organizations such as the Independent Voters of Illinois–Independent Precinct Organization (IVI-IPO) also endorsed Washington and provided a campaign structure in the white wards of the city.

William Grimshaw describes the Washington campaign as three campaigns rolled into one:

> First, there was the formal campaign organization, which was structured and conducted along conventional campaign lines. Full field operations were mounted in over half of the city's fifty wards, including all the black, Hispanic, and white lakefront liberal wards. Partial operations existed in another dozen wards. . . .
>
> The campaign also contained an elaborate network of interest groups that worked largely outside of the formal structure . . . from Artists for Washington to Women for Washington to just about everything else in between. . . .
>
> The campaign's third principal component was . . . a group of black nationalists, whose idealistic, "separatist" goals clashed with the more practical and "integrationist" goals of the formal campaign. . . . The nationalists' preferred form of communication was the spectacular event: big rallies and large parades that drummed up a powerful emotional response.[23]

Washington's campaign theme was "reform," but this reform had three different meanings to his different supporters:

- Good government reform—efficiency, openness, and honesty in government
- Affirmative action—more minorities and women in positions of political power
- Community control—participatory democracy in local government, including more government money given to neighborhood groups, neighborhood government, and decentralization of government by creating local school councils with authority over local schools[24]

As Grimshaw put it, "Washington thus campaigned as a reform candidate for mayor as well as a messiah for the black community. Without the capacity to encompass both roles, he could not have won."[25] The campaign was not only the normal election effort but became a crusade as well. This is possible when social movements and electoral campaigns combine.

Mayor Byrne's campaign unwittingly helped Washington do an even better job of mobilizing the black community. Three days before the election, Democratic Party chair and Byrne ally Chicago alderman Edward Vrdolyak spelled out the Byrne's campaign message and the ballot choices in racially charged language: "A vote for Daley is a vote for Washington.... It's a racial thing. Don't kid yourself. I am calling on you to save your city, to save your precinct. We are fighting to keep the city the way it is."[26] The Byrne campaign thus attempted to gain the white vote by racist appeals, but media reports of the Vrdolyak statement instead mobilized the black community and progressive whites and Latino/as behind Washington.

When the primary was over, Washington won with 37 percent of the vote to Byrne's 33 percent and Daley's 30 percent. Washington received 80 percent of the black vote, or 92 percent of his citywide total vote. On the other side, 78 percent of Byrne's vote and 90 percent of Daley's vote were white.[27] Washington did what minority candidates must do: mobilize their racial and ethnic support base and appeal sufficiently to other racial and ethnic voters to guarantee the extra votes needed for victory.

CAMPAIGNS FOR WOMEN CANDIDATES

Despite electoral victories by many women candidates, political science researchers conclude that women remain the "most underrepresented major social group in America."[28] However, this is beginning to change. Women such as Shirley Chisholm, Geraldine Ferraro, Sarah Palin, Michelle Bachman, Carly Fiorina, and Hillary Clinton have run campaigns for the highest offices. Nonetheless, as of 2015, despite being 51 percent of the population, women held only 20 percent of the seats in the US Senate and 19 percent in the House of Representatives. They held a similar 22 percent of statewide elected positions, and 24 percent of state legislative seats. Only 12 percent of the mayors of the 100 largest cities were women.[29]

The Pew Research Center has done important research on who runs for elected office. Although there are more than 90,000 government elections for more than 500,000 positions in a six-year cycle, only 2 percent of US citizens have ever run for federal, state, or local elective office. This includes running for more minor offices on school or library boards.

Of the 2 percent who have run for office, 75 percent have been men and only 25 percent have been women, who obviously cannot win if they do not run. The numbers are even lower for minority candidates. Whereas 82 percent of all candidates have been white, only 6 percent were Hispanic and 5 percent were African American despite those groups making up 15 and 12 percent of the population, respectively.[30]

This underrepresentation of women in elected office is caused by a number of factors. For instance, women have traditionally been barred from prestigious educational institutions and occupations or admitted only in limited numbers. The greatest barrier to more women in power remains not their education or rank in professions but the incumbency of men currently in office and the reluctant attitude some women themselves hold about running for office.

R. Darcy, Susan Welsh, and Janet Clark conclude in *Women, Elections, and Representation*: "The political system and cultural milieu no longer present barriers to women state legislative candidates they may once have. If more women run, more women will be elected. And as more women begin gaining tenure in legislatures, the pool of women candidates for higher office will also increase."[31]

However, the deeper social and psychological barriers must still be overcome. In their chapter in *Women and Elected Office*, Jennifer Lawless, Richard Fox, and Gail Baitinger note:

> The gender gap stems from the fact that women are more likely than men to doubt their qualifications and perceive a biased and highly competitive electoral environment and less likely than men to receive support and encouragement to run for office, both from political gatekeepers and personal contacts. In addition, women's more demanding household and family roles add complexity to the decision to run for office.[32]

Moreover, when women do run for office, "voters pay closer attention to the physical attributes and mannerisms of female candidates than those of their male counterparts."[33] In all campaigns, there is a tendency by the media and voters to focus on style over substance, but this is accentuated when the candidate is a woman. In the view of Susan MacManus, this "makes the job of political consultants considerably more difficult, the need for more female voices among their ranks even more critical, and the effectiveness of microtargeting the female electorate markedly more essential."[34]

GAY CANDIDATES

More than ever, lesbian, gay, bisexual, and transgender (LGBT) candidates are being regularly elected to positions in city councils, state legislatures, and Congress. In 2014, one of the most high-profile campaigns was that of Brett Smiley, an openly gay candidate, running against former Providence, Rhode Island, mayor Buddy Cianici, who although convicted of bribery and other crimes was eligible to run once again for mayor. Smiley eventually dropped out of the race and endorsed another candidate. Candidates who are gay or lesbian can now compete for higher office.

Openly gay and lesbian candidates do well in liberal districts where a sizable number of LGBT members live, but they also win when they are endorsed and supported by traditional political parties. For instance, in relatively conservative Chicago wards and districts, lesbian Debra Mell was elected first to the state legislature and later to the Chicago City Council to replace her father, former alderman Dick Mell. Bernie Frank was the longtime powerful US representative from Boston, and Tammy Baldwin was elected US senator from Wisconsin in 2012 after several terms in the House of Representatives. LGBT candidates can run and win if they convince voters that they will represent their districts well.

LATINO/A CANDIDATES

As Atiya Kai Stokes-Brown notes, "The increasing population of racial and ethnic minorities, particularly Latinos and Asian Americans, is transforming America's political landscape. . . . The success of [minority] candidates today has been attributed to the manner in which these candidates run their campaigns, adopting successful . . . electoral strategies designed to encourage greater support among white voters while maintaining electoral backing in minority communities."[35]

Before the 2014 elections added to their numbers, there were 5,850 Latinos/as serving in elected office, including 2 US senators, 24 members of the House of Representatives, 9 in statewide offices such as governor, 68 state senators, and 183 state representatives. Between 1996 and 2011, there was a 53 percent increase in the number of Latino/a elected officials, and that number will continue to grow as the population expands and more Latinos/as become citizens.[36] Like women officeholders, Latino/a officials are both Democratic and Republican.

Therefore, being Latino/a is no longer a barrier to holding public office. Latinos have served as mayors of major cities such as Miami, Denver, San Antonio, and Los Angeles. In some districts with large voting blocs, being Latino/a is even an advantage when running for office.

Most Latino/a and other minority candidates still have to build an effective electoral coalition beyond their racial or ethnic group. "As part of a strategy designed to attract white moderate voters, deracializing candidates project a nonthreatening image, avoid employing direct racial appeals, and avoid emphasizing a racially specific issue agenda. . . . They adopt a 'mainstream' strategy to appeal to white voters . . . but simultaneously make appeals to minority constituencies through political surrogates and tailored messages in racial and ethnic media."[37]

As with other campaigns, Latino/a candidates are more frequently using not only traditional media and door-to-door precinct work but social media as we discuss in Chapter 7. Beyond the mainstream Anglo media, they are making heavy use of Latino/a print, radio, and television media to get their campaign messages to their voters in Spanish. In many households, Spanish media are the main source of outside news and entertainment, and political messages there are most effective.

Anglo candidates in districts with a significant Latino/a population are advised to print their campaign literature in Spanish as well as English, to use social media in both languages, and to buy ads on Spanish media. It is also important to highlight Latino/a staff and supporters working for a candidate's election.

ASIAN AMERICAN CANDIDATES

Like other minorities, Asian Americans are gaining office in ever greater numbers. When the University of California–Los Angeles (UCLA) Asian American Studies Center first published its political almanac, it listed just more than 100 Asian Americans elected or appointed to public office. By June 2014, the almanac listed 4,000 officeholders in thirty-nine states and the federal government. This is in part because the Asian American population has grown to 18 million and is currently the fastest growing racial group in the United States.

Asian American elected officials include a US senator, 13 members of the House of Representatives, and more elected governors than any other minority. They also are mayors of cities such as San Francisco and Oakland.[38]

One successful Asian American candidate was Chicago alderman Ameya Pawar. He was the first Indian American to be elected in Chicago. He was elected in a ward that has few Asian American residents. Like other Asian American candidates, he won by door-to-door contacts, social media, and strong support of neighborhood leaders. His race did not matter as much as his persona, ideas, youth, and energy. He was also helped by circumstances. The long-term incumbent dropped out of the race and tried to substitute the head of the party organization. That did not work, and because Pawar was already running, he was able to succeed. As they say, succeeding in life is, in part, just showing up, but winning requires showing up with determination, a campaign plan, and supporters.

A Postgender, Postracial Era

The election of President Barack Obama in 2008 and 2012, along with the slow but steady growth in the number of women and minority public officials, is said to mean an end to the racial segregation and racial stereotyping that characterized earlier US history. Unfortunately, race and gender still matter in elections as in other aspects of life, as the demonstrations about police brutality in 2014–2015 illustrated.

Women, minorities, and majority white, male candidates have to take continuing racial and gender discrimination into account in running their campaigns. White, male candidates must learn to appeal to women and minority voters without patronizing, and minority and female candidates must learn how to appeal to white males and minority groups other than their own.

There may not yet be a level playing field, but women as well as men, minorities as well as whites, can run and win elections. It is up to progressive campaigns to lead the way in doing this in a positive and affirming way.

Reaching Voters

No matter the race of the candidate, she must still get her message to the voters. There are many different ways for a candidate to do this. Free media coverage and paid ads are important. Direct mail, phone calls, and social media reach voters as well. However in the end, petition drives, an effective voter registration campaign, and an in-person door-to-door effort are the hallmarks of participatory campaigns. They remain essential to winning elections in the twenty-first century.

Campaigns have to be adjusted based upon the characteristics of candidates and the district in which they are run, but as long as a campaign's message about the candidate and her platform can be sent to the voters, including through a neighbor-to-neighbor, door-to-door effort, any qualified candidate with a positive platform and dedicated supporters can be elected.

Chapter Six

Winning the Traditional Media War

....

Public relations play a critical role in campaigns. In every political campaign, publicity is used to get name recognition for the candidate. Public relations are employed in participatory campaigns to attract workers and money as well as to get candidate name recognition among voters. The images and theme of a campaign must therefore be powerful enough to attract supporters and be successfully disseminated through press conferences, news releases, campaign literature, the Internet, and social media. All of these activities must occur within time limits set by a tyrannical campaign schedule and be governed by a sure knowledge of the different types of media if they are to be effective.

In participatory campaigns, public relations serve three basic functions: (1) to create name recognition and a positive perception of a candidate, (2) to attract workers and financial contributions, and (3) to distinguish a candidate and his programs from his opponents. Negative campaigning is the dark side of public relations. An opposing candidate might have to be discredited before voters will vote for a candidate. Any negative campaigning opponents use to discredit a candidate must be countered forcefully and quickly. In between the positive publicity and negative attacks are compare-and-contrast public relations and advertising that compare the political and governmental actions of an opponent with the stands and promises of your candidate.

Developing a Media Strategy

A candidate's image and a clear campaign theme are inevitably developed as a part of a larger campaign publicity plan. One way to create such a plan is to answer the following questions:

1. Which voters are likely to vote for your candidate, and which are likely to vote for your opponent?
2. Beyond your base of support, who else can you get to vote for your candidate, and what will persuade them to do so?
3. What are the images you wish to project of your candidate and his opponent?
4. What is your campaign theme and definition of the political situation?
5. How will you inform the electorate that there is an election, get the voters to recognize your candidate's name, sell the campaign theme to them, and mobilize them on Election Day?
6. How can you counter your opponent's images and definition of the issues?
7. Given budget constraints, how can direct voter contact, media publicity, social media, and paid media advertising be employed to get the campaign message to the voters?

If you had unlimited funding, then manipulating the media to sell your candidate to the voters would not be a problem. Joe McGinniss documented this in *The Selling of the President, 1968*.[1] He provided the inside story of how Richard Nixon was sold to the voters using Madison Avenue advertising tricks. Nixon's media people carefully crafted television commercials and programs to win that election.

As McGinniss writes, television was the way to present the "new Nixon":

> But not just any kind of television. An uncommitted camera could do irreparable harm. [Nixon's] television would have to be controlled. He would need experts. They would have to find the proper settings for him, or if they could not be found, manufacture them. . . .
>
> So this was how they went into it. Trying with one hand to build the illusion that Richard Nixon, in addition to his attributes of mind and heart, considered . . . "communicating with the people . . . one of the great joys of seeking the Presidency"; while with the other they shielded him, controlled him, and controlled the atmosphere around him. It was as if they were

building not a President but an Astrodome, where the wind would never blow, the temperature never rise or fall, and the ball never bounce erratically on the artificial grass. . . .

And it worked. As he moved serenely through his primary campaign, there was . . . a new image of him on the television screen. TV both reflected and contributed to his strength.[2]

The technique developed for the Nixon campaign was for a panel of eight "ordinary people" to question Nixon live in front of a selected audience of 300 supporters on television. The program was created and telecast in ten different regions of the country even though Nixon's answers to the questions might remain much the same each time. This along with the carefully controlled production of more ordinary political commercials was the heart of the packaged 1968 Nixon campaign.

Nixon's technique of media manipulation has been repeated thousands of times since the 1960s. With enough money for polls and focus groups to sharpen the message, and television advertising to sell candidates the same way Madison Avenue sells soaps, mass media have been manipulated to sell candidates from city hall to the White House. Voters have often made pretty good choices between officials despite the hype. However, at times money, polls, focus groups, and paid media techniques have triumphed in electing less-qualified candidates. Now that the Internet and social media are in widespread use, they have become similarly controlled as we detail in Chapter 7.

Any candidate running for higher office must use public opinion polls, stage activities to get media coverage, send targeted direct mail and e-mails, employ the Internet to publicize the candidate and campaign themes, conduct phone campaigns, and spend considerable money on paid advertising in the media. So what is the difference between Nixon's campaign, in which a fake image and persona was sold, and a participatory campaign? More cynical readers may ask, is there any difference?

Phony campaigns since the 1960s have been defined by four elements:

- big money
- public opinion polls
- extensive use of thirty-second television commercials
- a carefully crafted and misleading persona of the candidate

In the twenty-first century, three additional elements have been added to synthetic campaigns:

- negative advertising attacking opponents in ways that cannot be answered successfully
- targeted communications using cable television, radio talk shows, direct mail, and phone campaigns to reach segmented audiences with particular messages
- the use of the Internet and social media to spread unfounded rumors and lies about an opponent

Phony campaigns distort the real personalities and qualities of candidates and pander to voters with a false presentation of issues. Elections are won with inaccurate or superficial information fed to voters through slick media ads and duplicitous targeted communications.

Participatory campaigns depend both upon grassroots support from volunteers and a receptive electorate ready to embrace change. They portray an honest image of the candidate, have less money, and depend heavily upon volunteers to get their message to the voters. Although participatory campaigns employ public opinion polls, paid media advertising, and targeted communications, including those on the Internet and through social media, this is not the heart of the campaign. Participatory campaigns at their best are about fundamental change in politics and government, and they mobilize a large number of people to get their message out.

These methods can be used by those with different ideologies including Republicans, Democrats, and independents. They can be used by ultraconservative and left-wing radical supporters alike. What all these groups have in common is a desire to mobilize citizens to challenge the status quo through elections.

USES AND ABUSES OF PUBLIC OPINION POLLS AND FOCUS GROUPS

In shaping a candidate's image, selecting a visual and verbal campaign theme, choosing a slogan, defining issues, and devising a campaign strategy, knowing the attitudes of voters in the district is crucial. Although your candidate, staff, and campaign advisors may have personal knowledge of the district, they have not talked to all the thousands of voters who live there. Thus public opinion polls and focus groups are used as a way of finding out what voters think about the possible candidates and important campaign issues, why voters hold the attitudes and positions they do, what might change their attitudes, and how they are likely to vote on Election Day.

According to Gary Selnow in *High-Tech Campaigns*, there are four categories of polls used in campaigns:

A *benchmark poll* accesses voters before a campaign is launched. It takes a
broad sweep of the issues and of the potential candidates. . . .

Follow-up surveys pick up on dominant themes . . . and track them through
a campaign. . . .

Panel surveys . . . monitor voters' movements through a campaign by re-
turning periodically to the same respondents . . . [to determine] how
thinking evolves over time. . . .

Tracking polls are conducted daily among small samples to sense emerging
problems or helpful trends that may evolve into significant factors.[3]

Obviously campaigns benefit from a benchmark poll at the beginning of
the campaign that provides the initial objective information about candidate
name recognition and voter views on critical issues. Any later public opinion
polls allow campaign leaders to tell how effective their various campaigning
and advertising efforts have been. In the more sophisticated *rolling-average
tracking polls*, a set number of voters are interviewed every night. Their views
are added to data from earlier polls. The oldest data is discarded in the new
totals. The results provide a constant track of changes in the public mood. As
William Hamilton characterizes them, they are like "Dow-Jones stock averages
for campaigns."[4]

Public opinion polls obviously have a variety of uses. *Benchmark polls* at the
beginning of a race tell you where you and your opponents would stand if the
election were held today. However, if a candidate is challenging an incumbent
or running for the first time, his name recognition will be so low that the poll
cannot provide a realistic idea of how the election will turn out. After months
of campaigning, he will be better known to the voters, and the election results
may be radically different from the predictions of any early polls. Even if the
horserace statistics are often unreliable as predictors of the final outcome of
the election, *benchmark* and *follow-up surveys* can be used to test name recognition and candidate image for each candidate over time. Campaign issues and
themes can also be tested in these polls to discover a theme or issue that would
win the election if exploited properly.

Unfortunately, the most sophisticated polling techniques, *panel* and *tracking polls* that monitor changes in voter attitudes, are affordable only if you are
planning to spend hundreds of thousands of dollars on television ads or direct
mail. A commercially purchased single poll can cost more than $15,000, and
four weeks of tracking polls will cost more than $50,000, so many campaigns
will decide these funds can be better spent on voter contact, direct mail, Internet communications, a website, or mass media ads. *Tracking polls* are especially

useful if your message in these media ads and flyers has to change from week to week. The Barack Obama presidential campaign in 2012 used tracking polls in the battleground states to target resources and voter contact efforts essential to winning the election, but few campaigns have the massive volunteer and financial resources of the Obama campaign.

If a candidate is leading or has stronger voter support than expected, or if the opponent is vulnerable, public opinion polls can also be used (1) to gain credibility with the media, (2) to win endorsements from interest groups (such as PACs), and (3) to garner contributions from donors. Nearly all campaigns that use polling conduct a *benchmark poll* at the beginning of the campaign. How many more polls they purchase depends on the money available as well as the need for poll information to direct the advertising campaign effectively.

Focus groups are also helpful in fine-tuning a campaign's media message or even defining it at the beginning of a campaign. Although public opinion polls can provide the campaign quantitative information, they are limited in the number of questions they can ask, providing only the broad contours of voter attitudes. Focus groups provide more in-depth information about why voters hold the attitudes they do. They also inform a campaign as to which images and arguments can take advantage of these attitudes or change them. With a focus group it is possible to show proposed television advertisements or websites to obtain voter reaction to them in ways that allow them to be edited to deliver the most effective and powerful message. It is important to begin using focus groups early in the campaign to help develop the campaign theme. Later sessions can refine the message as the campaign develops and even measure it against the quantitative message the polls provide.[5]

In addition to shaping the message, focus groups can be invaluable in developing the campaign's image, even with something as basic as use of colors and symbols.[6] On a more sophisticated level, they can evaluate through ad testing how your image and message are received. Obama's campaign leaders needed to find the right combination of image and message to convince undecided voters to vote for him. They used online focus groups of 400–500 participants, matched demographically to the electorate, to evaluate which proposed commercials were most appealing.[7] However, focus groups are expensive in time, effort, and money. One focus group of 10–12 participants can cost between $4,000 and $9,000 dollars per session, although often the costs can go down for more than one session.[8]

The problem with both polling and focus groups is, of course, cost. A *benchmark poll* with 500 valid responses from phone calls to randomly selected voters cost $15,000 in 2014. Estimates for a brief four-minute poll range from about $3,000 to $5,600 depending on the number of interviewees.[9] Two polls, including a benchmark poll at the beginning to develop campaign and public relations strategy and one at the end of the race to fine-tune the message for final media buys could cost about $30,000. *Panel* and *tracking polls* cost considerably more. Local campaigns run for $150,000 usually do not purchase commercial polls. The rule is that polling and focus groups should not cost more than 5–10 percent of your total budget.[10]

What are the alternatives to the high cost of public opinion polls? One alternative is to lower the cost. A political science or survey research professor can design a survey questionnaire or run a focus group for you. If he is a campaign supporter, he may do it free. If not, he will probably charge about $1,000 for designing, supervising, and interpreting a survey. A random dialing list of voters to poll in your district should cost less than $1,000, and if you are using an election data management system such as VoteBuilder, the phone numbers of many voters will be part of the package. Likewise, if you purchase voter lists separately for direct mail, phone canvasses, and precinct work, volunteers can randomize them easily enough at no cost.

Campaign volunteers can be trained to make the calls on campaign phone lines or using their own cell phones. Instead of $15,000 or more, a scientifically valid poll can be done for the campaign at a much lower cost. The poll may even have credibility with the media and with donors if the professor who designed it is willing to certify that it is valid.

There are a number of limitations to public opinion polling. Many voters in the district now own unlisted cell phones so that getting an accurate random sample of phone numbers is more difficult than previously. Second, voters are tired of endless phone calls from private telemarketers selling commercial products, charity solicitors, and previous political campaigns. Therefore many voters will no longer answer a public opinion phone call from political campaign volunteers or private polling firms. In addition, a recent National Health Interview Survey reported that 38.2 percent of American homes have only wireless telephones, and 15.9 percent of households with landlines still receive most of their calls on their cell phones. Because there are still legal restrictions on the dialing of cell phones, this makes it difficult to reach a growing population by phone.[11]

To overcome this problem, it is now possible to do public opinion polls using the Internet, although this works only if the campaign can compile or purchase a random sample of e-mail addresses of district voters. Polling existing campaign supporters by e-mail might be of some use, but they are clearly not a random sample of district voters.

Many campaigns do not have the volunteers or money to devote either to public opinion polling or focus groups. In these campaigns, it is still useful to test your candidate's popularity and the salience of important issues. The strength of a campaign can be judged by the number of voters signing petitions to get your candidate on the ballot. Recruitment of volunteers and the level of campaign donations are good measures of how well your campaign is going. Simple, unscientific polls can also be conducted by questioning people at grocery stores on a weekend or by sending questions to any list of e-mail addresses that can be obtained. None of these methods provides as accurate a reflection of public opinion as more scientific, random-sample public opinion polls or professionally conducted focus groups. New technology can help. Mobile-based app surveys are becoming available that will be able to reach more hard-to-reach supporters, especially young voters, and show videos and pictures to get immediate responses on images and messages before releasing them.[12] However, in the end, experience and judgment on the part of the campaign leaders will have to suffice for races without sufficient resources to conduct polls or focus groups.

It is important to remember that information obtained from impressions by the candidate and staff may be inaccurate. Many voters like to encourage a candidate when he meets them at transportation stops, grocery stores, events, and campaign rallies. A candidate is likely to overestimate the support he really has because voters are polite and do not tell him they are planning to vote for someone else.

No campaign ever has perfect information about the electorate and about how an election will turn out. Predicting election outcomes is always hazardous. If campaign polls and focus groups are not affordable, as much information as possible about voter attitudes should be gleaned from polls taken by the news media, universities, and other candidates. They will provide some information about the mood of the electorate even if they do not give precise information on a particular race.

CREATING A POSITIVE IMAGE

Public relations coordinators create an image for the candidate and the campaign. This is necessary in participatory campaigns as well as in those campaigns that attempt to project a false image of a candidate. A positive candidate image helps to accomplish the practical public relations goals of raising resources, informing voters, setting forth programs of change, and countering negative campaigns of opponents. Don Rose, a public relations political consultant, explains the process as follows: "The important thing is to establish early an identity for the candidate, a point of reference for the candidate, assuming, as with most [reformers], that this is a guy [or gal] without a broad public image or a well-known personality to begin with."[13]

It is crucial in building a candidate's image to begin with the real person, not some ideal type. A homebody cannot be made into a jetsetter or vice versa. Bernard Weisberg, a candidate for Illinois Constitutional Convention delegate, was a concerned, liberal lawyer long identified with the American Civil Liberties Union (ACLU). Therefore, his public relations coordinator emphasized Weisberg's capability as a lawyer and his concern for the bill of rights in the new state constitution. Because he was running independently of the Democratic Party, the image of an honest citizen battling the corrupt Chicago machine was also used.

Here is how Rose described the image projected for Weisberg:

> The other reality, that is, the image of a man of the people, as it were—ordinary citizen fighting against the political machine [was accentuated]. It's one that is necessary. . . . You do have a constituency of active people who are going to join such a fight, and you have to make clear that this is going to be one of those fights not only for all the good things in life and for constitutional reform, but a major battle, a chance to diminish or neutralize the machine that has been oppressing [Chicago] for so long.[14]

In Simpson's campaigns for Congress in the Democratic Party primary, he constantly highlighted the contrasts between the incumbent, Dan Rostenkowski, and himself. During both campaigns, the federal government was investigating Rostenkowski for corruption. Simpson therefore emphasized that he was an honest reformer who would serve with integrity. The media portrayed the incumbent as an arrogant official who ignored his constituents, whereas Simpson, as an alderman, had worked to encourage citizen participation. Citizens in a democracy are meant to control the government, and public officials are expected to answer for their conduct to both the media and the public, a point Simpson's campaign emphasized.

Simpson's campaign brochure emphasized his integrity and his record of courage and dedication to government ethics and reform. The differences were highlighted in "Three Reasons to Elect Dick Simpson":

- Dick Simpson will serve with integrity. . . .
- Dick Simpson has a proven record of courage and dedication to government ethics and reform. . . .

- Dick Simpson is tough enough, experienced enough, and practical enough to fight for change.

Rostenkowski countered Simpson's message by emphasizing that he was powerful and that his district, city, state, and president could not afford to lose his "clout" as chair of the US House Ways and Means Committee. With the endorsements of Mayor Richard M. Daley and President Bill Clinton, Rostenkowski's definition of the issues won the tough primary contest over Simpson's.

A key to any successful campaign is the ability to dramatize and distinguish it from other races occurring all over the state. This signals to the media, voters, and potential volunteers that a campaign is a major political battle worth fighting. Just getting better publicity than your opponent is not enough. First, the media and the public must be convinced the election is important—something significant is at stake. Then media coverage will follow.

Weisberg distinguished himself from the other candidates by filing a lawsuit charging that the Illinois secretary of state unfairly gave friends and party regulars valuable positions at the top of the ballot. This guaranteed them several hundred additional votes from voters who chose the first name they saw on the ballot.

Action attracts attention and coverage in the media. Before his campaign had barely begun, Weisberg jousted with one of the most powerful political bosses in the state. Winning his court case not only brought good publicity for months to come but also it opened up the electoral process for other candidates. Weisberg himself was moved up from fifth place to second in the drawing for ballot position. This kind of demonstrative action reinforces the image of a candidate and his campaign.

In Simpson's first aldermanic campaign, he introduced a citizen ordinance to curb the mayor's power in making school board appointments. Later, in his congressional campaigns, he began petition drives to reform Congress.

In developing a public relations plan, determining what image of the candidate to project is not enough, nor is it enough to state clear contrasts with your opponent. *A candidate must dramatize the differences between candidates by his actions.* Then press releases, press conferences, and campaign literature can reinforce the image projected.

A candidate's image must also be solid and truthful enough to withstand negative attacks. Michael Dukakis's 1988 image as the governor of Massachusetts, the "Economic Miracle State," in his presidential campaign could not withstand his opponent's Willie Horton television ads, which portrayed him as soft on criminals, and the advertisements showing a polluted Boston Harbor, which undermined his image as ecologically concerned. His own campaign even posed him foolishly like the cartoon character Rocky the Squirrel riding on top of a military tank in one campaign event, used in a Bush ad portraying Dukakis as weak on defense.[15] In the face of these negative campaign attacks and his own campaign mistakes, his image as a smart, able chief executive concerned with issues that mattered to the voters did not hold. Most political experts concluded that Dukakis should have quickly answered the negative ads from his opponent with a response in the same media. He failed to do so and lost the election.

Bill Clinton's 1992 image as a "New Democrat" governor concerned with the economy and the fate of common people withstood attacks on him as a womanizer and as a draft dodger in his presidential campaign. Despite the attacks by primary opponents and later by President George H. W. Bush, voters elected him. Quick response by him and his staff from the "war room" of his campaign to attacks as they came is one of the reasons his campaign prevailed.[16]

In a counterexample, in 2012 Mitt Romney was by all accounts a compassionate man and a successful business executive. He had also been an effective former governor of Massachusetts and head of the US Olympic Committee. Nevertheless in his presidential campaign, his Republican primary opponents and then the Obama campaign portrayed him as one of the richest 1 percent of Americans. His investment company, Bain Capital Management, had sold off US manufacturing companies in a way that cost thousands of workers their jobs. Neither Romney nor his campaign was able to counter this negative image of him as a ruthless, heartless capitalist. This was one of the reasons he lost the election.[17]

Before developing a campaign's stance on issues, a solid image for the candidate must be created and a clear theme for his campaign formulated. Shaping that image is the task of the candidate, campaign manager, public relations coordinator, and public relations consultants. Failing to do so, or allowing an opponent's portrayal of a candidate to go unanswered, will surely lose the election.

Despite a campaign creating a positive and truthful image of the candidate, the news media do not always buy it. The media mediate information rather than bringing it to their audience directly. In Simpson's aldermanic campaigns and after taking office he most often received positive coverage and was portrayed as a reformer. In his congressional campaigns, however, the media sometimes portrayed him as sure to lose because of Rostenkowski's power. Some political commentators agreed with his opponent's characterizations of

Simpson as a wild-eyed radical, out of touch with this working-class district. Although such media portrayals of a candidate cannot be entirely controlled, there is a much better chance of getting the campaign's message to voters if a consistent image is developed and projected clearly.

THE USES OF A CAMPAIGN THEME

A campaign theme unifies the campaign and defines the battleground. It briefly conveys information about the character of the candidate and the issues at stake. The theme might be simplified into a slogan, or it might remain implicit in the campaign literature and Internet postings. For example, in the campaign to elect African American John Stevens to the Chicago City Council, all his literature highlighted the simple theme "Stevens for Change." In a district represented by only white, conservative representatives of the entrenched Chicago Democratic organization, the slogan reflected the fact that he was an independent African American candidate who wanted to heal the racial breach in the ward and eliminate political machine domination.

An example of a similar campaign theme was Obama's in 2008 of "Hope and Change" and in 2012 "Forward," also short and clear. They were also effective in mobilizing thousands of volunteers and millions of voters to win both national elections.

As these examples illustrate, the choice of a theme is particularly important *in defining the issues in such a way that a majority of citizens can identify with a candidate*. Thus, a candidate is presented to voters as a qualified, good government candidate rather than as a radical out of touch with voters.

When a candidate takes stands on important issues, it is critical that he shape the issues and define the alternatives in a way that most citizens can support him. A candidate should be distinguished from opponents in strongly positive terms: an honest person versus a crooked politician; a reformer versus a corrupt political machine member; a peacemaker versus a warmonger; competent versus incompetent; a representative of the people versus a captive of special interests.

Although the emphasis is primarily placed upon a candidate's positive characteristics rather than on his opponent's faults, the contrast between candidates is important. These themes do not have to be made verbally explicit or sloganized in every case. Buttons, posters, and websites used primarily for name identification and encouragement of campaign workers often bear only a candidate's name and the office he seeks. Even in campaign literature, verbal slogans may not be necessary to make your point, although they will often be used.

If a verbal slogan is used, it should be the same phrase every time. Repetition is important, and conflicting themes undermine the entire effort. It is therefore critical to coordinate the graphics and campaign slogans on the website, Facebook posts, and all social media with the printed campaign materials, paid television spots, and mass media ads.

Joel Bradshaw in *Campaigns and Elections American Style* defines a campaign theme as the "*rationale for your candidate's election and your opponent's defeat.*"[18] He advises that there can be only one theme, not multiple themes, because "you can get [only] one point through to voters who think about this [election] five minutes a week or less." Your theme is your candidate's response to the question, "Why are you running?" Bradshaw concludes that a good campaign theme answering this question has six characteristics: "It must be clear, concise, compelling, connected, contrasting, and credible. It helps also if it can be communicated in an easily understandable and memorable way."[19]

Bradshaw also advises that the secret of your public relations plan is the "repetitive communication of your campaign theme."[20] The theme is repeated in campaign literature, paid commercials, debates, speeches, social media, and press releases. It is like a lawyer building a case for his client. You keep pounding it home in as many ways as possible.[21]

Joseph Napolitan in *The Election Game* argues that there are only three steps to winning an election:

First, define the message the candidate is to communicate to the voters.
Second, select the vehicles of communication.
Third, implement the communication process. . . .

A campaign can break down on any one of these three steps, but more likely it will break down on the first one: defining the message. Candidates often are unclear in their own minds precisely what it is they want to say to voters, or even why they are running.[22]

The failure to define the message or campaign theme is often the underlying cause of losing campaigns. Lack of resources to communicate the campaign message is the next most likely cause of defeat.

The theme of a campaign should be expressed visually as well as verbally. Although a campaign exercises only limited control over coverage by the media, complete control over the image portrayed by buttons, brochures, posters, and the campaign website is possible. Carefully selecting visual themes early and continuing to use them throughout the campaign for maximum effect is important. These graphic choices include color, typeface for the candidate's name, photographs, and general design. In making decisions about visual themes several rules apply:

- Keep it simple
- Emphasize the candidate's name
- Make all campaign materials easily identifiable
- Make your graphic designs distinctive but not wild

In Simpson's campaigns for Congress he used a large blue button with reverse (white) lettering (see Figure 6.1). The typeface is a slightly modified Bookman Bold. To make his name just a little different, the *i* in Simpson was dotted with a star. The result was a bold, clear, easily readable button identifiable at a distance. Like many campaigns, this one used red, white, and blue flag colors in various combinations in all campaign literature and posters. However, the blue was deeper and the red was brighter and softer than US flag colors. The campaign used only blue and white for the button and much of the campaign literature because it was distinctive and cheaper to print than using all three colors. In the Simpson campaign brochure, all three colors were used along with black for the photographs and some headlines. Whatever a campaign's selected typeface and selected campaign colors, it should use them consistently on all campaign materials. Colors and typeface should not be switched after a campaign begins unless the first efforts were totally amateurish and a standard is being established for the first time.

The Will Guzzardi for Illinois State Representative campaign in 2014 selected blue and green (along with black for text) on a white background for its brochures and mailers (see Figure 6.2). The addition of green stood out and emphasized his concern for the environment. These color combinations were used throughout the campaign and made his materials distinctive.

Publicity in the News Media

The battle to gain maximum publicity for a candidate involves two important restrictions. First, the publicity effort must be an integral part of the entire campaign, not a side activity in the hands of a single specialist. Publicity and the art of communicating through the media are simply other methods for recruiting workers and winning votes. Major publicity decisions, basic to the campaign as a whole, often involve the entire campaign leadership because there cannot be one campaign theme and another set of public relations themes. The best cam-

6.1. Simpson Campaign Button.
Courtesy of Dick Simpson.

paigns have a single unified theme, developed and exploited by publicity and social media as well as by other campaign efforts.

Second, in developing a media publicity campaign the single most important asset, in addition to a worthy candidate, is good judgment as to the newsworthiness of any event or announcement. News worth only a column note should not be sent as a major press release. Press conferences should not be called when an exclusive interview with a single reporter is more appropriate. Information developed for internal campaign use or for direct contact with the voters might be inappropriate for public announcements. Targeted direct mail or e-mail appeals to particular voters are not sent out as general press releases to mass media.

The news media publicity effort in a campaign requires a series of careful judgments as to what information is worth communicating, to whom, when, and through which media. Information about stupid things your opponent has said, or marvelous things your candidate has done, must be released in ways that have the maximum effect in building your campaign, communicating its purpose, and, most of all, winning on Election Day. Without a thorough knowledge of the peculiarities and potential of different media, including social media; without experience with what the media considers worthy of coverage; and without the advice of a professional public relations expert, these judgments will be difficult.

Participatory campaigns are not won by press conferences alone. With thousands of campaigns occurring simultaneously and with Federal Communications Commission (FCC) rules requiring equal time for candidates in

6.2. Guzzardi Flier: front of mailer (this page), back of mailer (facing page). Courtesy of State Representative Will Guzzardi.

WILL GUZZARDI'S PRIORITIES

STRENGTHENING OUR SCHOOLS

- Demand an immediate moratorium on school closings
- Push for an elected school board in Chicago
- Fight for the return of TIF surplus money to public schools to fund the restoration of arts, foreign languages, and physical education

FIXING OUR STATE'S ECONOMY

- Fight for a more progressive income tax
- Put an end to loopholes and tax breaks that allow 60% of Illinois corporations to avoid paying any income tax at all

CREATING JOBS

- Put people back to work through investments in public infrastructure
- Support small businesses through increased access to lending

MAKING GOVERNMENT ACCOUNTABLE

- Push for stronger rules prohibiting legislators from voting on bills that could directly benefit their own financial interests
- Work for campaign finance reform to limit the influence of money in politics

KEEPING OUR NEIGHBORHOODS SAFE

- Fight foreclosures in our neighborhoods
- Support community policing efforts
- Offer counseling and services to first-time, non-violent teenage offenders to help them get back on the right track

FIGHTING FOR LGBT RIGHTS

- Ensure all married couples get access to full state and federal benefits
- Fight workplace discrimination against LGBT employees

ADVANCING WOMEN'S RIGHTS

- Defend reproductive health services and a woman's right to choose
- Enforce federal labor law requiring equal pay for equal work

PROTECTING OUR ENVIRONMENT

- Work for job-training programs that put people to work weatherizing buildings and learning new trades
- Promote bike and public transportation
- Fight for an immediate moratorium on fracking

IMPROVING IMMIGRATION LAW

- Advocate for comprehensive immigration reform centered on safe routes to citizenship
- Partner with community organizations on English language training, job-training, and citizenship classes

DEFENDING OUR SENIORS

- Fight for reforms to our nursing-home laws
- Restore funding to Illinois Cares Rx

Guzzardi for State Representative
2642 W. Fullerton Ave
Chicago, IL 60647

PRSRT STD
U.S. POSTAGE
PAID
TAMPA, FL
PERMIT NO.345

some media situations, constant coverage is impossible to obtain. Therefore public relations coordinators also rely on the more ordinary news release, interview, column note, and letters to the editor to keep a candidate's name in the news. Today many campaigns have a link on their websites making available all press releases to both the public and the media.

The public relations process begins long before the first press conference, even before the first newspaper story is written about a candidate. After a public relations plan has been agreed upon, the public relations coordinator assembles a press packet in an attractive folder with the candidate's name and the campaign logo on the cover. The press packet usually contains the following items:

- A one-page biography of the candidate.
- A campaign button. Despite their "neutrality," reporters are particularly fond of collecting buttons, so one should be included. In addition, having a button demonstrates that a campaign has graphic expertise, volunteers to wear the buttons, and the money to pay for at least the basic campaign materials.
- A press release or full statement of a candidate's declaration of candidacy.
- Campaign literature (a brochure, campaign newsletter, or website address).
- One- or two-page position papers on central issue(s) of the campaign.
- A black and white glossy photograph (head or "mug" shot) of the candidate. (Television stations require a color photo.)

For those reporters and editorial writers to whom you cannot personally deliver the press packet, the same information should be on the campaign's website along with any recent news stories that have positively featured your candidate.

After these press packets are given out at the announcement press conference and delivered to select political reporters likely to cover the race, they are then updated with new material and news clippings as background briefing materials for the press throughout the campaign. Of course, the campaign website is updated with new materials every few days, useful for reporters as well as potential supporters.

After the announcement press conference, the candidate and public relations coordinator meet separately with the major news media and with the political reporters covering campaigns. The public relations coordinator arranges for these visits and ensures that the reporters get the updated press packets, which provide background information and a photograph for future articles.

After political editors and reporters meet the candidate, and the campaign has obtained information about their deadlines and news needs, a steady stream of press releases, usually two or three a week, are sent (usually by e-mail) to the media. Any special media needs are also met. For instance, television stations need color photographs of the candidate if this is a race they are covering in depth. Internet bloggers will need at least one breakfast or lunch meeting with the candidate outside of the usual press conference milieu.

The key to getting coverage by the media is to supply effective news releases. The media will only use a release if it contains "news." The best news is that someone *did* something provocative or original. The following are examples of the kinds of actions around which Simpson's congressional campaigns built press releases that became news stories:

> Former Alderman Dick Simpson today called for a federal investigation of Congressman Dan Rostenkowski for making $37,750 in illegal campaign donations just prior to the Democratic primary election last March. . . .
>
> Former Chicago Alderman Dick Simpson today launched a drive to collect voters' signatures on a petition calling for three new laws designed to help eliminate corruption in Congress. . . .
>
> Former Alderman Dick Simpson today announced his candidacy for Congress and challenged incumbent Congressman Dan Rostenkowski to make full disclosure of his personal finances, including what is hidden in Rostenkowski's secret "blind trust." Simpson, who today made public his income tax returns, his assets, and his liabilities, said he was entering the campaign "not just to weed out one corrupt Congressman but also to change Congress."
>
> The National Organization for Women's Political Action Committee, Cook County Democratic Women, and numerous women political and community leaders today endorsed Dick Simpson for Congress for the 5th District of Illinois.

After some action is taken or announced, there are a few simple rules for writing a news release in the form most likely to be accepted by the media. Hank Parkinson in his article in *Campaign Insight* suggests these simple rules:

1. Make sure the release carries a name and phone number in case additional information is needed.
2. Include release instructions. (Is the editor to hold it for a day or two, or can it be used immediately?)
3. Include plenty of white space between the release instructions and the copy start so a headline or instructions to the back shop can be jotted in.
4. Keep the margins wide.
5. Double space. (Never turn in a release that isn't typed.)
6. Never continue a paragraph from one page to another. (Use the word "More" when continuing a story to the second page.)
7. Keep the lead paragraph under 30 words in length, and never use more than three sentences per paragraph.
8. End the story with 30 (this is journalese for "The End").[23]

After reading these simple instructions, it might seem that an inexperienced volunteer could be put in charge of publicity, but public relations is more than just calling press conferences or drafting news releases. Successful public relations results in your candidate being interviewed by reporters and appearing on TV and radio programs, in blogs and Internet news sites, and campaign notes appearing in society or gossip columns. Success requires knowing members of the working press and, more importantly, knowing the way the press works—both the mass media and the Internet media. A professional public relations person is much more likely to have personal contacts and to know deadlines and normal media procedures. With lots of perseverance and hard work a nonprofessional can make contacts, learn the trade, and get some coverage, but it will be harder than it would be for an experienced, fulltime professional in the field.

In mounting a professional publicity campaign, simple and natural techniques that can gain great exposure for a candidate should not be overlooked. Drawing your opponent into a debate is often advantageous. Begin with simple debates in front of community organizations. Many groups will be only too pleased to hold a debate. After all, they have the problem of dull meetings to overcome, and holding a debate is a public service rather than a partisan effort. Opponents will find it difficult to turn down a request from a legitimate organization. Later, a candidate may be able to use the debate format to get television and radio exposure.

In Simpson's campaign to unseat Rostenkowski, the incumbent refused to debate before community organizations and turned down invitations for formal television debates. However, the television stations did force him to agree to separate back-to-back television interviews in which Simpson and Rosten-kowski appeared with the same TV reporters. This allowed Simpson to gain considerable positive publicity and credibility from these "debates."

Letters to the editor are often overlooked as a source of publicity. A candidate or his campaign workers can write several letters to all the newspapers in the district. Often more people read these published letters than the news or the editorials. As with everything in a campaign, there are successful and unsuccessful ways of doing the job. For best results the Stevenson for U.S. Senate Campaign suggested that campaign volunteers abide by the following Do's and Don'ts:

Do's

1. Use the Stevenson brochure and other materials sent to you by the Citizens' Committee as your reference material.
2. Always be sure of your facts.
3. Always be polite and objective. An earnest, honest statement with the ring of conviction can draw respect even from those who disagree with its content.
4. Write your own letter, in your own words. Make it brief, neat, and clear. Get your point across, then stop. The best letters run between 100 and 200 words, no longer. Long letters will not be printed.
5. Sign your name and address.

Don'ts

1. Don't write hot-tempered letters or engage in personal attacks on the editor or reporters. Avoid extreme statements.
2. Don't mail any letter that is unsigned. If you can't sign it, don't send it.
3. Don't copy other letters. Organized write-in campaigns have no effect. They can be detected instantly.
4. Do not assert as a fact anything that you cannot document.
5. Do not attack the newspapers. They always have the last word.[24]

It is also useful, when possible, to refer to a recent news story in the particular paper where you wish your letter to be published. Do not neglect to have campaign workers send letters to the editors at smaller publications, such as community or small town newspapers, or to comment on political blogs following the same basic rules.

6.3. STEP-BY-STEP GUIDE TO HOLDING SUCCESSFUL NEWS CONFERENCES

I. Advance Preparation

1. Arrange a location for the news conference that is somewhat close to where the news offices are located so that it's easy to get to, which will enable more reporters to attend.
2. Choose a room large enough to accommodate five to ten reporters plus TV cameras unless you are certain fewer reporters will attend. Don't select a space so large that the news conference turnout will appear to be negligible.
3. Several days prior to the news conference, email or fax a news advisory to broadcast, print, and on-line news media. Send the advisory to news assignment editors, political reporters, and columnists. Also notify those reporters and editors who the candidate or campaign knows from previous contacts.
4. Prepare a news release and a statement, and produce enough copies to distribute at the press conference.
5. The day before or morning of the news conference, the candidate or spokesperson should anticipate questions he or she will likely receive and prepare quotable responses. Following is an example of a quotable response preceded by one that is dull and therefore not quotable.
Question: Are the issues you are

NEWS CONFERENCES

The news conference is especially useful as a communication tool because it allows television and radio coverage of a candidate. However, remember that unless the candidate is an incumbent governor or president, coverage will be limited. Some campaigns might never develop sufficient news to call a legitimate news conference. In most major cities, where the large number of simultaneous campaigns makes the battle for media attention fierce, one or two well-covered news conferences are all that can be expected. A simple news assignment memo on campaign stationery telling the time, place, and purpose of the conference should announce it the day before or the morning the news conference is scheduled. In major cities this same information must also be sent by e-mail to every political reporter and news assignment editor. Other than conferences requiring a special location, such as the opening of a headquarters, most news conferences are held at a downtown hotel or in the pressroom at government buildings such as city hall or the state government office building. After the memo has gone out, all major media are called and reminded of the conference. At early morning news conferences coffee and pastries should be provided.

Campaign communications consultant Tom Gradel covers the basic rules for conducting a news conference in his step-by-step guide (see Figure 6.3). News conference preparations begin with the judgment that something the candidate has done (introducing a citizen's ordinance on an important issue or filing suit in federal court) or has had done to him (the campaign headquarters has been bombed) is of sufficient importance to justify a news conference. In addition to preparing the news assignment memo announcing the news conference, the public relations coordinator prepares a statement to be read by the candidate and a news release written as if it were a news story about the conference. A candidate should know the content of the statement so thoroughly that he can deliver it without having to read it line by line. A formal statement saying exactly what the candidate wants to tell the press and the public is handed out to the reporters even if the candidate paraphrases parts of it in his presentation.

Immediately after answering all the questions of the media reporters who attend the news conference, the candidate calls radio stations that take news interviews over the phone. The public relations coordinator calls television stations that failed to cover the conference and asks if they would like to interview the candidate from the campaign office or in the television studio later in the day. Television coverage is golden, and usually television stations use footage made with their limited crews, so any opportunity to redo the news event for television is instantly agreed to by the public relations coordinator even if it means an extra effort on the part of the candidate.

In a news conference, the "news" aspect should be viewed from the perspective of the reporters who cover it and their editors. *Does this action affect the lives of many people?* For instance, when the president, governor, and mayor announce new taxes they propose to enact, it is always news. *Is the action real or is it just words?* The impact of new taxes is felt by everyone, but slogans about fiscal responsibility are only words. Statements about procedural reforms of government are even less interesting to most news consumers. *Finally, is there a human interest aspect to the story?* People do not often challenge party

raising really important enough to receive the kind of priority attention from the government that you say are necessary?

Dull Response: I (we) believe everything we outlined today is important and of great concern to all Americans.

Quotable Response: No civilization can survive if life in its cities is unaffordable, or fraught with fear and destruction. It is imperative, therefore, that we substantially improve the health and safety of communities if we hope to preserve the viability of our nation.

II. The Day of the Conference
1. Early in the day send e-mail reminders to all media including online news sites and bloggers. Make phone calls to TV and radio news assignment desks and to key reporters. Besides reminding media of the time and place of the news conference use the phone calls to ascertain who will be covering the news conference. If you have been told a TV crew will be covering, you can delay for a few minutes the start of the news conference until they arrive. If you find out that a news outlet will be shorthanded and can't send a crew or reporter, you can arrange for a telephone interview after the news conference.
2. Well before the news conference is scheduled to begin, put a lectern deep into the room facing the entrance and with a blank wall a few feet behind

it. The back wall need not be blank as long as what's on it will not be distracting in photos or on TV. Arrange chairs for reports facing the lectern with a wide middle aisle so the TV cameras can have unobstructed sight lines to the candidate or spokesperson at the lectern. Make sure you have enough chairs but not so many that an abundance of unfilled chairs will make the event seem to be poorly attended.

3. If you are expecting a large crowd of reporters or if there will be supporters or others present, and if the room is large, make sure you test the microphone and sound system well before attendees start arriving. If you plan to use a computer or other projecting equipment, make sure you test it well in advance and again when you are checking the sound equipment.

4. Use a mult box so those recording sound can plug in. This will eliminate the need for a cluster of microphones attached to the lectern or front table. It will also help avoid feedback and distortion from multiple microphones. Many venues will have a mult box, or you can rent one.

III. The News Conference

1. The candidate or spokesperson should arrive at least thirty minutes ahead of time to make sure the room is arranged properly and that all the electronic equipment is working.

leaders, so such a challenge is newsworthy. A real battle between two political personalities is often more newsworthy than the merits of any proposed law. It may be unfortunate that personalities are more interesting to readers and viewers than substance, but this is a fact that must be recognized in planning to win media coverage. The human interest aspects increase the importance of a news story.

The news assignment memo, the statement to be read, and the news release must be written around the best "news pegs" from the perspective of the media. The strongest words and the most far-reaching action must be placed in the first paragraph, even in the first sentence.

The whole news conference should not be given away in the news assignment memo. The questions of the reporters who call in advance to get the story for their deadlines should not be answered if a candidate wishes to avoid an angry press corps "scooped" before the press conference.

Once again, if campaign volunteers do not have a lot of experience holding news conferences, the campaigns will be better off hiring a professional public relations person to coordinate at least these key press events.

PAID ADVERTISING

For local races, mass media advertising might be too expensive because the media broadcast to a much larger audience than the residents of one district. The bulk of the readers or viewers cannot vote for the candidate. One way of overcoming this handicap is to advertise only in neighborhood newspapers, on targeted cable television stations, or on specific Internet sites or community blogs.

If your campaign also advertises on radio, first pick station(s) with the most listeners from the district and purchase thirty-second spots immediately before the election. By narrowing the audience reached through the media, or by limiting the period in which a candidate advertises, a campaign saves money and still has the greatest impact. Of course, with early voting and mail ballot options getting great use in many states, radio ads may need to run for at least a month before the election.

Of all the media, radio is one of the cheapest for reaching large audiences. Cable television and Internet advertising are also inexpensive, but they do not usually reach as many district voters. Three to five candidates running on a similar platform can purchase joint media ads to cut costs. However, to be effective, one must buy "saturation time" on the stations selected. That means as many as ten replays a week on a single station at various broadcast hours and prices. A campaign can probably buy two weeks of spots on each station for $1,000 or less. Advertising rates, of course, vary according to the size of the audience. One advantage of radio ads is that FCC regulations require both radio and television stations to play campaign ads, so they are guaranteed to get on the air. Political advertisements have priority and the least expensive commercial rates.

An example of a simple radio ad used to support three alderman candidates (all three won their elections) is shown in Figure 6.4. Writing such advertisements is tricky and usually requires a specialist. The images evoked and the phrasing are important, and these writing tricks are not quickly learned. Only a few concepts can be transmitted in a single advertisement, so the message has to be carefully crafted. A professional announcer, the candidate, or an "important person" whose voice endorsement is helpful tapes the ad.

2. Assign a staffer or volunteer to stand at the front door of the room to pass out copies of the release, statement, and supporting materials. Have a sign-in sheet for reporters to print their names, news organizations, email addresses, and phone numbers. This list will enable you to determine who didn't show and therefore needs to be called after the conference. And you can add any new names to your campaign's media contact list.

3. Wait up to five minutes after the scheduled starting time if it looks as though more media may be on the way. Start as soon after the scheduled time as practical.

4. Begin the conference by having the campaign manager or other clear-speaking staffer or volunteer ask the reporters if they are ready to begin. Announce that the candidate will deliver a short statement followed by a time for questions and answers.

5. Then introduce the candidate and any other persons who will be speaking.

6. After reading the statement, the candidate should answer questions until all important points have been made and clarified. When the conference appears to have run its course, thank everyone for coming and state that the candidate will remain for a few more minutes in case someone still has questions. If you wait too long, some reporters—especially those on a close

deadline—will be uncomfortable and may get up to leave, distracting the others.

IV. Follow-up Work

1. Immediately following the news conference, the candidate should phone the news outlets who could not attend but requested phone interviews.

2. Email or fax copies of the release, statement, and supporting material to those who could not attend. Copies or especially prepared stories should be emailed to key contributors and supporters and posted on your website.

3. Check all online news sites, watch and record broadcast news reports, and read print editions of the news. You do this to assess the extent, quality, and accuracy of the coverage. If necessary, e-mail or phone clarifications or corrections for any important errors. News organizations are as interested in accuracy as you are but only do this if the errors are significant.

4. The candidate, campaign manager, communications consultant, and/or publicity staffer should do a postmortem after the news conference to discuss aspects that could be done better at the next news conference.

Source: Thomas J. Gradel, a longtime campaign communications consultant based in Chicago. He revised and updated a version that he and Ronni Scheier prepared for an earlier edition of *Winning Elections.*

Television advertisements are too expensive for most candidates unless they are part of city, county, or statewide campaigns. The same is generally true of downtown newspaper ads, although those costs vary according to the size of the city or town. Most campaigns, however, do place ads in specialized community newspapers. Even so, an ordinary campaign advertisement is a waste of money because political ads look the same and appear at the same time as advertisements supporting dozens of other candidates. As with every other aspect of the campaign, imagination and people should be the hallmark of the advertising. For instance, simple testimonial ads can be scattered throughout the neighborhood paper at modest expense but maximum effect. These smaller advertisements are not consigned to the section of the paper with the usual political ads. Because they are statements of real citizens rather than concoctions of a public relations firm, they are read more often, and their message is more convincing. They have a simple message and a striking graphic layout.

Different quotes from different citizens can be scattered in small ads throughout the newspaper for less than the cost of a single standard quarter- or half-page ad. Similar "testimonials" are ideal for Internet advertising as well. They also complement the comments supporters write on a candidate's behalf on political blogs.

If a campaign is fortunate enough to have enough money to purchase television ads, it is important to make sure they do not look like all the other political ads. Bill Hillsman made the classic Paul Wellstone for U.S. Senate advertisements in Minnesota (see Figure 6.5). Along with the Ronald Reagan for President advertisements in 1984, they are often cited as among the best political advertising because they reached voters at an emotional level. Hillsman's principle is, "If a political ad looks like a political ad—too preachy, too serious, too cautious, and, worst of all, dull—then it is a failure."[25]

In the first Wellstone ad, called "Fast-Paced Paul,"[26] Hillsman's goal was to "introduce Wellstone and give viewers a feel for his unconventional campaign, and it would warn people to look with suspicion on [incumbent Senator] Boschwitz's commercials."[27] It succeeded by being so different from the standard advertisements that it caught the audience's attention. Only creative ads such as this one allow low-budget, participatory campaigns to win the advertising war against candidates with greater funds and therefore more television commercials.

In recent years, buying ads on cable television has become much more frequent. One example was from Calabasas, a Southern California community at the northern end of Los Angeles County. The costs of thirty-second cable ads for Councilman James Bozajian were affordable enough to be incorporated into his campaign. A primetime *FOX TV News* ad cost him only $17 each time in 2005 and is not much more costly today if it is confined to small districts served by cable TV. As Todd Blair and Garrett Biggs write:

> There are three major rules to cable television advertising: time element, product quality, and strength of buy. The world of cable television is a marathon, not a sprint. It takes time for viewers to accumulate substantive viewings of campaign TV spots. Therefore, it is best to begin earlier rather than later. Start advertising 12 weeks before the election, so that voters, especially those who will vote by absentee ballot, have enough time to see your TV spots and digest your message.[28]

6.4. SCRIPT FOR ALDERMAN ELECTION RADIO AD

I'm Alderman Dick Simpson. This February 27 and April 3, Chicago will elect a mayor, city officials, and a city council. The question is: Will we elect good people, or the same old machine? Unless a lot of people get out and register to vote, Chicago will be stuck with the same old machine. Three honest, independent candidates don't want this to happen. That's why Alderman Marty Oberman of the Forty-Third Ward, Bruce Young of the Forty-Fourth, and David Orr of the Forty-Ninth Ward urge you to register to vote. Low voter turnout works for the machine but hinders the independent candidates who provide a voice of reason in the chaos of the city council. If the independent vote doesn't get out, the machine will win out. You can still register. If you're a new voter, or a new Illinois resident, or have changed your address, register Tuesday, January 30 at your precinct polling place. Only if you register can you help elect good people, not the same old machine. To volunteer, get registration information, or the address of your precinct polling place, phone 312-248-7979. That's 312-248-7979.

6.5. PAUL WELLSTONE FOR U.S. SENATE COMMERCIAL

The ad begins with Wellstone standing outside in a short-sleeved shirt and tie. Addressing the camera, he immediately takes on Rudy Boschwitz instead of Jim Nichols, his Democratic primary opponent. "Hi, I'm Paul Wellstone," he starts, "and I'm running for United States Senate from Minnesota. Unlike my opponent, I don't have $6 million, so I'm going to have to talk fast."

Then Wellstone literally races through the commercial, stopping for a breather and a few words, such as "I'll lead the fight for national health care," in front of an appropriate backdrop before he rushes off to the right and enters again from the left for the next scene. By the end of the thirty-second spot, he's running across the screen at fast-forward speed. He looks like a blurred hybrid of Harpo Marx and a Keystone Kop as he jumps into his campaign bus, which speeds away as the narrator says, "Paul Wellstone won't slow down after he's elected." You can view this commercial at https://www.youtube.com/watch?v=aTiW0YCMM0g.

Source: Dennis McGrath and Dane Smith, *Professor Wellstone Goes to Washington* (Minneapolis: University of Minnesota Press, 1995), 152.

CAMPAIGN LITERATURE

Whether a campaign succeeds in getting front-page newspaper stories or coverage on the 10:00 p.m. television news for the candidate, it can distribute its own campaign information to all the voters in the district. It accomplishes this by sending volunteers door to door, by direct mail, and via e-mail.

Different types of campaign literature have different purposes. Campaign buttons, small window posters, and yard signs are employed to gain name recognition and to encourage campaign workers. Hundreds of citizens wearing campaign buttons are more impressive than hundreds of dollars of paid advertisements in local newspapers. Buttons are among the least expensive of all forms of campaign advertising, and many campaigns recover the cost of printing buttons by selling them for a dollar each. Of course, buttons succeed only if the campaign has hundreds of supporters wearing them.

It is equally effective if hundreds of campaign supporters post endorsements of the candidate on their Facebook pages or tweet their support to their friends and followers.

Small posters have maximum effect when they go up in the windows of homes or on lawn signs in private yards. They demonstrate that citizens of the district support a candidate, for an impact money cannot buy. Some campaigns augment posters and buttons with bumper stickers, car tops, and yard signs. A special visibility campaign can also put stickers on every utility pole in the district. Well-financed campaigns purchase billboard space or posters for commuter buses and trains. For local campaigns, buttons, small posters, Facebook posts, campaign websites, tweets, and yard signs create sufficient name recognition and a good campaign image. Larger campaigns will supplement this with more expensive paid campaign advertising as well.

Convincing supporters and campaign workers to wear buttons or to make Facebook posts or tweet requires mentioning the need for such visibility at all campaign functions. Getting hundreds of posters into windows or signs into yards is more difficult. A visibility chair or team of workers must call or e-mail every potential campaign supporter listed in the headquarters files, asking that they put up a poster or yard sign and get others to do so. Posters and yard signs are dispatched immediately by car to the homes of those willing to take them, and a careful record of each poster is kept on a map of the district on the campaign headquarters wall or in an office computer. As posters and yard signs go up, special efforts are made to get them into the weakest areas and into at least one home or yard near every polling place in the district.

Buttons, stickers, posters, Facebook posts, tweets, and yard signs are primarily used to improve name recognition and create a positive campaign image. They can be simple—perhaps containing only the name of the candidate and the office he seeks. Literature dropped door to door, passed out on street corners, or mailed and e-mailed to voters must be more complete, supplying information about the candidate's history, platform, and the groups endorsing his candidacy. The literature may also contain photographs of the candidate with his family, with prominent supporters, and with voters to tell the campaign's story visually as well as verbally. A study of campaign brochures has concluded that the most frequently used photos were individual shots of the candidates themselves and that the next most frequent were of other people including politicians who endorsed a candidate.[29]

The basic piece of campaign literature is a simple threefold brochure that can be mailed in an envelope, put through a mail slot, or easily handed to voters at transportation stops or grocery stores. A campaign creates such a brochure by answering a series of questions voters might ask if they were talking to the candidate in person.

1. Who are you and against whom are you running?
2. Why should we vote for you?
3. What is your platform (or what will you do if we elect you)?
4. What have you done before running for this office?
5. When is the election, and how do I vote for you?
6. Who endorses your candidacy?

The answers to all these questions and more are provided in this single brochure.

Whatever media are used to promote a candidate, the information presented will, of necessity, have to be brief. Photographs and graphic design replace endless words in conveying the campaign's message to the voters.

The general rule is to highlight only the positive aspects of the candidate and completely ignore opponents in campaign literature. The exceptions are what are called "comparative" brochures, mailers, or Internet posts. In these communications, the record and platform of the incumbent or opposing candidate is explicitly compared with your candidate's. This is done to demonstrate why voters should vote for him.

The best method of distributing campaign literature is by precinct workers going door to door.[30] Using this method, campaign workers can talk to the voters, answer their questions, and learn voter preferences. Even so, there will be some precincts in the district that will not be worked because there are not enough campaign volunteers. Those precincts should receive a blitz of campaign literature at the door or in the foyer. An experiment attempted by Byron Sistler in Evanston, Illinois, indicates that just leaving literature for a slate of candidates endorsed by the Independent Voters of Illinois affected a limited number of voters. He found that in precincts not covered, an average split-ticket vote for six endorsed candidates (both Democrat and Republican) was 6.1 percent of the total vote. In the precincts in which he left campaign literature, they received 8.2 percent of the vote for all six candidates across party lines. The difference, 2.1 percent of the total vote or about ten votes per precinct, was affected by his literature blitz.[31]

More recent studies confirm the effectiveness of door-to-door canvassing. They find, however, that quality conversations with potential voters are far more effective than simply a large number of doors knocked on with perfunctory conversations.[32] These results demonstrate why personal contact is more desirable, but why blitzes, direct mail, e-mail, and social media are used to contact voters in otherwise unworked precincts.[33]

Misusing the Media

In the modern era, both the mass media and more targeted media can be used to mislead voters. A candidate's persona can be altered even more easily than in the past when many voters knew local political candidates personally. Public opinion polls, focus groups, and analytics can be used to find out what the voters want, and various characteristics of the candidate and campaign issues can be constantly tested by techniques such as tracking polls. With this information, sophisticated media advisors can manipulate the candidate's image to deceive voters.

Style and image have become more important than substance in too many campaigns. Negative attack ads are used heavily to discredit opponents. These techniques are too often used in campaigns.

The real danger is that media manipulation has the potential to undermine the campaign process by creating a false persona for the candidate, an untrue stand on issues, or an inaccurate portrayal of one's opponents. Democracy only works if the voters have accurate information to make a decision on the best person to elect.

Chapter Seven

Getting the Word Out
in the Digital Age

....

In 1998, former professional wrestler Jesse Ventura threw his hat in the ring to run for governor of Minnesota against two heavy-hitting politicians, Democrat Hubert Humphrey III and Republican Norm Coleman. Both of Ventura's opponents were well known, with good records in the state and solid financial backing from their parties and supporters.

Nonetheless, Ventura won. Why? The other candidates were better known. Regular party loyalists worked and voted for them.

Ventura's campaign team had decided to put together a set of irreverent commercials to appeal to Minnesotans tired of politics as usual. To counteract Ventura's trademark wrestling tag of "Jesse the Body Ventura," they created ads with Ventura posed as Rodin's statue of the Thinker. They also made a commercial that showed children playing with Ventura action figures defeating a suit-clad figure representing old-style politics.[1]

A website highlighting Ventura's background and his stand on major issues supplemented these ads, which simultaneously solicited funds and volunteers. Jesse Net, an interactive e-mail system, provided a new twist for campaigns at that time: two-way communication with the public to keep them updated on campaign events. By November, more than 3,000 people had signed up. Finally, although Ventura's web page had traditional political information, it also had a shopping link to buy Ventura action figures, Ventura for governor T-shirts, and other campaign paraphernalia.[2]

The Ventura campaign did not have the money to run a saturation advertising campaign. What Ventura had was a well-known name, and what he could do was make a website to let his supporters (many of whom were young, white males) know that they could register to vote even on Election Day. Ventura's candidacy brought an overall increase in voter turnout of 7.4 percent.[3] Although his mass media ads successfully spoke to voters alienated by run-of-the-mill politics, he also presented his message inexpensively on his website and raised money through its online sales.

At the time, Betty O'Shaughnessy was teaching about campaign websites, which in 1998 had few links, were not updated often, and seldom were used except by the national party committees and major candidates. O'Shaughnessy suggested to her students that they access the Ventura website. These students were similar to Ventura's young Minnesotan supporters; both groups liked his rebellious, outspoken approach to politics.

The Ventura campaign was an example of how, in the late twentieth century, Internet technology was changing how we communicated with each other. It penetrated all aspects of society, and political campaigns were no exception. Today, campaigns use websites to provide voters information about candidates, issues, and campaigns. Through the Internet, a campaign can reach potential supporters more personally by presenting photos of the candidate, accounts of recent events, and the candidate's most recent statement on issues.[4] Contributions are made online. Social media encourage followers to access campaign websites and make campaigns more transparent because they become open to everyone.

Even the most local campaigns are now using voter analytics and social media techniques developed by presidential campaigns and national political parties. It is important to understand, however, that these new methods are being used to accomplish the same tasks performed by Cicero in Rome millennia ago and Abraham Lincoln 150 years ago. Nonetheless, it is critical to master these new technologies.

To be effective, techniques such as analytics and social media must be fully integrated with the rest of the campaign. Software analytics programs should incorporate data directly from voter contacts to be successful. Social media must amplify the same campaign messages developed in the overall publicity campaign, and interactive responses via social media have to be passed on to campaign strategists and traditional media advisors to guide campaign message adjustments and strategies. This is especially useful in responding to negative voter perceptions of a candidate or weaknesses in an opponent's campaign.

These new techniques, from interactive websites to tweets, having been perfected in national campaigns for president and members of Congress with their budgets from $1 million to $1 billion, are now being scaled back for use in more local campaigns run for a few thousand or a few hundreds of thousands of dollars. Candidates and campaign leaders less familiar with analytics and with only a passing knowledge of social media such as Facebook and Twitter will need the assistance of more experienced staff and volunteers to use these new campaign techniques. However, the payoff will be better targeting of voters and more effective advertising across all media. In short, analytics and social media are new ways to win elections by lowering the cost of getting campaign messages to the voters most likely to vote for a candidate.

In Chapter 9 we will describe how all the techniques, both old and new, came together to win the Will Guzzardi state legislative race. For now, we will confine ourselves to a general description of the way these techniques were developed, have evolved, and have been adapted to local campaigns in general.

The Internet Revolution

In 1994, thousands of people began accessing the World Wide Web when Netscape made its browser available free. Within ten years, more than 70 million Americans would be logging onto the Internet to use e-mail, get news, find product information, and pursue other activities.[5] By 2015, there were almost 300 million users, or 87 percent of the US population.[6]

EARLY USE OF THE INTERNET
IN CAMPAIGNS

Before Internet use became widespread, a campaign's communication with potential voters was generally one way only—campaigns sent messages to voters, who found it difficult to contact a candidate directly. Also, campaigns were party centered. Although the media routinely covered party-slated candidates, anyone who wanted to launch an independent candidacy had to find potential supporters on her own. The same went for news about the campaign. News coverage of any campaign was limited to print and broadcast media; for a local campaign this meant free media coverage was limited to announcement of candidacies, tight races before the election, and returns on election night.

Internet use changed election campaigns. Early on, the Internet was used mostly to put a campaign website online, create a supporter list from those who accessed it, and contact these voters for further support. Results were impressive, and Internet use in campaigns gradually became widespread. As early as 1998, a survey revealed that more than 63 percent of political strategists used campaign websites.[7] The Internet had shown that it could change how people got information, limit the power of the mainstream media, and potentially cancel party candidate advantage. Internet communities allowed people to become politically active online, interact with each other, and campaign through political websites and e-mail.[8]

Campaign managers and candidates perceived that one of the Internet's main functions was to find and keep supporters by building large e-mail lists of potential adherents. For instance, while running for governor in 1998, Republican Jim Gilmore of Virginia ran on a platform of abolishing the state automobile tax. His campaign compiled an e-mail list of about 2,000 supporters and added 3,000 more by obtaining the 1996 Dole presidential campaign e-mail list. Gilmore's campaign e-mailed updates on campaign issues regularly—including opposing a car tax—and encouraged supporters to forward this message to people on their own e-mail lists. That way thousands of voters learned of Gilmore's proposed tax cut in a quick, inexpensive way, and Gilmore won by 13 percentage points.[9]

PRESIDENTIAL CAMPAIGNS GO ONLINE

LaCrystal Ricke holds that the first national politician to really understand how to use the Internet in politics was Howard Dean. He believed that those who made use of the Internet would have the upper hand in future elections. In 2004, Dean's presidential campaign drew attention with its novel use of online campaigning to reach voters and raise funds. His was also one of the first to make use of blogs and e-mail to get rapid feedback from his supporters and to use the Internet to coordinate the work of his volunteers. Dean's online approach to elections attracted young, tech-savvy workers. Although his campaign ultimately was not successful, it changed the way candidates approached campaigns.[10]

Internet campaigning rapidly became more widespread and sophisticated. After the Dean campaign, candidates in all types of elections began hiring professional web consultants who suggested improvements such as embedding videos in websites. Videos helped to hook viewers emotionally. Campaigns still used traditional media to "drive" voters to their websites. However, after voters came there, the campaign encouraged its new supporters to e-mail friends about the candidate, a practice known as *viral marketing*.[11]

EARLY SOCIAL MEDIA IN PRESIDENTIAL CAMPAIGNS

After going on the Internet, e-mail users discovered they could use new social media to get in touch with both friends and strangers more conveniently. The number of Americans on social media networks increased rapidly. Whereas in 2005 only 8 percent of all Americans on the Internet were social network users, by 2013 the percentage had climbed to 73 percent.[12] Use of the Internet and social media in political campaigns increased correspondingly.

Businesses know that when marketing a product, it is important to have a brand and to use different outlets to appeal to different audiences. Inevitably, these marketing strategies reached the political sphere, and campaigns learned to employ social media along with traditional news outlets. This was the case with the 2008 Obama presidential campaign, which political analyst Leonard Steinhorn argues became a model for future campaigns by turning every "media tool, new and old, into an instrument to promote his 'brand' and emotionally connect it with the American public."[13] That is exactly what local campaigns attempt to achieve today.

Obama's campaign used eighteen separate social networking sites, enabling activists to network, organize, fund-raise, and build his campaign at the grassroots level. Those who accessed his sites on social media interacted not only with the campaign but also with each other. Participants felt emotionally engaged, which became the key to winning donations, workers, and votes.[14]

PRESIDENTIAL CAMPAIGNS EMPLOY DATA ANALYTICS

With the rise of the Internet, the amount of unstructured data increased exponentially. To make sense of this *big data*, the business community used mathematical or statistical analysis of data, now called *data analytics.* Such analytics are used to drive decisions based on information gathered from large amounts of data. Knowing that social media site users put all sorts of information about themselves online, the business community figured out a way to transform site users into customers.[15] Marketing specialists used data analytics to study social networks, gleaning names and information from membership lists, alumni directories, and league rosters.

By the early 2000s, political strategists sought data analytics experts to develop technology that could sell a candidate online just as the business community marketed products. The presidential campaigns of George W. Bush in 2004 and Barack Obama in 2008 and 2012 were pioneers in these efforts. Their developments using analytics in campaigns are now copied everywhere. Today, campaign analytics specialists combine massive amounts of data found on social media sites with other data. They employ everything from census figures to the car one drives to contact voters according to their interests.[16]

Microtargeting and Nanotargeting

Today, campaign analytics specialists use *microtargeting* to channel massive amounts of data found at online social media sites. By combining this with other data, such as organization memberships or consumer purchases, they can build statistical models to predict a voter's support for a candidate. [17]

In order to get enough voters to the polls to win, campaigns mobilize their base of supporters, persuade swing voters of the superiority of the campaign's candidate, and address the specific issues that concern them.[18] In the past, campaigns would probably target voters broadly. For instance, if campaigns wanted to get the African American vote, they might place an ad on a network that programs mainly for African Americans. To reach younger voters, the candidate might speak on a college campus.

Campaigns could also target specific neighborhoods and towns. By looking at voter records, a campaign would know whether a town or neighborhood voted predominantly for the Democrats. If so, it might place ads in the local paper showing that the candidate supported Democratic issues.

There were two problems with this approach. For instance, Republicans might bypass a Democratic-leaning precinct, thereby not capitalizing on any support that might be there. Alternatively, a Democratic campaign might emphasize an issue not important to the Democrats in a specific area or ignore one of their main concerns.

By comparison, microtargeting finds voters and the issues they care about regardless of where they live. A campaign can get the voter records in thirty-nine states plus the District of Columbia that record a voter's party affiliation and voting choices in party primaries. This information allows it to target independent voters with a message specifically designed to persuade them to vote for their candidate. In addition to existing information on voter preferences, a campaign can send a random survey to voters asking about political views and consumer habits. Cross-referencing the survey information with the voter list, a campaign then buys the credit history of these voters. With all this information, a campaign creates an ideal voter profile and uses it to target specific voters most like the supporters found in the survey.[19]

In a practical example of how this works, Bill Brady was the Republican candidate for governor of Illinois in 2010. While still serving in the Illinois General Assembly, and immediately after he won the Republican primary, Brady introduced a bill allowing for mass euthanasia of dogs and cats, reversing a ban enacted the year before. Through their data management system, Illinois Democrats found that the heaviest concentration of pet owners lived in the suburbs. The Democratic gubernatorial candidate's campaign then put together a very unflattering ad describing Brady as a supporter of dog and cat "gas chambers" and spread this story heavily in the suburbs. Although Brady had quickly retracted his support of the euthanasia bill, this became an issue Brady could not shake. He went on to lose the election by less than 1 percent of the vote.[20]

Microtargeting became even more refined by 2012, when campaigns mined data found over the Internet and used this information to *nanotarget*. With nanotargeting, candidates choose the issues they want to emphasize to specific social media users.[21]

Al Franken's campaign for US senator from Minnesota in 2008 used nanotargeting by placing online ads on users' screens based on words that appeared in their Google searches. When Minnesotans did a Google search for fuel-efficient cars or inexpensive gas, they saw ads about how Franken proposed to lower the price of gasoline. Those who did a search for farm supplies found on their homepage an ad describing Franken's support for farmers.[22] Using analytics and online advertising, Franken won a close, recounted race.

Adjusting the Message: Dynamic Modeling

Data analytics experts are constantly refining ways to find specific target audiences. By 2012, *dynamic modeling* made it possible for a campaign to constantly survey and recalibrate the level of support from an individual. Such adjusting meant that as an individual's support score changed, a campaign could adjust the message sent to him or her accordingly. By 2014, it was possible for campaigns to target audiences through information obtained through their cable TV boxes, and local campaigns could also use cookie-targeted online advertising to reach voters.

The technology developed by the major political campaigns can now be used in local campaigns. Wise use of the Internet and social media gets the word out to potential supporters and obtains volunteers, donations, and votes. Even the smallest campaigns use Facebook to find voters and bring in donations through online messaging and ads specifically tailored for them.[23]

Making Use of the Internet in Local Campaigns

Now that local campaigns can take advantage of the online strategies developed by presidential campaigns, they should take steps to maximize their effectiveness. Campaign experts have several suggestions.

When planning an online campaign, it is best to begin by building an integrated system in which all the components of a campaign, including its website and other social media, reinforce each other. It is important not to forget campaign fundamentals even while adapting new methods. Using newer digitalized tools and the Internet only succeeds if the basics are covered, such as making sure the candidate meets the legal requirements to run for office, studying the district's demographics and voting history, selecting a target number of votes needed, taking advantage of special aspects of a particular election year (presidential election, off-year election, etc.), and carefully developing an overall campaign message and strategy. All the online aspects should be coordinated with traditional buttons, brochures, graphics, posters, direct mail, and media advertising.[24]

E-MAIL IN LOCAL CAMPAIGNS

Before undertaking any other steps, a campaign should start collecting e-mail addresses to build a list from a candidate's personal contacts and then add campaign contacts.[25]

One technique used by local campaigns today includes tapping into national party databases to find voters. In 2004 a Colorado state senator got more than 5,000 Democrats and 6,000 independents from the Democratic database for his small state senatorial campaign. His campaign e-mailed these 11,000 voters, asked them to complete a survey, sent them a targeted message based on their answers, and used the list for a get-out-the-vote (GOTV) effort. To get more votes, the campaign encouraged supporters to cast absentee votes by e-mailing them a link to the Colorado Absentee Ballot Request Form with the voter's information already filled out. Not only did this allow the campaign to lock in votes but to find out which voters downloaded the form.[26]

BUILDING A WEBSITE FOR A LOCAL CAMPAIGN

The second step is to build the campaign website. Although online software can help design a good website, it is best to hire a professional. The website should be built in harmony with all other media such as the campaign's Facebook pages and Twitter accounts. Yet the webpage is central. A good website is attractive, easy to navigate, interactive, and updated regularly. It has attractive photos and videos of the candidate. It gives voters information about the candidate's background, why she is running, and her positions on issues.[27] It provides background information for reporters doing media on the campaign as well as information directly to voters.

Political strategist Colin Delany advises you to ask yourself, if you wanted to learn about a candidate, could you find her website easily? After you got there, how hard was it to sign up for e-mail updates, and how easy was it to find information on how to volunteer?

Other suggestions on constructing a campaign website include:

- Have helpful information easily available, such as how to register to vote.
- Include a calendar of upcoming campaign events.
- Make certain your website has easily found links to its social media sites.
- Supporters should be able to find a campaign blog from the website. A blog gives a campaign the ability to shape its own story and answer opponents.[28]
- Two vital pieces of a campaign website are its "donate" and "volunteer" links.
- Post information to the campaign website consistently, whether once a day or once a week.[29]
- Many potential supporters, especially younger voters, will access your website on smartphones, so integrate mobile-friendly apps into the campaign plan. Design your website so that it is attractive and readable on a smaller screen.[30]
- Use *search-engine optimization* (SEO) to improve the ranking of a website in online searches. Change information on the website frequently. Include brief campaign information in your domain name (i.e., 50th Ward or 10th District), which will cause a website to appear ahead of opponents' if people search for the district or community rather than the candidate's name.[31]

Figure 7.1 shows the 2016 campaign website of Mandy Wright when she ran for Wisconsin's 85th Assembly. This website was user-friendly and attractive when viewed on a computer but also easy to read and access on a smartphone.

MAKING THE BEST USE OF BLOGS

"In the age of tiny cell phones and audio recorders nothing is really 'closed press.'"[32] Weblogs—or blogs for short—have become an integral part of political campaigns. One development is that people increasingly handpick their news sources to mirror their ideological preferences. Traditional media no longer have as great an agenda-setting power as they had in the past. Because blogs often have taken over much of this influence, campaigns must develop ways to monitor and respond to bloggers.[33]

Today local campaigns need to be prepared to work within the blogosphere. First get to know the bloggers in your area. Do a blog search, using a blog

7.1. Mandy Wright for Wisconsin's 85th Assembly Campaign Webstite. Courtesy of Mandy Wright.

search engine, such as Google's blogsearch.google.com. This will help a campaign estimate which bloggers will have the biggest impact on your election.[34] Local bloggers often have a huge influence on the outcome of local campaigns such as school referenda.

Alan Rosenblatt recommends that after identifying the blog posts and bloggers to which you need to respond, you post comments on the blogs that have articles that concern your candidate. Also ask bloggers directly to cover a campaign story from the candidate's viewpoint. Many campaigns hold special breakfast briefings just for bloggers to encourage them to cover the campaign. Putting a paid advertisement on a blog can make interactions go more smoothly.[35] Candidates should consider having their own blogs. Phil Van Treuren in Figure 7.2 gives more detailed information on how best to do them.

USING SOCIAL MEDIA IN LOCAL CAMPAIGNS

A report by the Pew Research Center found that in 2014 almost three-quarters of adults online used at least one social media site, and 42 percent used multiple networks. Facebook was accessed the most, followed by LinkedIn, Pinterest, Twitter, and Instagram. Each of these social media networks often targets a different audience, so recognizing the audiences and functions of each helps a

7.2. LOCAL POLITICS: HOW TO START A SUCCESSFUL POLITICAL BLOG

The blogosphere is home to thousands of politics websites, thanks in large part to the development of user-friendly, inexpensive blogging platforms. . . . Most local political blogs, though, are only read by a small audience. . . .
If you want to ensure that your politics blog quickly becomes a popular online hub for the local political community, there are some simple steps you can take to help ensure success.

Optimize Your Blog for Local Political Keywords to Generate Relevant Organic Traffic

Many local political bloggers make the mistake of jumping right into their first website without doing any . . . planning. If you want more free traffic for your politics blog, then you need to make sure it's optimized to rank highly in search engines like Google for phrases that locals are actually searching for.

One of the most powerful things you can do to rank highly for a specific keyword is making sure that it's included in your website's domain name. If you're kicking off a politics blog that focuses on Cleveland, Ohio, for example, then you want to make sure that you try to include the keywords "Cleveland," "Ohio" or "Politics" in the URL. . . .

Don't stuff your domain name with too many keywords and

campaign know which strategies work best in targeting voters.[36] This trend is growing; because 61 percent of members of the millennial generation (as opposed to 39 percent of baby boomers) get their news primarily from Facebook, command of social media in campaigns is becoming more crucial than ever.[37]

Connecting with Facebook

Today, Facebook remains the social media network of choice for the majority of adults online. Because more than 70 percent of Internet users access Facebook, it is an important resource for local campaigns that have fewer resources for field organizing and advertising.[38] Facebook can work as a virtual campaign office and a place for supporters to gather virtually in support of a local candidate. It is a powerful tool for sending a campaign's message because it can keep supporters involved, and its content can be easily shared with other Facebook "friends."

One advantage of Facebook is that it is easy to create a campaign Facebook page by "friending" people a candidate already knows, such as personal friends and longtime supporters. Then a campaign can add party activists, local bloggers, and local elected officials. Even small campaigns can use Facebook to find voters and bring in donations through online messages and ads specifically tailored for them.[39]

Facebook favors images and will attract more followers if a campaign posts photos and other visuals such as logos and charts. A campaign should ask people to repost campaign information on their own profiles, which exposes it to their networks. The best postings are engaging and include photos.

Twitter Accounts

Unlike Facebook, Twitter acts more like a news channel, with every "follower" having the role of reporter. Anyone who has a Twitter account can post and read other "tweets" from anyone else in the network. For campaigns, Twitter keeps influential leaders or writers from dominating a conversation. Sometimes what an average person tweets can end up appearing in national media. Consequently, tweets can become a major source of communication for a campaign. In a campaign, it is best to actively engage the Twitter community regularly. Keep hashtags simple but catchy, and make sure your campaign hashtag has not been used by someone else, especially anyone opposing your candidate. Have a Twitter editor in the campaign check each tweet before it is sent. As with Facebook, political ads can also be purchased through "promoted tweets."[40]

Send Information via YouTube

YouTube gives users opportunities to access but also to make and send videos concerning a candidate. It has become an exciting and important communication tool. Appealing to most voters but accessed mostly by the young, it allows campaigns to send a video message inexpensively that is longer and more viewed than a conventional political commercial. By putting its YouTube link on its website, a campaign can share personal video narratives about a candidate. Because anyone can make a video about a candidate and put it on YouTube, a potential problem is that campaigns have to constantly watch out for third-party videos that send negative messages about the candidate.[41] In 2014, an estimated 300 hours of video were uploaded to YouTube every minute and were accessed by 72 percent of

make it difficult to remember. . . . A blog that has a short URL is much easier for new readers to remember and recommend to their political friends. . . . [Also] make sure that you intersperse your targeted keyword phrases throughout your site, in sidebars and footers, to help your site rank higher and faster. And when you're writing posts, put some thought into your titles. Always include keyword phrases that locals might type in if they're looking for information about your post topic.

Build Backlinks and Followers by Forming Relationships with Other Local Political Bloggers

Building good links back to your political blog is vital to driving new traffic and subscribers, and not just because people will click on the links and find your site. . . .

If you want to make your politics blog popular fast, then you should be aggressive in building high-quality backlinks. You can do that through link exchanges with other like-minded political websites, by guest posting on other blogs, and by publishing shout-outs to other local bloggers in hopes of a reciprocal link. . . .

Gossip and Scoops Are Good, but Libel and Slander Are Downright Dangerous

In order to generate attention, there's nothing better than being the first to break some local political news . . . However . . . you need to be very careful that your juicy posts don't stray into the realm of libel and slander. If you're publishing a scoop about a politician, candidate, group, or organization, then you had better ensure it's substantiated . . . or make it clear that your information is unconfirmed. The best practice is to never publish anything on your politics blog unless you've done your homework and can provide proof of your claims.

Don't Damage Your Career with Careless Writing or Publicity Stunts

Here's the thing about the Internet: you can safely assume that everything you write online is going to be there forever. . . . Even if you decide to publish as an "anonymous" blogger, you always run the risk of being outed by someone online and being forever associated with all of the stuff you posted on your site.

Source: Phil Van Treuren, "How to Start a Successful Political Blog," 2014, http://www.politicalcampaigningtips.com/.

all Internet users aged eighteen through thirty-four, 58 percent of users thirty-five through fifty, and 48 percent of users fifty-one through sixty-nine, making it a critical social medium for campaigns.[42]

Videos on the Internet are a powerful political tool as demonstrated by videos of police actions in places such as Ferguson, Missouri, during 2015. Anyone with a smartphone can now make and post videos on sites such as YouTube.

Videos have been used in political campaigns ever since they were posted on the Internet or on cable TV. Now, candidates and volunteers can easily make their own videos and embed them on the campaign website and post them on YouTube. In 2006, a video showed US Senator George Allen referring to an opponent's supporter as "macaca," which was seen as a racial slur. It cost Allen the election. Likewise, in the 2012 election, Republican presidential candidate Mitt Romney was videoed speaking to rich supporters saying that many Americans were welfare cheats. It reinforced his image as only caring about the wealthy. He also lost.

Since about 2006, e-videos and now YouTube videos are cheap enough to be used in local campaigns to good effect. For example, that year Plano, Texas, mayoral candidate Ken Lambert produced two videos for about $6,300 and forwarded them to friends and family. Although airtime costs ranged between $7 and $100 per spot, e-mailing a link to the videos was free. Yet even producing the video was free for his opponent, Mayor Pat Evans, because friends recorded her campaign video, and like Lambert, she e-mailed it to supporters and posted it on her website. Mayor Evans got an additional boost when a high school student made a campaign video supporting her and posted it on Google

Video. Without costing Evans's campaign anything, it got at least 4,700 hits before the election.[43]

ANALYTICS AND MICROTARGETING IN LOCAL CAMPAIGNS

Depending on their expertise and budget, even local campaigns can make some use of microtargeting and analytics.[44] Because both Democrats and Republicans have their own national voter databases and make them available to party candidates, campaigns often do not have to put together their voter files from scratch. For instance, the Democratic National Committee makes access to VoteBuilder available to all state parties, with training and support.[45] In addition, private companies provide validated voter files for purchase as well as voter-mapping and mobile-canvassing apps. Nonetheless, although the data are available, they may be difficult to use effectively unless a campaign has someone who knows how to employ the software properly.

Phone calling and precinct walking lists once painstakingly built are now run off automatically with the old-style personal contacts added into the system (see Figure 7.3). Every voter contact provides new information for the database. For instance, if during a door-to-door canvas, a volunteer finds someone who would like to work for the candidate, her name is put on the "new volunteer" list as soon as a worker enters that information into the system. On a GOTV call, after a person called says she has already voted, she is removed from the call list. A well-funded campaign can feed such constantly updated voter information into its automatic calling system.

Cost-Effective Ways to Use Analytics

Even on a small budget, a candidate can make use of analytics. Campaigns may hire a digital political consulting firm, often at a fairly low cost. Such firms can help a campaign run smarter and more efficiently by showing the campaign how to use analytical tools to microtarget supporters most successfully. These digital consulting firms place and create digital ads; help a campaign grow its list of supporters (not every potential supporter is in the party database); run media campaigns, including placing online ads; and even write and send campaign e-mails and tweets.[46]

For instance, in 2014 David Brat, a little-known Tea Party–backed economics professor with no political experience, challenged one of the most powerful men in the US Congress. Republican House majority leader Eric Cantor was running for reelection in the Republican primary in Virginia. Having served for seven terms, his victory was expected to be a shoo-in. His budget was

WalkList / Precinct 325 / Wall Township / Dems>=1 / Page 4

Name	Address	Phone	Age	Sex	Reg	Primary					General					Notes
						'14	'13	'12	'11	'10	'14	'13	'12	'11	'10	
Andrew Allen	102 Green ST	8472621201	58	M	1981			D			V				V	
Beulah Allen	102 Green St	8472621201	65	F	2007			D			V		V		V	
Carl C. Carroll	106 Green ST	8472621202	44	M	2004	D		D			V		V		V	
David D. Davis	108 Green ST	8472621203	45	M	2004	D		D			V		V		V	
Ellen E. Davis	108 Green ST	8472621203	39	F	2004	D		D		D	V		V		V	
Frederick Fallon	112 Green ST	8472621204	60	M	1986										V	
Georgia Fallon	112 Green ST	8472621204	58	F	1987						V				V	
Henry H. Fallon	112 Green ST		25	M	2012	D		D		D	V		V		V	
Isaac I. Ignatius	120 Green ST	8472621205	71	M	2007			D		D	V	V	V		V	
James J. Johnson	124 Green ST		67	M	1978			D		D	V		V		V	
Kevin K. Johnson	124 Green ST		66	M	1990						V				V	
Louisa L. Leoni	130 Green ST	8472621207	42	F	1995							V	V		V	
Michael Mikowski	134 Green ST	6302345679	29	M	2005	D		D		D		V	V		V	
Nora N. Nelson	138 Green ST	8472621209	36	F	2002			D					V		V	
Olivia O'Rourke	142 Green ST	8472621210	33	F	2004	D		D		D	V	V	V	V	V	
Peter P. O'Rourke	142 Green ST	8472621210	34	M	2004	D		D		D	V	V	V	V	V	
GROVE AVE																
Quinn Q. Quincy	203 Grove AVE	8472621211	23	F	2012			D			V		V		V	
Rose R. Quincy	203 Grove AVE	8472621211	52	F	2012			D			V		V		V	
Steven S. Smith	207 Grove AVE	8472621212	39	M	2004	D				D	V		V		V	
Timothy T. Turner	207 Grove AVE	8472621213	42	F	1995	D		D		D		V	V	V		
Ulysses Unger	211 Grove AVE	8472621214	60	M	1980	D				D	V					
Violet Unger	211 Grove AVE	8472621214	61	F	1980	D		D		D	V		V		V	
Wayne W. Unger	211 Grove AVE		30	M	2006	D										
Yvette Youngman	215 Grove AVE	8472621215	76	F	1962	D		D		D	V		V		V	
Zelda Zimmerman	219 Grove AVE	8472621216	71	F	1975	D		D		D	V		V		V	

$5.4 million; Brat's was $200,000. Cantor's pollsters had him ahead by 30 percentage points. However, Brat won. In an election with a low turnout in a district with more than 758,000 people, the final tally was Brat 36,105 to Cantor 28,912.[47]

Political analysts variously attributed the upset to Cantor's ignoring his district, having "sold out" to Washington moneyed interests, his stand on immigration, the rise of the Tea Party, or an increase in ideological primary challenges. Regardless of why people voted for him, Cantor lost because Brat's campaign found supporters by using analytics and got more of his supporters out to vote.[48]

Brat is one of many candidates who have used data analytics to win elections. Running on a shoestring budget, Brat bought rVotes for only $1,500. This program is an Internet-based data management system that provided his campaign the information needed to find those voters in the district who might vote against Cantor. Brat's volunteers then made phone calls, kept up with followers on social media, and rang doorbells of the potential supporters rVotes found. His campaign tailored its message to address specific voters' concerns and updated its social media scripts to provide Brat's views on recent political issues and events where he would be speaking. Brat got his anti-Washington message out with the help of dedicated volunteers. As a result, unlike the voters who said they would back Cantor, supporters whom Brat's campaign contacted actually went to the polls.[49] Brat went on to win the November 2014 election with more than 60 percent of the vote.

Campaigns with even smaller budgets can use these new technologies. After the primary, a local campaign of a party-nominated candidate can generally get access to the state party's voter data file and correlate it with the campaign's Facebook friends, using tools such as Constant Contact. Although many local campaigns prefer to rely on traditional methods of targeting voters, such as direct mail and canvassing, they should research if online advertising might be cost effective for them. Local campaigns also sometimes use microtargeting during primaries even when there are no party voter files available or when a campaign must depend primarily on personal voter contact.[50] Such rudimentary targeting and voter analytics can help campaigns decide which voters to visit or mail.

For a few hundred dollars campaigns that cannot afford a consultant can use online social media tools as an alternative. Google Analytics can help a campaign perform some microtargeting tasks with minimal technical expertise. With this tool, a campaign can learn who is accessing its website and which pages they are accessing and create daily GOTV reports. Other social media tools include Facebook Insights and Twitter Web Analytics, which can help campaigns test and refine their messages and place targeted ads.[51] Facebook automatically provides information on how many people visit a campaign's Facebook page and whether that number is increasing each week. This lets a campaign know which of its Facebook posts are having the most effect.

Another way to use microtargeting is to make use of microsites, small temporary sites tailored to get your message across to niche voters. Microsites are also often used to send negative messages so that a campaign can avoid the blame.[52]

Local campaigns can also nanotarget their messages. To do so they combine all the information in their data file with what they find about voters on social media networks, voter Internet browsing activity, and even supermarket membership cards and consumer purchases. With this data, campaigns can nanotarget specific groups of voters and contact them accordingly.[53]

Campaigns with a small budget also find that tweeting a message with a hashtag directly linked to its Twitter page is effective and inexpensive. It is important, however, to make sure your hashtag is issue specific. Marking tweets with niche-specific hashtags allows a campaign to reach activists outside the campaign's geographical area and possibly bring additional attention, support, and donations to the campaign. Campaigns with greater resources can access the list of Twitter followers on specific sites. Thus, regardless of its resources, a savvy campaign will examine which social media users are interested in specific issues in order to make sure that environmentalists hear the candidate's stand on oil spills or that parents hear about school referenda.[54]

Adapting Techniques from Major Campaigns

Finally, local campaigns can adapt practices that experts in the 2012 presidential campaigns developed, but at a lower cost. For instance, they can test their messages for the best possible wording before sending them. Amelia Showalter, Obama's 2012 director of analytics, recalled that she constantly tested Obama campaign messages for e-mails by splitting the e-mail list into groups and sending differently worded messages to each. The message with the best response was then used for later e-mails to larger lists. She suggests that instead of the large number of variations she used, a local campaign could test two messages.[55] This helps a campaign fine-tune its message to get the best response.

Moreover, just as the 2012 presidential campaigns sent and received voter information online, local campaigns can get their messages out and use their online connections to listen to voters in order to gauge enthusiasm for the candidate and her positions on issues that concern voters.

Finally, the 2012 presidential campaigns monitored interaction persistently. A local campaign should also monitor the data that comes in through e-mail and social media constantly.[56] This is a good use of volunteers you can train to enter data from phone bankers and door-to-door canvassers about support, issues, donations, and potential new volunteers.

Effects of Social Media on Elections

Political scientists and media experts are continually reassessing the effects of online media on campaigns. Research shows that social media can be an indicator of public opinion and a predictor of voter preferences.[57]

The use of social media for state and local elections has lagged behind that of presidential and congressional campaigns because of lower funding and fewer state party commitments to the latest technology. As late as 2014, many successful state campaigns used only Facebook and did not blog except on their own websites. Because many candidates were well known and already had Facebook friends, they found it an effective means to present themselves in a positive way and to send people to their websites.[58] However, they made less use of tools such as YouTube or Instagram. Candidates in local elections, however, increasingly use social media. With each election their campaigns are becoming more tech savvy.

Although online politics brings many benefits both to the voter and the candidate, it also brings potential problems. One problem is with a candidate's unearned recognizability. In the past, people became well known, even famous, in their communities because they were trusted. People earned their prominence. Currently with politics online, prominence may come before a person gains credentials or experience. This is especially true in the world of viral politics, where a catchy, "buzz-worthy" campaign of a candidate with no gravitas can gain notoriety quickly. In the worst-case scenario, she can displace a worthy candidate with less online presence.[59]

The extent to which social media increase political knowledge and political participation is problematic. Recent studies of digital media show only a limited effect. Just as in the predigital age, what matters more for political learning is political interest, prior political knowledge, and attention to politics in traditional media formats. Although political party websites and social media sites can lead to increased political participation, they do not necessarily do so.[60]

This is partly because viewership of candidate information, like most information on the web, is self-selective. Although a majority of Americans still gets news offline, studies show that when people go online to get news, they view sites that agree with their ideology and partisanship. Likewise, when candidates use the Internet to find supporters, they are more likely to contact people who support them anyway.

Of course, Internet users can still find alternative political news if they "surf" online.[61] However, Internet search engines refer users to websites similar to those they have already seen, without the users knowing it.[62] The use of social media in today's hyperpartisan atmosphere encourages "ideological cocooning," especially through the blogosphere. Partisan blog communities may encourage higher political participation, but they often lack the objectivity of traditional media.[63] Therefore although social media and analytics are essential campaign tools, they do not automatically promote informed voter participation.

The final issue for campaigns is the discrepancy between how social media users perceive and use the political knowledge they find online. A study during the 2010 election cycle found that although users went online to find political information, they did not necessarily find the information they sought. Additionally, all forms of information were lumped together by many Internet users as "not credible information" because so much information on the Internet is biased or of doubtful authenticity. On the campaign side, political strategists necessarily use social media only as a way to encourage supporters and get contributions rather than as an accurate communication platform.[64]

Despite these issues, the Internet and social media have become a permanent part of political campaigns. More citizens have become participants, even if only by tweeting about debates, sharing satires of political ads, or campaigning for or against a candidate on Facebook.[65]

Like other election strategies, wise use of digital media gives an advantage to a candidate. Smart campaigns use social media to reach voters inexpensively. Thus, it is important that digital media be harnessed to improve informed, democratic participation as well.

Chapter Eight

Canvassing the Voters
and Election Day

....

A careful canvass to locate a candidate's voters and get them to the polls wins elections despite differences between wealthy and poor precincts, urban and rural areas, and national and local elections. The work is hard, but the results on Election Day justify it.

The canvass usually takes place three or four weeks before the election. With early and absentee voting becoming more prevalent, the effort to reach early voters should begin at least a month in advance.

The function of this precinct canvass is to locate all voters favorable, or potentially favorable, to a candidate. A secondary, but still important, function is to "mobilize lukewarm supporters."[1] The importance of locating a candidate's voters is emphasized in the written instructions given to precinct workers (see Figure 8.1).

The "sales" pitch is really a smokescreen to conceal the worker's true intent, to find out for whom the voter plans to cast his or her ballot on Election Day. Elections are won by locating and identifying the vote and, on Election Day, being sure those voters who intend to vote for us actually do vote.[2]

In practice, precinct workers affect voters as well as learn their preferences simply by providing information about the election and their candidate: "The issue content of the canvasser's appeal is far less important than conveying the most elementary facts: first, that an election is about to take place, and second, that the name of one of the candidates is the one you are working for."[3]

Precinct workers tell voters during the canvass what a candidate is doing about issues that concern them, from mundane matters like street sweeping to ideological questions such as freedom of speech. They answer any questions the

8.1. CANVASS INSTRUCTIONS FROM IVI-IPO: HOW TO WIN ELECTIONS

Most people think of precinct workers as strong-arm salesmen. Actually, nothing could be further from the truth. What you say in a minute or two is unlikely to decide a voter's choice for the top of the ticket (president, governor). However, your recommendations for local or less well-known candidates are more likely to have an effect. Therefore, our aim is to locate and identify voters supporting our candidate and to be sure that those favorable voters actually do vote on Election Day.

Your canvassing material will include:

- A list of registered voters in the precinct (poll sheet or walk sheet)
- Literature
- Buttons, posters, etc.
- Volunteer cards

Locating the vote and selling our candidates:

1. Before you knock or ring the bell, make sure you know the names of the people who live there. Introduce yourself to the voter. You are a neighbor and/or a volunteer for the Independent Campaign Committee or for a particular candidate.
2. Hand the voter the basic piece of literature and one or two supplemental pieces. "Sell" our candidates, emphasizing those most important to your

voter may have. Because a precinct worker is the personal representative of the candidate, many voters judge a candidate by his workers. Because reformers normally represent better-qualified candidates and ask voters to decide to vote based on the issues, they often beat regular party precinct captains and overcome costly mass media or direct mail appeals by their opponents, but it takes lots of hard work.

Canvassing the Voters

After a precinct worker talks to a voter about a candidate, he determines a voter's position on the election by politely asking, "May we count on your support for our candidate on Election Day?" Based on the voter's response, in the simplest system a precinct worker marks a plus (+), minus (−), or zero (0) beside the voter's name on the poll list, computer printout, or on his tablet or smartphone. When he is finished with the canvass he will have a list of *plus voters* who favor his candidate, *minus voters* who favor his opponent, and as many as one-half who are *zero voters* because they will not say how they will vote or have not yet decided. Unless the voter says differently, all members of the family will probably vote the same way and are recorded accordingly. The results of the canvass are reported back twice a week to the area chairman and the campaign staff so adjustments in strategy can be made (see Figure 8.2).

Some campaigns use more complicated scoring systems; the most common for local elections is a 1–5 scoring system with 1 being those most likely to vote for a candidate and 5 those absolutely voting for the opposing candidate. Campaigns with large datasets such as the Obama for President campaign use complicated voter analytics to assign a score from 0–100 on the probability of a voter voting for the candidate. Factors such as race, geographical area, past voting history, commercial purchases, and family income go into assigning a score. Any voters assigned a score of more than 65 are then definitely canvassed. Based upon the canvass information, their scores can be adjusted or confirmed by precinct work.

Catherine Shaw in *The Campaign Manager* calls the various voters "Saints," "Sinners," and "Saveables." Because Saints will vote for a candidate no matter what, you only have to get them to the polls after you identify them. Because Sinners will not vote for a candidate no matter what, you "do not have to spend campaign resources activating them: Don't canvass them, call them, or send direct mail to them." The Saveables, who have not made up their minds, can be located by precinct analysis and then contacted by direct mail, social networking, phoning, and finally by precinct workers who can then persuade them to become supporters.[4]

For the purpose of simplicity we will use the +, −, 0 scoring system in this book. However, the key remains the same regardless of which scoring system is used: precinct workers find out which way voters are likely to vote and report this information to their campaign headquarters. This valuable information is then entered into the campaign database and used to plan the next steps in the campaign and to organize the effort to get a candidate's voters to the polls on Election Day. No matter how simple or sophisticated the data record keeping becomes, these are the essentials for a winning campaign.

Whichever scoring system is used, each worker develops his own way of talking with voters. Generally, the presentation will be organized around the following points:

campaign. About two or three sentences should be enough. If the voter wants to know more about any of our candidates, offer her/him any additional literature you have as you answer his/her questions.

3. Determine the voter's attitudes by asking a subtle but sufficiently direct question. For example: "May we count on your support on Election Day?" Usually, it is only necessary to ask one person in a family. Mark the other family members as you marked the voter you talked with.

4. Evaluate the voter:

   a. Mark a plus (+) in front of the voter's name on the poll sheet if s/he is for your candidate.

   b. Mark a minus (−) in front of the voter's name on the poll sheet if the voter definitely will not vote for the candidate.

   c. Mark a zero (0) if the voter is undecided or refuses to tell you.

5. Leave as quickly and courteously as you can. NEVER argue.

6. Continue in this manner until every voter has been located, persuaded, and evaluated. If no one is home, leave literature and call again.

7. Don't fake. If a voter wants further information or asks questions you are unable to answer, note the question, ask your ward or area chair for the

answer, and then go back to the voter once you know.

8. If you reach a voter who will be out of town on Election Day, let them know that they may vote at a country clerk's office or at the Chicago Board of Election Commissioners during normal business hours and Saturday mornings, 9 a.m. to 12 noon. There will also be "early voting" from Monday, January 31, through Thursday, February 17, at various locations throughout the county. You may call the office to request absentee ballot applications, which voters can use if there is adequate time before Election Day.

9. Recruit as you work. If anyone seems enthusiastic about our candidate, ask them to help you with the canvass. If they are too busy to do that, ask them to help on Election Day. If they can't do that, perhaps they can do office work or make a contribution. Ask them to fill out a volunteer card. If they won't volunteer for the campaign, ask them to let you put a sign in their window. Be sure to tell your precinct captain or area chair about any possible helper, including address and phone number.

In order to gauge voter response to our campaign, periodic checks will be made by your area chair or precinct captain. You will be asked for a count of plus, minus, and zero on report nights, which are the four Thursdays and

- Introducing oneself ("I'm Joe Smith, a volunteer working to elect Jane Doe as our state representative")
- Handing the voter a piece of campaign literature and discussing the candidate's virtues in two or three sentences
- Asking if the voter's support may be counted on for your candidate
- Thanking the voter and leaving as quickly and courteously as possible

The entire discussion with a voter should take only five minutes. If 100 registered families live in a precinct, a canvass of every family can be completed in fewer than ten hours. With three workers in the precinct, each will have to work only slightly more than three hours. A precinct worker can finish the job if he follows these guidelines:

- *Do not engage in long discussions.* If the voter has numerous detailed questions, have him call your campaign headquarters for the answers. A worker has hundreds of voters to see. In the hour he spends talking to a single voter he could canvas twenty others.
- *Do not engage in arguments.* A worker may win the argument, but his candidate has lost a vote and the votes of all the voters the worker now will not have time to see.
- *Start early.* Do not put off the job. Begin as soon as you have received canvassing instructions and materials.
- *Work systematically.* Divide the list of voters among the workers available. Divide the list so that a worker can canvass a portion of the voters each week.
- *Recruit new workers to help.* As workers go

to each home, they should watch for potential workers, even more valuable than *plus voters*. If they find citizens interested in the campaign, they should encourage the new recruits to work along with them. After anyone has recruited more than two or three coworkers, they can turn in any extra names of potential workers to the campaign headquarters so that they can be employed in some of the uncovered precincts. In sharing workers, the point of the campaign is to win the election, not simply to carry one precinct.

Accuracy is crucial in a good canvass. To achieve accuracy, workers must understand the +, −, and 0 symbols and the reason for them. On Election Day, workers will work hard to get the *plus voters* to the polls. They will need to ignore the *minus voters*. Unless there are special considerations such as racial or ethnic identification with the candidate, strong support for a candidate in the rest of the precinct, or too few *plus voters* to win the election, workers will also ignore *zero voters*. Campaign volunteers work from 5 a.m. until at least 7 p.m. on Election Day to ensure that every one of the *plus voters* votes.

While canvassing, precinct workers must be careful in their evaluation of voters. Voters who can be counted on to vote for a candidate, not necessarily voters who smile in a friendly manner, are the ones to be identified with a plus. Precinct workers should mark as *plus voters* only those who answer "Yes" to the question "May we count on your support?"

The canvass is the most crucial phase of the campaign. If the canvass is done well, the chances of winning are good. If workers fail to contact enough voters, discern their preferences,

three Sundays prior to Election Day. Report your totals cumulatively on these dates.

Work systematically. You should have:

- One-quarter of the precinct completed by the 1st Sunday report night.
- Three-quarters of the precinct completed by the 3rd Thursday report night.
- The entire precinct completed by the 4th Thursday report night.
- After you have finished your part of the canvass, return the marked poll sheet (the Plus List) to your precinct captain or area chair. Keep the weekend before Election Day open to deliver sample ballots to all the voters and reminders to each "plus" voter as well as to contact those voters whom you may have missed during the original canvass.

It has been said many times that elections are won in the precincts. Personal contact with the voters is the required ingredient for victory. You must realize that you, the precinct worker, will determine who will win and who will lose on Election Day.

GOOD LUCK!

Source: IVI-IPO *2010 A–Z Campaign Training Manual,* Independent Voters of Illinois–Independent Precinct Organization, 2010.

8.2. Canvass Report Form. Courtesy of Independent Voters of Illinois-Independent Precinct Organization.

CANVASS REPORT FORM FOR COORDINATORS, AREA CHAIRS AND PRECINCT CAPTAINS

CUMULATIVE CANVASS COUNTS

AREA

PCT

Name/Address	Phone/email	Thursday Jan 27			Sunday Jan 30			Thursday Feb 3			Sunday Feb 6			Thursday Feb 10			Sunday Feb 13			Thursday Feb 17			Sunday Feb 20		
		+	-	O	C	+	-	O	C	+	-	O	C	+	-	O	C	+	-	O	C	+	-	O	C
Cumulative Totals																										

or serve as good representatives of a candidate, not enough *plus voters* will go to the polls on Election Day, and all will be lost. No candidate wins on good looks, publicity, or issues alone. To win the election, campaign workers must contact voters personally, ask for their vote, and remind them of their civic duty on Election Day. The other side will be working, too, but can be beaten if enough volunteers are willing to put in the time and if they work effectively. Over a period of several campaigns, dramatic results can be achieved by good precinct work, and information about the voters and their preferences can be accumulated to make precinct work easier in future elections.

While the door-to-door effort is occurring in the precincts, the candidate is not idle. He continues his schedule of three or four house parties each night to win over campaign volunteers, additional fund-raising breakfasts and luncheons to raise money, news conferences to get publicity, and staff meetings to develop campaign strategy. He now adds meeting voters at bus stops each morning from 7:00 to 9:00 a.m., shopping center appearances every weekend, and walking tours of precincts in the afternoons. By talking with voters at bus stops, at stores, and in their homes, the candidate demonstrates his interest in their problems and makes the job of his precinct workers much easier. Word will quickly get around when a candidate personally visits a neighborhood, something previous candidates and even incumbent elected officials may not have done.

CANVASSING HIGH-RISE BUILDINGS IN CITIES

Difficulties in running campaigns in poor and minority communities were covered in Chapter 5. The opposite end of the socioeconomic spectrum poses a different set of problems for campaigns. Upper-middle-class and wealthy citizens in cities often live in large, high-rise apartments. In suburbs, many live in restricted "gated communities" with guards at entry points. Both high-rise buildings and gated suburban communities include condominiums, cooperatives, and townhouses closed to the outside world.

Some mammoth high-rise buildings contain more than a thousand voters. Restricted, gated, suburban subdivisions contain so many voters that these communities cannot be ignored. Yet residents of high-rises and gated communities are surprisingly isolated. Seldom do they know their next-door neighbors, and even more rarely do they know residents in other parts of the building or in the outside community. Their privacy is zealously protected by watchful door attendants, apartment managers, and security guards.

The first problem for a campaign in reaching these voters is finding volunteers living in these high-rises or restricted suburban compounds. Holding house parties allows the residents to meet the candidate and allows the campaign to recruit volunteers. Alternatively, many of these communities are willing to sponsor candidate forums. If you do not have workers in the development, sponsoring house parties or arranging for forums may be difficult. In such cases, area chairs or house party coordinators must call their own contacts, friends of campaign volunteers, or the list of registered voters until a willing host can be found. Then all residents must receive an invitation and be personally invited to attend. After all these efforts, attendance might still be disappointing. Hopefully, enough resident workers can be signed up to work their own building or development.

In a city district with dozens of high-rise apartments, holding successful house parties or candidate forums in all the high-rises will not be possible. The remaining buildings will have to be worked by outside volunteers. Obtaining entry into high-rise buildings or residential compounds to canvass will be difficult. Four practical methods of gaining entrance are (1) to have a contact who lives in the building let in the canvasser, (2) to walk in at the same time as someone who lives in the building, (3) to call people listed on the precinct poll list over the speaker system until someone willing to talk about the election lets in the canvasser, and (4) to walk up to the doorman, say hello, and act as if you expect him to open the door for you, and often he will.[5] If none of these techniques work, ask the manager for admittance or, at least, permission to place campaign literature in the mailboxes.[6]

After trying every trick, a canvasser may obtain entry to the building or gated community only to find irate residents calling the manager to have him thrown out. Three tactics remain to be tried. Five or more workers can enter the building or community to canvass different floors or sections simultaneously. By the time the management throws them all out, the bulk of the building or community will have been canvassed.

Alternatively, a door-to-door canvass can be replaced by a direct mail piece and a telephone canvass. The results are less desirable but are superior to no canvass at all. A successful telephone canvass is best preceded by leafleting or mailing campaign brochures to each resident.

As in a door-to-door canvass, the campaign worker introduces himself by phone to the person he calls, gives a brief statement of the candidate's virtues, finds out the voter's preference, and marks the appropriate symbol on the poll list or in the campaign data program. In phone canvassing, as in face-to-face canvassing, the critical element is the kind and quality of interaction between the worker and the voter. Most voters will vote for a candidate if they feel that his campaign worker is trustworthy and well informed. The worker must sell

CHAPTER EIGHT

himself in order to sell the candidate. His own good judgment, politeness, and helpfulness will win over many voters.

In this regard, relying on a standard script is absolutely self-defeating. It makes you seem insincere and uncaring, as if you were only going through the motions. Your most difficult job will be to maintain your own authenticity, to continue to be yourself, time after time, call after call. Your own genuineness and spontaneity, whether quick and enthusiastic, serious, or bashful, are your strongest assets. Of course, the voters will want you to listen to their views as well, respond appropriately, and answer their questions.

Even without the volunteers for a telephone canvass or the money to hire a professional telemarketing firm to do the job, a direct mail or literature blitz can still be made, although more limited results can be expected. As discussed in Chapter 5, direct mail is likely to be most effective if more than one piece of mail is sent. Therefore the unworked high-rise or gated suburban community should be part of the direct mail campaign as early as possible.

RURAL CAMPAIGNS

Rural campaigns differ from those run in either cities or suburbs, but the intent is the same: Voters must be personally contacted. The differences between urban and rural campaigns are (1) money, (2) tools for campaigning, and (3) distances.[7] Although it is still generally true that rural races are cheaper than a contested race in a major city, they are becoming more and more expensive. These elections "tend to be much more candidate-driven than [by] party loyalty. ... These large rural districts play a lot more to local issues than larger races and much more depend on relationships and friendships."[8] Who the candidate is and who supports him is critically important in rural campaigns.

The campaign tools and political information easily available in urban districts might be completely lacking in rural areas. In this case, the first task of the campaign will be to develop a list of registered voters, determine their party affiliation from assorted public and private records, and find precinct maps and canvassing routes. It is also necessary to assemble kits of registration information and campaign literature. All of this must be done before the registration drive or the voter canvass can be launched.

Greater distances involved in rural canvassing require automobiles and create transportation problems not faced in urban districts. It also takes longer to canvass voters. Coordination and planning is required in scheduling and holding meetings in the larger districts and transporting the candidate. Time becomes a scarce commodity just because it takes canvassers, the candidate, and campaign personnel so long to traverse the district.

Recruiting sufficient volunteers to canvass rural areas can also be a problem unless there happens to be a college within the district. Volunteer canvassers seem to produce good results in spite of the legendary rural distrust of outsiders. The regular parties tend to be weaker in rural districts and to hold voters by primeval rather than modern ties. For instance, in Bloomington, Indiana, liberal Democrats won contested races for precinct committeeman simply by canvassing all the voters. Many rural voters, just like urban voters, have never been visited by a campaign worker before. Their votes are available almost for the asking, but reaching them requires a greater effort.

Finally, rural communities frequently are conservative. The organized anti-government movements in the rural areas of some western states and the conservatism of the rural South are two examples. In any campaign, the attitudes of the constituents must shape any effective campaign platform. Nonetheless, liberal, populist candidates often do well in rural areas if they are able to campaign on important issues affecting the lives of these constituents.

Winning Party Caucuses

In many states party nominations for higher offices are won not by direct election but by party caucuses and conventions. Everyone is familiar with the well-publicized Iowa caucuses in presidential campaigns. Caucuses are also used in other states. Paul Wellstone's campaign in Minnesota for the US Senate and later Jesse Ventura's campaign for governor are classic participatory campaigns within the caucus system.

Wellstone was a political science professor at Carleton College, a liberal and labor union supporter, cochair of Jesse Jackson's campaign for president in Minnesota in 1988, and a member of the Democratic National Committee. He won the party nomination over the opposition of many state party leaders who thought he was far too radical to defeat an incumbent Republican senator.

The process within the caucus system is similar to other elections, but the electorate comprises only voters who show up at precinct caucuses to elect delegates to higher-level party conventions.

The Wellstone campaign began by contacting voters, local Democratic Party leaders, and interest groups such as labor unions. These grassroots contacts from meetings, events, and door-to-door canvassing created a list of several thousand potential supporters throughout the state. The campaign then followed up with a massive phone canvass. Dennis McGrath and Dane Smith in *Professor Wellstone Goes to Washington* described the Wellstone phone canvass this way:

The phone callers would ask people who [sic] they supported in the Senate race and note the answer on the computer printout of names and phone numbers using a rating system. [This is a variant of the +, –, 0 system.] A person who was solidly behind Wellstone was rated five, a person leaning toward him was assigned a four, an uncommitted person was given a three, a person leaning toward another candidate was given a two, and a person strongly supporting another candidate was awarded a one. To the people who were uncommitted or were favoring another candidate, the volunteer would make a short pitch for Wellstone. "If someone was uncommitted, we would try, if we had money in the budget that week, to send a piece of literature."[9]

While the phone callers were finding Wellstone supporters to attend precinct caucuses, the campaign staff recruited a network of precinct coordinators. "In addition to being responsible for one night of phone calling every week the [precinct] coordinators were asked to organize their neighborhoods, get supporters to the caucuses, . . . and then lead the formation of Wellstone subcaucuses that night."[10]

By the night of the caucuses the campaign had about a thousand precinct coordinators signed up. On the weekend before the caucus, several thousand of the identified Wellstone supporters received at least one phone call urging them to attend the precinct caucuses. On the basis of the campaign's straw poll of 207 precincts, Wellstone won a major victory with 43 percent of the delegates to his opponents' 14 percent and 7 percent respectively.[11]

Wellstone's campaign returned to the phones and called as many as they could of the 40,000 delegates and alternates elected to the county and legislative district conventions. Finally, they out-organized their opponents on the floor of the statewide convention, whose delegate votes chose the Democratic Party nominee for the US Senate along with a number of other offices.

Wellstone's campaign was a case of field operations and grassroots efforts winning over party officials who preferred other candidates. He was also a candidate with a message and a cause. As McGrath and Smith describe it,

Wellstone laid out a program featuring a demand for universal health care, much heavier tax burdens on the wealthy, more spending on education and social programs, tough new environmental and energy standards, and radical reforms of the money-polluted political campaign system. And he delivered this vision to Minnesota voters with a new attitude—anger and good-humored irreverence and hope all at once. . . . Wellstone claimed to be offering real change and not just accommodation.[12]

Committed ideological factions often win when they organize in caucus states. This was proven by Tea Party candidates within the Republican Party and Barack Obama in the Democratic Party caucuses of 2008. In Wellstone's case, he went on to win the Senate seat with the same type of grassroots organizing and the creative television commercials such as the one described in Chapter 6.

Election Day

Election Day activities complete the process of winning elections. To win, three functions must be performed by campaign workers in as many precincts as possible: (1) distribution of sample ballots, (2) poll watching to prevent fraud and to check on who has voted, and (3) getting *plus voters* and other voters most likely to support a candidate to the polls. Other activities, such as troubleshooting and putting up campaign posters, support these basic functions. If a campaign's message has reached the voters and the precincts have been canvassed, a good job on Election Day will ensure victory.

This single day is the climax of each election. Months of effort are focused on this one opportunity. A candidate's workers and those of his opponents will devote at least twelve hours to the battle on Election Day, and when the polls close a binding verdict will have been rendered. Any votes not obtained Election Day are lost forever, so if you do not want hopes raised among the electorate to be dashed, work on Election Day must ensure victory for your candidate and for participatory politics.

GETTING OUT THE VOTE

Other than direct mail, social media, e-mail efforts, and radio and television commercials, the last hours, days, and weeks of the campaign depend upon the field operation. This stage of the campaign is called *get out the vote*, or GOTV.

Any field operation has three principal purposes. Will Robinson in *Campaigns and Elections American Style* describes them this way:

1. Repetitively move the campaign's message to key groups, areas, and individuals in an effort to persuade them to support your candidate.
2. Create programs to identify the key demographic groups, geographical areas, or specific individuals who are most likely to support your candidate.

3. Set up the structure and program to get those identified supporters out to vote on Election Day or during the early voting period.[13]

The 2012 Obama campaign leaders used the information collected through VoteBuilder to organize their grassroots effort. Obama for America opened local offices throughout the nation that called potential volunteers, reminded or helped voters to register, contacted wavering supporters, and got out the vote on Election Day. From these volunteers, Obama for America recruited team leaders who organized other volunteers from that particular office to canvass locally and call wherever needed. The local Obama campaign offices also coordinated with the national campaign office to get their volunteers to go to nearby states as needed, with team leaders notifying their workers where to meet to carpool or climb on chartered buses. They also worked with local campaigns to help those candidates win.[14]

In addition to sending the campaign message and finding *plus voters*, the GOTV campaign culminates by getting those *plus voters* to the polls. In addition, Election Day activities also influence uncommitted voters and prevent election fraud. Ideally, this work is divided between three different types of Election Day workers, but in understaffed precincts each volunteer may have to perform several functions.

The three jobs are (1) the *distributor*, who passes out sample ballots to voters on their way to the polls, (2) the *poll watcher* or *checker*, who observes the opening, operation, and closing of the polls while keeping track of exactly who has voted (see Figure 8.3), and (3) the *runner*, who goes door to door reminding *plus voters* to vote. Of these three functions, running is by far the most crucial to a winning campaign. Elections are won or lost on Election Day, and determined and persistent running will win the election for a candidate.[15]

If early voting occurs at a few centralized precincts, distributors and poll watchers would ideally be present during those days as well. Staff and volunteers would call voters who have said they plan to vote early to remind them to do so, but runners would not be used at this voting stage.

State and national campaigns cannot cover every precinct in the same depth on Election Day. Instead, they divide their precincts into low-performance and high-performance precincts. High-performance precincts are those in which precinct workers have done a canvass and found a significant number of *plus voters*, those precincts that have voted heavily for candidates from the same party in the past, or those precincts in which voters have demographic characteristics that match the strongest supporters of a candidate. All voters in high-performance precincts will be visited by precinct workers on Election

8.3. OPENING THE POLLS INSTRUCTION SHEET FROM IVI-IPO

Poll Watchers with credentials are allowed in the polling place as early as 5:00 a.m. to observe the setting up of the polling place. The ESC (Election Supply Carrier) is marked for Ward/Township and Precinct to assure that is the correct precinct. There should be a green seal that the poll is being prepared in accordance with election law. Establishing a polite and professional relationship with the judges can be essential. Voting booths should be arranged to allow for the greatest privacy for the voter. A voter's ballot should not be able to be seen by anyone in the polling place. As with all communication with the judges of election, politely point out your concerns if any. If this is ignored, contact your Area Chair at the campaign office.

There are two balloting systems in the polling place, one using paper ballots and the other using a computerized touch screen. The systems are similar, and verification of proper setup is required by both.

The Ballot Scanner is the electronic machine voters will use to submit their paper ballots after marking them in the polling booth. This machine has a back door that provides access to the control panel and memory pack. At the start of the day, the back panel should be secured with a red seal. There should be a mem-

Day, called by volunteers, or reached by professional telemarketing firms to remind them to vote. In low-performance precincts, only *plus voters* are phoned and reminded. In city, county, statewide, and congressional campaigns without enough precinct workers to cover all precincts, it is not unusual to use several hundred volunteer phone callers on Election Day.[16]

DISTRIBUTING AND POLL WATCHING

In more local campaigns with a well-developed field operation, *distributors, checkers*, and *runners* will be used in all precincts. The *distributor* puts up posters near the polling place and passes out leaflets such as the endorsement palm card. By encouraging votes for a particular candidate, the *distributor* can sway at least ten to twenty votes in most precincts. If there are not enough volunteers for a *distributor* at each polling place all day, *distributors* will be used during the hours when polls open and close because most people vote at these times. In a close race the few extra votes won by distributing endorsement palm cards in each precinct can make the difference between victory and defeat. Influencing these still uncommitted voters is important enough that the distributor will have the company of the opposing precinct captains in front of the polling place. Needless to say, opposing workers should not make payoffs to voters, and workers from both campaigns stay the same distance from the polling place.[17] (In Illinois, campaigners are required to be at least 100 feet from the polling place; in Massachusetts, it is 150 feet.)

The palm cards volunteers distribute on Election Day include endorsements a candidate has received and the appropriate number to mark on a Scantron voting system or to select on a computer touch screen to vote for a candidate. Often there are so many offices to elect that some voters get confused and fail to vote for candidates without this information.

Poll watchers perform dual functions on Election Day. They keep the election honest, and they keep track of which *plus voters* have voted so that the *runners* know which of a candidate's supporters they still have to get to the polls. When reform candidates lose, they usually do so because they have not worked the precincts and have not located their *plus voters*. However, having *poll watchers* in every precinct ensures that no votes are stolen. Election results are more often incorrectly reported because of honest errors rather than through intentional fraud. However, in some precincts hundreds of votes may be stolen if campaigns fail to watch the polls. Losing by a few votes is tragic if you know that the stealing could have been prevented.

Poll watching ensures that votes are not stolen. It guarantees that an opponent will not get votes he does not deserve. Most vote fraud is perpetrated by five methods: (1) stuffing the ballot box with false votes, (2) improper voter instructions and "assistance" by election judges, (3) buying votes, (4) getting voters to fill out fraudulent absentee or mail ballots before Election Day, and (5) recording inaccurate election results. The best protection against such vote fraud is an alert *poll watcher*:

Poll watching is the only known means of safeguarding honest, democratic elections on Election Day. Your responsibility as a poll watcher is to detect and report any misconduct in the polling place. *You, as a poll watcher, are responsible for any errors that are made in the conduct of the election in your polling place if you do not call adequate attention to them.*

ory pack installed in the machine. The machine will be plugged in, and it will automatically begin its initiation sequence. The Poll Watcher will observe the judges printing a "zero tape" indicating the correct date, Ward/Township, Precinct, and most importantly that no ballots have been cast. The tape is to remain on the roll attached to the machine; it is not signed by judges or removed.

The touch screen machine(s) will have a data cartridge installed, and a red seal should be secured and unbroken. The judges will turn this machine on, and just as the Ballot Scanner printed its zero tape, so will the touch screen. You will need to verify the same information with the importance of no ballots having been cast yet. The zero tape will remain on the machine.

The Poll Watcher will record information for both voting methods on their morning report sheet. If there are any irregularities, specifically if the ward/precinct doesn't match or there are ballots already registered, contact the campaign office immediately.

Source: IVI-IPO *2010 A–Z Campaign Training Manual*, Independent Voters of Illinois–Independent Precinct Organization, 2010.

Poll watching is a very serious and important job.

You can be an effective poll watcher only if you are adequately informed. When you accepted the responsibility of being a poll watcher, you accepted also the responsibility of becoming informed. Therefore, before Election Day, you should know:

1. Correct election procedure.
2. Your rights.
3. Your duties.

Your effectiveness as a poll watcher depends upon you being more informed than the Judges of Election.[18]

Stuffing the ballot box or hacking electronic voting systems does not happen as often as it once did. The penalties are stiff, and fraud is relatively easy to detect. If the polls go unwatched, however, there is danger that fraud will still be used to steal elections. A precinct captain can falsely fill out voter affidavits and then mark additional votes for his candidate before the polls open, during a lull, or after the polls have closed.

In the old days when paper ballots were used, a "paper ballot chain" was employed. A precinct captain or campaign worker stole the first ballot and marked it appropriately. He gave it to a voter with the promise of several dollars if the voter would vote with it. The voter went into the polling booth and pulled the curtain. Then he took the marked ballot from one pocket and put his new unmarked ballot in the other. After voting with the precinct captain's marked ballot, he took the unmarked ballot back to the captain and received his payoff. To break the "chain," a poll watcher had to see it being used and get officials from the state's attorney's office or the US Justice Department to order an arrest. Paper ballots are almost never used in elections anymore (except when voting by mail or absentee), but more sophisticated methods of stealing elections have been developed, especially after many claimed that the Bush-Gore election of 2000 was stolen in Florida as both sides fought over obscure "hanging chads" and other marks on ballot punch cards of that era.

Absentee and mail ballots can be either a blessing or a curse to a campaign, especially in a tight race when the number of absentee or mail votes cast by the supporters of either side might determine the winner. On the one hand, effective phone banking and canvassing can discover supporters who will be out of town on Election Day, so the campaign can ask these voters if they would consider taking an absentee ballot. Campaigns should familiarize themselves with their state's mail balloting procedures well before Election Day. In some states, campaigns themselves can provide a ballot application to a potential supporter, who can mail it directly to the state board of elections, which will then mail the voter the ballot.

On the other hand, it is harder to prevent improper use of absentee and mail ballots than to prevent fraud at the polls on Election Day. In many states now, precinct captains are using legal absentee and mail ballots to guarantee votes for their party's candidates before the election. In places such as nursing homes, it is easy for campaign workers to convince voters to fill out the forms for absentee ballots and then to go back and "help" the voters fill out the ballots the way the precinct captain wants. Only legislative changes guarantee that absentee ballots are used for proper reasons and that the voters, not the precinct captains, do the voting. Challenging unduly large numbers of absentee and mail ballots is the necessary first step in curbing the improper use of these ballots.

A similar problem occurs with improper voter "assistance" by election judges on Election Day. Some election judges, even some party precinct captains, simply do the voting for citizens under the pretext of giving them assistance. Only citizens with disabilities or who cannot read may have election judges mark the ballots for them, and only if there is a signed affidavit that attests to the reason this assistance is needed. Voters may ask for instructions on a voting machine model or computer system, but any such instruction must be given in the presence of at least one Democratic and one Republican judge in full view of the poll watchers. The demonstration must be given neutrally. If not carefully controlled by a *poll watcher*, incorrect absentee or mail voting assistance can cause a candidate to lose a sizable number of votes.

Recording election results incorrectly causes even greater losses (although this is less likely to occur with newer computer systems used in most precincts today). To prevent recording errors, two poll watchers are needed when the polls close. One watcher stands behind the judge recording the figures and sending them electronically to the election board while the other observes the judge who calls out results from the machine or ballot box. Lawsuits and recounts in elections have shown that recording errors happen frequently. It is the job of poll watchers to make sure that errors do not happen in elections and that if mistakes are made, recounts remedy the errors.

Early Voting

Early voting and mail-in ballots pose a number of difficulties for campaigns, and they become more pronounced as electronic voting is adopted in more states. Today, there are usually only one or two early voting sites per ward or township. They are open during regular work hours five or six days a week for several weeks. They are used to attempt to increase turnout.

One advantage for campaigns of early voting is that all campaign workers can now vote early and thus be free to work all day Election Day. Volunteers no longer have to take time off to go back to vote in their home precinct. People who will be out of town or are unable to vote Election Day because of their jobs can also vote during the early voting period.

In general, campaigns try to get as many of their *plus voters* and strong supporters to vote early to ensure that they vote and their votes are counted. However, it is difficult to have poll watchers, much less other campaign workers such as *distributors*, at the early voting sites over so many days. Therefore each campaign must work out in advance how much effort it will put into encouraging early voting and protecting against vote fraud during this longer period. It also moves up the precinct work timetable to be sure that potential early voters are contacted by the campaign.

Unfortunately, there is still no uniform voting system across the states. Many election jurisdictions after the debacle of the 2000 election were able to use the funding provided by the federal government to install new voting systems such as Scantron and touch-screen voting. All of these new systems are capable of being hacked in order to rig election outcomes. Moreover, because these systems are more than a decade old, they need replacing again, but there is no federal funding this time to assist in their upgrading. Getting an election system that does not break down and is safe, secure, reliable, and hard to hack is going to cost billions of dollars nationwide in a time of government cutbacks.[19]

In addition to new voting systems, many election jurisdictions now have lists of eligible voters computerized along with copies of voter signatures. The Presidential Commission on Electoral Administration has recommended the five following broad reforms to improve all elections:

- modernization of the registration process through continued expansion of online voter registration;
- expanded state collaboration in improving the accuracy of voter lists;
- improving access to the polls through expansion of the period for voting before Election Day, and through the selection of suitable, well-equipped polling place facilities;
- state-of-the-art techniques to assure efficient management of polling places; and
- reforms of the standard-setting and certification process for new voting

technology to address soon-to-be antiquated voting machines and to encourage innovation and the adoption of widely available off-the-shelf technologies.[20]

The consensus of experts at a conference on implementation of the report's recommendations was that

- online voter registration and early voting would continue to expand;
- Internet voting was not yet ready for primetime;
- registration along with driver licenses and license renewals was greatly increasing voter registration; and
- the Electronic Voter Registration system (ERIC), now used by more than ten states, would allow more accurate and timely voter registration in all jurisdictions.

With all this technology being used in electoral administration, different forms of election fraud become possible, so campaigns must carefully study the systems used in their jurisdictions and train their poll watchers appropriately.

Election Day Training Session

Election Day scheduling is a massive task requiring special coordinators who call and e-mail potential volunteers and schedule them for each precinct polling place that needs to be covered. Scheduling several hundred volunteers is not enough. They must also be trained and given their election materials.

On the weekend before the election, a training session or multiple training sessions are held. For each precinct, a packet is prepared with all necessary materials: a *plus* list, additional poll lists, posters, buttons, leaflets, written instructions, assignment sheets, and report forms. At the meeting, instructions for Election Day work are given, the candidate speaks, and materials are handed out. If possible, poll watchers are given the opportunity to practice voting on the system being used in this election.

Later the same afternoon or evening, area chairs may hold parties in their homes to reinforce what workers learned at the larger training session, to answer questions more fully, to make a final check on preparations, and to give the workers a sense of being part of a team effort. Through both large training sessions and smaller area parties, morale is boosted for the final push toward victory.

The Day before the Election

The day before the election, precinct workers visit all their *plus voters* to give them an Election Day leaflet or endorsement palm card with the candidate's name and ballot number. This reminds voters to vote and tells them how to vote for a candidate. Precinct workers can remind anyone who is not home by leaving the card in the mailbox or under the door. If additional time remains after all *plus voters* have been alerted, a few minutes can be spent talking with the most promising *zero voters* to convert them.

The night before the election in better-funded and better-staffed campaigns, a group of high school and college students is brought together to go throughout the district to put up posters on main streets, around polling places, and at major intersections. This activity is directed by the same visibility chair who has coordinated the placement of window posters and yard signs throughout the campaign. The workers first have a pep talk by the candidate and then disperse to put up the posters. This blitz bolsters the morale of campaign workers, discourages opponents, and, by sheer visual repetition, makes voters aware of a candidate on Election Day. This work cannot be done before Election Day, because the opponent's workers might tear these posters down quickly.

Election Day

Election Day begins for a handful of volunteers with the visibility blitz at 2:00 a.m. As the students finish their job at 3:00 or 4:00 a.m., the precincts remain unstaffed. At 5:00 a.m. the new day begins as workers throughout the district arise and prepare to do battle. If the polls open at 6 a.m., precinct captains and volunteers arrive at each polling place in the district at 5:30 a.m. After placing campaign posters along the walks leading to the polling place, at least one of the workers goes inside, introduces himself to the judges, shows his poll watcher credentials if necessary, and watches the opening of the polls. As each voting machine is readied, whichever system is used, he reads the "public counter" to make sure that no votes have yet been cast. If no votes have been cast before the election begins, then the first step in ensuring a fair election has been taken.

Despite fears of election fraud, voting machines and computers usually have not been tampered with. The election begins without incident. By 6:00 a.m. or the official opening time, five election judges (two of one party and three of the other) are seated behind the desks as voters begin to arrive. Poll watchers and precinct captains working for various contenders are also present.

The election judges have complete authority over the conduct of the election in each precinct. They should be treated with respect and courtesy because it will do a candidate no good to have his workers thrown out of the polling place.

A poll watcher's primary responsibility is to stay in the polling place, not to be thrown out for causing trouble. Thus, a poll watcher can only suggest to the judges how a situation might best be handled, reinforcing her request with citations from the judge's handbook. If judges fail to take a suggestion, a campaign troubleshooter (usually a lawyer or campaign staff member) is called by cell phone to handle the problem, and the poll watcher continues her role as a watcher.

By 7:00 a.m. the number of voters increases slightly, and the *distributors* in front of the polling place are busy handing out literature and keeping the opposition from tearing down posters. By 9:00 a.m. most voters will have gone to work, so the number of citizens going to the polls slows to a trickle. In many precincts, a campaign volunteer will begin to visit the homes of *plus voters*, encouraging them to vote or leaving reminder slips if they are not at home. In other precincts, that process will not begin until after 2 p.m. in the afternoon. If the precinct has a busy bus stop or a commuter train station, an additional volunteer might be stationed there to remind voters to vote before they leave for work. If a campaign has sufficient volunteers or a hired telemarketing firm, all *plus voters* who have not voted by the afternoon will be called by phone and reminded to vote as well.

All morning the *checker* or *poll watcher* inside the polls has been carefully drawing lines through names on a computer-generated precinct poll list as each voter casts his or her ballot. A voter comes into the polling place and signs an affidavit that two judges check against names of eligible voters in the precinct binder or a computerized list of registered voters. If the voter's name is found, the judges call it out in a loud voice so that *poll watchers* may also check it. No challenge being made, the voter proceeds to the voting booth, casts his or her vote, and leaves. During slack periods, the *checker* or *poll watcher* compares his precinct poll list with his *plus list*, kept safely in his pocket or tablet until now. He then makes out reminders for *plus voters* yet to vote. These are the slips or computerized lists that guide the *runners* as they convince voters to come to the polls. In larger campaigns for higher offices, the *plus voters* on the list are once again called from phone banks by volunteers to remind them.

Ten hours pass. After 4 p.m., the number of voters increases. Fifteen minutes before official closing time, the two *poll watchers* assigned to watch the count are inside waiting for the polls to close at exactly closing time. When the last voter leaves, the ballot boxes are opened, and the ballots are counted. In

8.4. CLOSING THE POLLS INSTRUCTION SHEET FROM IVI-IPO

Make sure you are in the polling place before 7:00 p.m.; even if you have a credential filed and have been working all day you will be locked out if you aren't inside the polling place at 7:00.

There are two voting systems to be tallied and consolidated, the paper ballots and the touch screens.

Ballot Scanner

The judges will access the panel in back of the machine and set it to close the polls; this will start the printing of the results tape. Copy this information to a campaign tally sheet, updating your evening report sheet with the number of paper ballots cast. After completing the results tape, the machine will be powered down and the data cartridge removed; the judges should be in possession of the data cartridge at all times.

Touch Screen Machines

The judges will break the red seal and "close the polls" on this machine. It will begin to print a results tape. Copy the number of ballots to your evening report sheet and the vote totals to the campaign vote totals sheet. The judges will remove the paper roll, sign it, and place it in the ballot carrier. The memory cartridge from the touch screen machine will be removed to be consolidated with the Ballot Scanner votes.

The consolidation of the two systems is facilitated by the card activator (this is the machine the

most modern precincts the votes are automatically tallied and sent electronically to the board of elections commission. *Poll watchers* (following instructions like those in Figure 8.4) carefully check the count while the votes for their candidate and his opponents are recorded and totaled. As soon as the election judges have sent their reports, the *poll watchers* fill out their own reports and call, e-mail, or text them to the campaign headquarters. They go to the campaign party ready to share in the victory celebration. If the judges make an error or their reports are later falsified, the *poll watchers'* records, as signed physical documents, make future legal action possible.

The Challenges to Canvassing and GOTV

The most important advice to participatory campaigns, whether engaged in primaries, nonpartisan elections, or caucus battles, is to *organize*. A volunteer army must be trained and deployed in precincts and on the phone contacting voters. Free news coverage, paid media ads, and direct mail campaigns are necessary, but systematically canvassing voters in person and by phone has to be a campaign's focus. This is the hard, but certain, road to victory.

Only by combining analytics, social media, and precinct work can the necessary volunteers be recruited, *plus voters* be found, and GOTV effort succeed. Reminders to vote can now be sent by e-mail and tweets, and campaign messages can be packaged in videos on YouTube, but reaching voters, convincing them to vote for a candidate, and getting them to the polls remains the heart of any participatory campaign.

The Victory Party

After months of effort, the victory party can be an exciting and satisfying experience. The spirit of camaraderie, the beer and wine, the laughter, and the sense of accomplishment are heady stuff. Even a losing campaign can be important if people have come together to participate in elections for the first time, and they see for themselves that winning is a real possibility in the next election. A successful party in victory or defeat should provide refreshments, reports of election results as they become available, television monitors to show supporters television coverage of the election, and a final appearance of the candidate.

Win or lose, the workers need to come away from the evening with a sense of pride in what they have accomplished and dedication to remain active in future campaigns.

As one writer puts it, "Everyone's got a defining moment in their life if they do anything worth a damn. Something good or bad that shapes every day of your existence from then on."[21] Often, especially in first political campaigns or later critical ones, campaign workers experience something that feels like a defining moment in their lives and shapes their political actions for years to come.

judges used to issue the plastic "credit" card to voters for the touch screen machine). The data cartridge from the touch screen will be plugged into the left side of the card activator; the cartridge from the Ballot Scanner is plugged into a small device connected to the card activator. Once all cartridges are consolidated and transferred, a final election tally will print.

There will be 12 results tapes run; the judges use 7 for their reports, post one on the wall, and have 4 remaining to give to poll watchers. They may also run extra tapes but are not required to. It is a good idea during the day to cultivate a friendly relationship with the judges and let them know you will want a tape after the polls close. Remind them of this when the tapes are run. If you cannot get your own tape, copy the number of total ballots and the election results onto your closer's report from the tape posted on the wall.

The judges will take the data cartridges, paper ballots, applications for ballots, affidavits, and the touch screen printer rolls to the election data return point. All other materials will be locked in the ESC.

Do not leave the polling place until the judges have signed the certificate of results. If possible, stay until the judges close and pack everything and take the results to the receiving station.

Source: IVI-IPO *2010 A–Z Campaign Training Manual,* Independent Voters of Illinois–Independent Precinct Organization, 2010.

Chapter Nine

The Campaign to Elect
Will Guzzardi

....

After graduating from Brown University with a bachelor of arts degree in comparative literature, Will Guzzardi moved to Chicago to find work as a journalist. His victory in 2014 is proof that grassroots campaigns using new high-tech tools can win in the twenty-first century.

Guzzardi worked for the *Huffington Post*, an online news agency, covering the local political beat. Through his investigative reporting, he discovered a restrictive and cynical political system. As a result, he began to discuss with friends the harm that lack of true representation in his neighborhood created for average citizens.

He asked why residents did not challenge the political status quo. As part of his job, he reported on the local 39th District state representative race, in which Green Party candidate Jeremy Karpen unsuccessfully challenged incumbent Democrat Maria "Toni" Berrios for a second time in 2010. In 2008, Karpen had received only 21 percent of the vote, but his vote total climbed to 35 percent in 2010 (see Table 9.1). That was still a long way from enough votes to win, however.[1]

Guzzardi, who had written stories headlined "The Greening of Logan Square" and "Green against the Machine," watched the Democratic machine wear Karpen down. He kept reporting, but he was frustrated. He became "in-

The first draft of this chapter was written by Elise Doody-Jones. Much of this chapter comes from her original draft. It was then fact-checked and corrected by campaign manager Erica Sagrans and candidate Will Guzzardi.

Table 9.1. Illinois General Election Results, State Representative, 39th District, 2008 and 2010

Candidate	2008		2010	
	Number of Votes	*Percentage of Votes*	*Number of Votes*	*Percentage of Votes*
Berrios (D)	19,569	79.16	10,487	65.49
Karpen (G)	5,176	20.84	5,526	34.51

Source: Illinois State Board of Elections, http://www.elections.il.gov/ElectionResultsState HouseSet2.aspx?ID=22; http://www.elections.il.gov/ElectionResultsStateHouseSet2.aspx ?ID=29

creasingly aware of the ancient system of favors that Chicago is run by, but [he was] no nearer to making it stop."[2]

Unseating the five-term 39th District incumbent would be difficult because she was the daughter of Joseph Berrios, Cook County assessor and powerful chair of the Cook County Democratic Party. The district had been gerrymandered to make a safe district for her ten years earlier.[3] Despite the public's distrust of the Berrios family because of recent revelations of nepotism in the assessor's office, voters were reluctant to vote against Berrios's daughter. Fear of retaliation from the Chicago machine kept voters voting for Democratic Party candidates regardless of whether they effectively served the citizens.

Guzzardi and a small team of activists saw an opportunity to challenge the incumbent when the district was remapped in 2011. Redistricting resulted in one-quarter of the district containing new voters unfamiliar with either the incumbent or challenger. All candidates would have to focus on name recognition and introduce themselves to win over these new district voters. An ideal time to run for office is when there is an open seat with no incumbent. The next best opportunity is when there is a redrawn district with many voters unfamiliar with the incumbent. Still this was a seat considered unwinnable by nearly all Chicago political observers. As we emphasized earlier, it is important to carefully analyze any district in which a grassroots candidate is considering running to determine the "target number" of votes needed to win and to have a realistic plan to run a winning campaign.

Guzzardi and his earliest supporters developed just such a campaign plan, cultivated a grassroots army of volunteers, and began the effort to disprove the long-held belief that "you can't beat the Chicago machine." They believed instead that old-fashioned, face-to-face voter contact was the most important element in a local campaign. Guzzardi's 2012 campaign manager, Rebecca Reynold, had a mantra: "If only 9,000 people are going to vote, then you only have to shake 4,501 hands to win."[4] Thus Guzzardi announced his candidacy for state representative in the summer of 2011 prepared to shake those hands.

After developing his campaign strategy, Guzzardi knocked on doors of nearly every primary voter multiple times prior to Election Day. His chances were better because he ran as a candidate in the Democratic Party primary, not as an outsider Green Party candidate as Karpen had. Almost all political insiders with whom he spoke told him that as much as they wanted the Berrios family out, they thought he did not stand a chance. "I sat down with a lot of people when I was getting started," Guzzardi said, "and I remember one of those conversations like it was yesterday. Someone said to me, 'You'll get 20–30 percent, and you'll be out of Chicago in three months.'"[5] However, that is not how it turned out.

On election night in March 2012, twenty-four-year-old Guzzardi took the stage to make a speech he had not prepared. His two prepared speeches were for winning or losing. On that primary election night, however, he announced that no winner had been declared. "When we saw the results come in, we realized how tight it was going to be right away," Guzzardi told *Hoy*, the largest Spanish newspaper in Chicago. "At the end of the night we were seventy-six votes behind. I'd been up to 49 percent this whole time. . . . Ultimately we decided not to concede on election night because it was simply too close to call."[6]

In the discovery recount, the Guzzardi campaign chose one-quarter of the eighty-four precincts in the 39th District to be recounted. The Illinois Supreme Court would then review the results of this partial recount to decide whether to call for a full recount. The cost to the campaign was only $10 a precinct, so $210 was minimal. In contrast, the cost of a full recount would have been much greater and probably not change the result.[7]

The six weeks following Election Day in 2012 were spent in a warehouse counting ballots with incumbent and challenger workers both present. One by one the votes were recounted. Despite possible discrepancies at several polling locations, the Guzzardi campaign chose not to continue a costly legal battle over the results. In the end, the incumbent reclaimed her seat by only 125 votes (see Table 9.2). It was a painful loss to come so close but fall short, but in politics you cannot win every campaign.

Guzzardi announced his loss to his supporters via e-mail and social media. Yet by coming so close, he proved that the powerful Chicago political machine was vulnerable. Whenever a grassroots campaign gets more than 40 percent of the vote, the same effort next time can win because the political circumstances

Table 9.2. Illinois Democratic Primary Results, State Representative, 39th District, 2012

Candidate	Number of Votes	Percentage of Votes
Berrios	4,021	50.79
Guzzardi	3,896	49.21

Source: Illinois State Board of Elections, http://www.elections.il.gov/ElectionResultsState HouseSet2.aspx?ID=32

change, and the next campaign can build on a base of voters and volunteers. After his defeat, Guzzardi took time off to reflect, sent his resume out, and took a day job.

The 2014 Campaign

Months went by. Guzzardi's core campaign team disbanded. His campaign manager became the executive director of a new nonprofit, Chicago Votes, that focuses on voter registration policy and encourages civic participation of young people. It has become a successful new political organization in Chicago and an example of one result of a good campaign.

Meanwhile, Guzzardi remained active in the effort to pass new online voter registration legislation but was undecided if he would run for office again. Nonetheless, he was engaged in local public school issues because more than fifty Chicago public schools were being closed. He was a member of a neighborhood coalition that helped keep the Brentano Math and Science Academy in Logan Square open. This kept him visible and in touch with the concerns of district citizens. He helped organize volunteers to gather signatures for an elected school board nonbinding referendum as well.

Six months after the 2012 primary, supporters began to ask if Guzzardi was considering running for the two-year state representative seat again. Local schools were hurting for funds, the pension crisis continued to loom over the state, and the incumbent state representative still did not seem to be part of the solution. In addition to the pressure from past supporters to run again, his inner circle of previous campaign workers urged Guzzardi to try once more. Even though some previous campaign leaders would not be available to work for his next campaign, they convinced him that too many people put their time, energy, and money into the race for him to quit now. Moreover, it would be a big blow to the progressive grassroots movement to get so close and not try again. The problem this time was that the incumbent would see him coming, and the machine would go all out to defeat him.

Small-group and one-on-one discussions were held to determine the level of support people would provide to a second campaign. At the same time, Guzzardi continued taking intensive Spanish courses to better converse with the voters in this Latino/a-heavy district. As a Latina, Berrios had an advantage among Spanish-speaking voters in the previous election.

In the early summer of 2013, an intimate group assembled at the home of a Guzzardi supporter. Each attendee had already had individual lunches or coffees with Guzzardi prior to this meeting. Fifteen people met on a roof deck on a warm afternoon with an assortment of beers, sodas, and snacks. It only takes a dozen or so people to start a campaign, although it takes hundreds to win it. A Chicago Transit Authority train rumbled past in the background before disappearing downward into the Logan Square subway tunnel. The group was a mix of supporters from the previous race and new ones. It was diverse, reflective of multiethnic Chicago. Roughly 40 percent spoke Spanish as well as English. The group represented both long-term and new residents. There was only a loose agenda for the meeting, but attendees had filled out an online survey prior to this gathering about whether Guzzardi should run a second time.

The group spent nearly three hours discussing the lessons of the prior race. What should be kept and what should be altered in a second run? This was the start of many separate brain-trust meetings that helped determine the campaign's message, strategy, early funders, and volunteers. Guzzardi was able to develop a solid campaign plan from these meetings. He then hired a few part-time, local campaign staff members. The candidate loaned initial seed money to begin, and fund-raising started as soon as the decision was made to enter the race. A volunteer scheduled coffees and house parties in order to recruit volunteers and solicit donors. House parties are the secret weapons of grassroots campaigns, and Guzzardi fully utilized them.

One innovation in his second run was to encourage small, automatic, monthly Internet donations, especially from early supporters. These funds were easy to ask for and guaranteed a vote by the donor. Most importantly, these early contributions covered the basic overhead costs. The rent, utilities, Internet, and part of the first full-time staff member's salary were paid by early fall, long before the March 2014 primary election.

By August 2013, a campaign office was rented, but only one full-time field organizer and one part-time staff member were hired at this stage of the campaign. These first hires had not worked formally on political campaigns in the past. One of the young, eager new office staff members later showed strengths in organizing people and became the campaign field director, and the other took on the responsibilities of deputy campaign manager later in the campaign.

At this early stage the campaign focused on essentials only. The candidate's task was to knock on doors and meet voters. He was not scheduled to attend events other than coffees to meet voters, donors, and potential volunteers. The campaign targeted voters who were prior supporters or who had been identified as voting in the previous three Democratic primaries. The goal was to identify a minimum of 6,000 Guzzardi voters needed to win and to ensure that they got to the polls. Every weeknight the candidate set out with a walk sheet at 5:00 p.m. and continued until just before 9:00 p.m. On Saturdays, he left the campaign office around noon and returned from knocking on doors after 9:00 p.m. Sundays he attended coffees and also knocked on doors. Weekdays before walking, he made fund-raising phone calls. His dedication inspired volunteers to work harder and kept their energy high. The priorities at this early stage of his second run for office were fund-raising and voter contact, all according to the campaign plan.

In October 2013, the candidate hired Erica Sagrans as the campaign manager. She had only volunteered a little in the previous race, but at the recommendation of the candidate's inner circle, she had been encouraged to apply for the job. Although she had no campaign management experience, she had extensive experience from serving as Speaker of the House Nancy Pelosi's digital manager and the Obama for America paid digital team in Virginia and Chicago. Her expertise allowed the campaign to run a data-focused, highly efficient effort.

Sagrans was a young progressive who lived in the district in the Logan Square neighborhood. She had volunteered to be part of the digital brain trust for Guzzardi's campaign and had helped select NationBuilder, the database system the campaign purchased. After she was hired, she had the task of hiring other staff.

Guzzardi and his campaign made a conscious choice not to demonize the incumbent. The campaign goal was simply to cultivate voter support by connecting with voters on the values they shared rather than letting the incumbent define Guzzardi. This would be a ground-war campaign. The candidate and campaign leaders held to the belief that signs and mailers do not win elections, but that people reaching out to people, especially in this new highly digital world, win local elections. The campaign purchased window signs only for supporters who requested them. Different campaigns in other districts might use more buttons, bumper stickers, posters, and yard signs, but the most important ingredient of winning campaigns is to have the candidate or his volunteers contact voters personally.

The precinct campaign of voter contact began, as it most often does, with

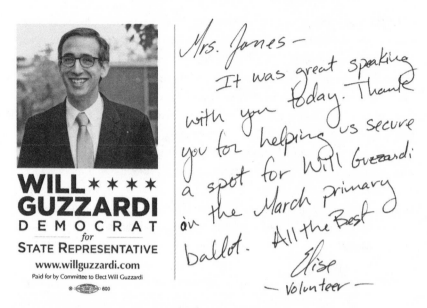

9.1. Handwritten Postcard Used in Will Guzzardi's Campaign. Courtesy of State Representative Will Guzzardi.

the petition drive. It was important that canvassing included sending hand-written thank-you postcards from the canvasser after a voter signed the nomination petition to get the candidate on the ballot (see Figure 9.1).

The ground campaign thus always starts most intensively at the early petition stage. Petition signatures were sought especially from voters who had voted in past primaries and from newly registered voters. Even at this early campaign stage, petition signers were asked the likelihood of their casting a vote for Guzzardi. This was the first phase of sorting *plus* from *minus* voters. Thus, counting positive votes for Guzzardi began before he had even officially secured a place on the ballot.

An experienced election lawyer ensured that the petitions were correctly filled out and notarized. Copies were made and numbered. Then volunteers examined the accuracy of the signatures at the Chicago Board of Elections. Line by line the volunteers compared the voters' signatures to the signatures officially on file and ranked them by grades A, B, C, and D. Only A and B signatures were submitted to the Illinois Board of Elections in Springfield in order to prevent a petition challenge from the incumbent. Many first-time candidates fail to be this careful in gathering and filing petitions and, therefore, get thrown off the ballot by more experienced and entrenched opponents.

During the campaign itself, political canvassers were invited to fun, theme-based Saturday morning or afternoon events. These events focused on a specific group with a title such as Women for Guzzardi, Latinos for Guzzardi, Progressives for Guzzardi, or Teachers for Guzzardi. A different speaker was invited to address the targeted crowd each week. Guzzardi's campaign was able to recruit many students to help canvass the precincts. Several student interns worked more than ten hours a week, each coordinating different campaign efforts.

In addition, Facebook invites, evites, tweets, and phone calls were made to supporters to get volunteers to commit to specific times. NationBuilder was used to manage canvassing and allow the campaign to accurately keep track of voters. The use of NationBuilder allowed the type of analytics developed by the Obama presidential campaign to be used to decide which voters to contact in this local election and enabled the campaign to begin with a list of voters and volunteers who had supported Guzzardi in the last campaign. It was possible to add to that list the voters who had voted in previous Democratic primaries and were most likely to vote this time. Then information collected from door-to-door canvassing, such as level of support for Guzzardi ranked from 1 to 5, was added to the NationBuilder file. Voters who indicated support for Berrios were ranked as 4 or 5 and removed from the canvassing list. Voters who indicated that they were "undecided" were ranked as 3 level of support and remained on the supporters list. They would later be contacted via door-to-door canvassing, phone calls, and mailers. This narrowed the number of voters to be contacted, connected, and reminded to vote early or on Election Day.

The campaign cultivated a volunteer team brought together by a common message:

- The current political incumbent is part of a system that does not serve us.
- Guzzardi lost by just 125 votes last time. If everyone reached just five additional voters and convinced them to vote for Guzzardi we would easily make up that difference.
- We all want the same thing regardless of where you are from: strong public schools, safe communities, and a fair economy that helps working families and asks the wealthy to pay their fair share.

The campaign made the serious work of politics fun. Part of this was creating a buzz on social media outlets. The campaign used social media tools to recruit volunteers, get small financial contributions, and get out the vote (GOTV) for Guzzardi.

The campaign had an easily navigated website and made good use of Face-

Dialogue on Reddit

✱ [-] di-xxxxxx **7 points 6 hours ago**

✱ As a new state rep (And a young one at that), how would you go about build relationships and respect among your new colleagues?

permalink

> ✱ [-] willguzzardi [5] **11 points 5 hours ago**
>
> ✱ This is really important to me. In my organizing efforts these past two years – pushing for an elected school board, successfully fighting to pass online voter registration in Illinois – I've developed some good relationships with a few state legislators already. I think the key is that I'm not going to agree with hardly anyone down there on every single thing. But I want to find individual issues where I can work with lawmakers from across the state to get some concrete things done. I think it's important to be uncompromising in your values, but not to be so dogmatic that you can't build bridges.
>
> permalink parent ...

✱ [-] de-xxxxx **11 points 5 hours ago**

✱ I'm in your district and you will get my vote again in March, Will. I'm looking forward to a rep who will actually do work on my behalf. What issue do you see as the highest priority in the 39th right now?

permalink

> ✱ [willguzzardi] [5] **10 points 5 hours ago**
>
> ✱ Fixing the state's economy is absolutely critical, for two reason: our families in this district and across the state are simply bearing too much of the burden right now; and we're also not funding the priorities that we all care about, like public education, safety, mental health, etc.
>
> I support a broad-based plan of economic reforms that would ease the tax burden on 94% of families in Illinois, hold corporations accountable to paying their fair share,... and generate billions of dollars in new revenues to pay down our pension over time, pay our backlog of bills to human service providers, and meet our funding targets for K-12 and higher ed. Can give more details if you care to hear....

✱ [-] gr-xxxxxxx   Logan Square **10 points 5 hours ago**

✱ Hi, Will – just popping in to thank you for giving it another go. Now go get Toni Berrios. I'll be voting for you again...

9.2. Dialogue on Reddit between Will Guzzardi and Some Voters. Courtesy of State Representative Will Guzzardi.

book posts and tweets not just from the campaign but from volunteers on their own accounts.

The candidate conversed with voters on newer social media sites, such as Reddit, for which he prepared as if he were being interviewed face to face (see Figure 9.2). Some Internet questioners were clearly from the opposition's campaign, but those plants were called out by others on the site.

Entering 2014, the campaign effort ramped up. Door-knocking by volunteers was hampered by one of the deepest, coldest Chicago winters in more than thirty years. On the coldest days, the campaign shifted to phone banking to reach voters. While the ice and snow blocked volunteers from going door to door, voter contact by phone volunteers rather than robo-calls continued to reach voters and build the *plus voter* list in NationBuilder.

CHAPTER NINE

Our campaign is proud to have been endorsed by a number of organizations and

community leaders. Will Guzzardi for State Representative has been endorsed by:

State Senator Willie Delgado (2nd District)

Alderman Joe Moreno (1st Ward)

Alderman Bob Fioretti (2nd Ward)

Alderman Scott Waguespack (32nd Ward)

Alderman Joe Arena (45rd Ward)

SEIU Health Care Illinois and Indiana

SEIU Local 1

SEIU Local 73

AFSCME 31

National Nurses United

The Chicago Teachers Union

Illinois Education Association

Illinois federation of Teachers

Fraternal Order of Police, Chicago Lodge #7

Northside Democracy for America

Progressive Democrats of America – PDA-Illinois and PDA-Chicago

The People's Lobby

Citizen Action of Illinois

Source: http://www.willguzzardi.com/endorsements

9.3. Endorsements for Candidate Will Guzzardi. Courtesy of State
Representative Will Guzzardi.

Campaign momentum sped up with the announcement that the Chicago Teacher's Union endorsed Guzzardi. After the organization made its support public, many other endorsements for Guzzardi were announced (see Figure 9.3). This was unlike his 2012 campaign, in which endorsements were hard to get. These endorsements brought more people and money to the campaign, allowing the purchase of television commercials to combat the steady flow of negative mailers and television, radio, and Internet ads from the opposition. The big-name support also allowed the campaign to hire full-time canvassers and GOTV staff. The 39th District race became, as *Sun-Times* columnist Carol Marin predicted, the "race to watch."

It is particularly critical that any successful campaign become one of the handful of races on which the media focuses during an election cycle so news stories reach voters in ways that change election outcomes. When hundreds of races are happening at the same time, becoming one of the handful of elections the media are watching is key to the additional publicity that drives candidate name recognition and convinces potential voters that this is a candidate for whom they should vote.

The negative mailers against Guzzardi by Berrios became so offensive that even the major newspapers took notice. In fact, "Berrios hammered Will in daily mail pieces showing little blonde girls getting lured into cars, scary men's faces lurking in the shadows, and one particularly disturbing piece with a young girl with large dirt-stained hands ominously placed on her shoulders from behind."[8] Candidates must respond to such direct mail and media attack ads rather than ignoring them.

The Guzzardi campaign responded with a flyer that refuted the charge that Will was soft on crime and supported laws that prevented prosecution of sex offenders. The campaign also sent a supportive direct mail piece from local aldermen. "But more important than responding to the attacks was the fact that Guzzardi had met and earned the support of many voters before the attacks even began."[9]

Because Guzzardi had built trust with voters ahead of time, few voters changed their opinions or voted against Guzzardi because of these negative ads. Voters already "touched" by the Guzzardi campaign in a positive manner were not converted to the Berrios campaign. The heavy flow of negative ads and direct mail late in the race boosted the recruitment of volunteers and the grassroots efforts for the Guzzardi campaign instead.

Even though the Berrios campaign sent forty direct mail pieces while the Guzzardi campaign sent only nine, the Guzzardi mailers were enough to neutralize the opponent's message. However, had the Guzzardi campaign not used direct mail at all, the negative Berrios campaign mailers might have won the day. Few hotly contested campaigns can win without using direct mail in addition to social media and door-to-door contact. A local campaign has to raise enough money to afford a direct mail effort, and sometimes, a mail/phone campaign. That is why the candidate must spend so much of her time fund-raising and why endorsements such as that of the Teachers Union, which come with additional funding, campaign workers, and expertise, are also important.

When Chicago's winter days finally warmed above subzero temperatures, the canvass effort shifted its focus to "commit to vote" postcards signed by voters (see Figure 9.4).[10] The voter-signed cards promising to vote were then

9.4. Voter-Signed Postcard Used in Will Guzzardi's Campaign. Courtesy of State Representative Will Guzzardi.

sent back to those voters a few weeks before Election Day reminding them of their pledge.

In the weeks immediately before the election, data-entry volunteers and top volunteer canvassers began to get paid for the first time for their efforts as their workload became more intense. A relatively new early voting option became available in Chicago, so phone-banking volunteers began to call voters to remind them they could now vote early. Volunteers explained that voters could go to any of fifty-one polling locations throughout the city to vote before Election Day. Educating the voters about this convenient option turned out to be fruitful. All Election Day volunteers were strongly encouraged to vote early, and a number of pro-Guzzardi votes were cast. This freed them to work all of Election Day and guaranteed their vote if they should fall sick.

Election Day preparations began in earnest more than a month before the election itself. In addition to two short-term rented locations and the campaign headquarters, one volunteer provided her home as the fourth Election Day staging location. Thus mini-headquarters were available throughout the district to coordinate the Election Day effort and rush help where needed. Large campaign signs were donated, giving a morale boost to canvassers who mostly saw large Berrios signs throughout the district. If signs won elections the incumbent would have won, but they do not. Yet the new Guzzardi signs boosted morale.

Berrios did not start campaigning until mid-January. She followed the old

Table 9.3. Illinois Democratic Primary Results, State Representative, 39th District, 2014

Candidate	Number of Votes	Percentage of Votes
Guzzardi	5,316	60.41
Berrios	3,484	39.59

Source: Illinois State Board of Elections, http://www.elections.il.gov/ElectionResultsState HouseSet2.aspx?ID=41

campaign timetable of gearing up in the last month or so to get reliable Democratic machine voters to the polls. It did not work this time. According to Guzzardi coordinator Joel Stopka, "The Berrios [campaign] spent money, but [was] still asleep at the wheel in terms of running a real ground crew."[11]

The Guzzardi campaign opted not to spend money on traditional palm cards. The campaign continually evaluated every campaign practice and modified it to fit their situation. Because Guzzardi had run before in this district, his managers could make wise and informed decisions about what worked and what did not.

Instead of palm cards, they spent their money on GOTV staff and training poll watchers. The Chicago machine is notorious for stealing elections, so Team Guzzardi's goal was to ensure that all polling places ran as honestly as possible. This turned out to be a wise strategic decision because several polling locations in the district experienced problems. Two polling places opened late. One opened so late that it was required to stay open an hour later than the usual closing time so all voters could vote. Television crews arrived to cover the location that opened late, and the presence of these cameras may have helped keep voter intimidation down at that polling place.

On March 18, 2014, Guzzardi won his second time around (see Table 9.3), and you can see the photograph of his cheering supporters on the cover of this book. Voters in the district reached a tipping point, and they overwhelmingly selected a young, progressive candidate over the traditional machine candidate. Guzzardi was elected with a near landslide of 60 percent of the vote.

Lessons Learned

We learned from Guzzardi's election that sometimes it takes an outsider with youthful zeal, a dose of naivety, and academic prowess to envision and implement a plan to oust a deeply entrenched, well-connected incumbent. The pattern of corruption and its harm is sometimes more clearly seen by those with a fresh perspective.

These are other lessons of the Guzzardi campaign:

1. *Start early with "house parties" or cocktail hours.* This is the way to recruit the volunteer army needed, help the candidate polish his or her presentation, and get the pledged money necessary to fund the critical early stages of the campaign.
2. *Use grassroots organizing to get the campaign message out.* As campaign manager, Sagrans wrote in an op-ed after the election that a big part of why Guzzardi won was having him and his volunteers

   > out talking to voters as much as possible, making the case for why they should support Guzzardi. . . . He set the example. . . . In contrast, the Berrios campaign seemed to hardly be out talking to voters. They spent money on piles of negative mail . . . and negative TV ads attacking Will. The people knocking on doors for Berrios were paid canvassers who often didn't seem very invested in the outcome of the race.[12]

3. *Have a clear campaign strategy early and stick with it.* Unexpected things always happen in a campaign, and it must respond to negative attack ads or to mistakes made by the opponent. Deciding early on a plan and then executing it well is the best way to win.
4. *Cultivate low-dollar monthly giving.* This creates steady campaign income and helps encourage more donors to give. Monthly givers are also guaranteed to turn out to vote, become regular volunteers, and gather the most accurate and up-to-date voter data. They literally have an investment in the campaign.
5. *Invest in people.* Signs and mailers do not win elections. Face-to-face contact and genuinely "touching" the voters early win votes. Moreover, "when big campaign donations started coming in towards the end, we didn't just do more TV and mail—we hired a street team made up of some of our top volunteers to talk to even more voters, plus extra data-entry volunteers to keep up with the piles of walk sheets."[13]
6. *Keep it positive.* Although it is fine to do comparative advertisements and press conferences comparing a candidate to his or her opponent, do not attack the opponent personally if it can be avoided. When the candidate or precinct volunteers find voters who provide support for the campaign, always send them a handwritten thank-you note afterward. These personal, positive touches cement their support.

7. *Use technology, target voters, and track them.* Do not contact the opponent's voters. The Guzzardi campaign

> took the research and cutting-edge technology from the Obama world and other large campaigns and applied them to our race. . . . We also adopted many voter outreach best practices from the Analyst Institute, a research consortium that runs experiments and centralized the latest research so that it can be put to use by progressive campaigns. . . . But while technology can help make campaigns more effective . . . talking to voters is first and foremost the most important part of a local campaign, and data and technology have to be used to support those efforts.[14]

8. *There are no shortcuts.* The candidate must do the footwork, start early, and surround him- or herself with good staff members and volunteers. The candidate must meet the voters one-on-one, cultivate volunteers through events, and spend endless hours raising money. Other people must invest countless hours as well to win a participatory campaign.[15]

Building Democracy

Participatory grassroots campaigns do not always win. Guzzardi lost his first campaign, as did the Green Party candidate who ran previously for this legislative seat. By persevering, Guzzardi and his supporters won this time. Guzzardi now serves in the Illinois legislature, is helping other progressive candidates to defeat political machine candidates, and is a strong voice for change.

The Guzzardi campaign is an example of how grassroots participatory efforts using the latest technology and social media can succeed. However, the financial resources still have to be raised to prevail. Participatory campaigns are generally less expensive than more synthetic campaigns driven by big money and superPACs, but they are still not cheap. They require a commitment of time and money by the candidate, volunteers, and financial supporters. Democracy is not free.

Chapter Ten

Challenges to Democracy

....

At the end of the movie *The Candidate*, Robert Redford's character, having won an upset victory, asks, "What do I do now?" This is not a trivial question for anyone who works in an election campaign. Whether you win or lose, there are important things to be done. Campaign promises must be kept, a permanent political organization created or maintained, and, most importantly, governmental and electoral reforms enacted.

Beyond winning or losing individual elections, there is a need to reform the electoral process. Both liberal and conservative participatory campaigns and officials can agree that democracy needs to be strengthened and protected.

Democracy is undermined when elections are won by the endorsement of closed party organizations, millions of dollars spent on thirty-second television spots, and distorted direct mail campaigns funded by outside organizations that do not disclose their donors. Some key challenges to democracy today are (1) the cost of campaigns, (2) the "selling" of candidates with false images, (3) the use of technologies that undermine democracy, and (4) the manipulation of mass media, "narrowcasting," and microtargeting campaign messages tailored to private rather than the public interests. Because of these obstacles, many good potential candidates currently choose not to run.

Electoral Reform

To judge which electoral reforms are necessary, we must consider what democracy requires. Representative democracy is based upon a paradigm of debate and discussion. Political candidates are supposed to present clear alternatives. Voters choose between these alternatives and empower their elected representatives to govern. After they enter government, these officials then convince a majority of other representatives to vote for the best government policies. All these stages require debate, deliberation, and discussion. Candidates and policies win by persuasion in a democracy.

Some scholars have concluded that the current political marketing of candidates undermines democracy. Nicholas O'Shaughnessy, in *The Phenomenon of Political Marketing*, concludes:

> American politics are shaped by the need to market candidates and parties as if they were soap powder, employing the techniques taken from the world of business. . . .
>
> Unfortunately, the . . . marketing [in] American politics has accentuated this preference of democracy for the likeable leader over the strong, the smart phrase over the smart idea, the common over the elegant; it has redefined democracy's criteria further along the path antiquity most feared since it vaunts appeals to immediate satisfaction and superficial, instantly communicable indices of worth. . . .
>
> Political marketing . . . makes politics more fickle and opportunistic.[1]

Representative democracy cannot be sustained in a system of media manipulation paid for by big money. When we are reduced to consumers being sold a product by slick advertising, we are no longer citizens deciding between alternative candidates and policies.

One reform often advocated is free media for candidates. However, as Randall Rothenberg has written in the *New York Times,* "A true cure . . . would require more than free [media] ads and earnest narration." In his article he quotes political science professor Larry Sabato as saying, "You cannot improve discourse [on television by merely requiring free time or by merely applying legal restrictions]. . . . Lack of education, lack of demands by the public that a certain level of discourse be reached, are the problem. That will not change with free time. That is corrected with more and better civic education starting from kindergarten."[2]

Paid political commercials, negative advertising, targeted e-mail messages, and cleverly packaged direct mail provide even less opportunity than the news media for honest discourse. Despite countertrends on cable news channels, PBS, public radio programs, and local public access channels, voters do not get enough information to make rational choices among candidates or policies. Although there is political news available on the Internet and websites such as Project VoteSmart that provide objective information on candidates, they cannot fill the void. Because younger voters obtain most of their political information from the Internet, they mostly view only brief news headlines or biased, short blog posts.

CHAPTER TEN

In recent years, there have been advances in the use of the Internet and social media in political campaigns, in neighborhood blogs to keep neighbors involved in their community's problems, and in the use of websites and e-mail by government officials to provide more government information. This has allowed more citizens to give campaign contributions and campaigns to better mobilize volunteers and reach voters directly with campaign messages. It has given community groups, civic organizations, and elected officials the opportunity to rally support for proposed legislation. However, despite the democratizing potential of the Internet and cable television, most communications remain top-down. Messages are sent from the owner of the website, blog, or e-mail list to consumers, customers, and voters. Social media and Internet communications can be manipulated just as mass media or direct mail can. In some ways the Internet has been a boon to campaigns and to citizen empowerment, but it has not been a panacea.

Under today's conditions, six reforms have the best chance of making elections and government more democratic:

1. Campaign finance reform
2. Term limits
3. Standards for analytics
4. Democratizing campaigns and government through citizen contact
5. Making voting easier and providing better voter information
6. Civic education and engagement programs in schools

These six changes provide an action agenda for winning or losing candidates and the volunteers and voters who support them.

Campaign Finance Reform

The arguments for campaign finance reform are simple. Better-financed candidates most often win elections. To obtain necessary funds, candidates have to appeal to political action committees (PACs) that represent narrow special interests, wealthy businesspeople, or superPACs funded by billionaires.

Because of the need for campaign contributions, our representative democracy is often reduced to representing wealthy special interests. These interests corrupt public officials, who have no alternative but to court PACs and wealthy individuals if they want to be elected.

The Supreme Court's *Citizens United* decision in 2010 determined that "political spending is a form of protected speech under the First Amendment, and the government may not keep corporations or unions from spending money to support or denounce individual candidates in elections. While corporations or unions may not give money directly to campaigns, they may seek to persuade the voting public through other means, including ads."[3] This was followed by *McCutcheon v. Federal Election Commission* in 2014, which struck down limits on aggregate totals of campaign contributions as a violation of free speech.[4] The net effect of these Supreme Court decisions was to open a floodgate of superPAC funding in elections.

By summer 2014, superPACs spent more than $21 million to influence congressional elections. Now superPACs operate in local elections as well. Outside superPACs spent nearly $5.3 million to influence Newark, New Jersey, elections, outraised even the mayoral candidates in San Diego, and raised more than $2 million in support of aldermanic candidates who would vote with Mayor Rahm Emanuel on the Chicago City Council.[5]

We already have an effective method for overcoming the undue effects of big money and PACs in the presidential campaign financing system. However, that system has been weakened because the top candidates in both parties have decided not to accept public funding because of contribution and spending limits in the crucial primary election season.

At the more local level, public funding and transparency of contributions to campaigns have been instituted. Many reform groups including the Illinois Campaign for Political Reform (ICPR) and Common Cause believe some form of public financing is the only cure for the current problems within the restrictions of the Supreme Court decisions. They conclude:

> Public campaign financing is a sound option for minimizing these problems [of donations by wealthy individuals and interest groups affecting election outcomes and scaring off potentially good candidates]. Under a public financing system, candidates meeting certain thresholds of public support could draw campaign cash from a state-operated fund. Candidates would not be required to accept such dollars, but this option would fuel qualified candidates who lack access to party bosses, special interests, or personal wealth. Public campaign financing has been applied successfully in at least 25 states, and new innovations are being studied around the country each year.
>
> Several options for campaign financing exist. States like Hawaii and Minnesota have implemented partial financing systems, so candidates can draw from both public and private sources of funds so they need to focus less on private fund-raising. Other systems are more expansive, completely

cutting out big donors. Maine is one of the states to have "clean elections," where qualified candidates fund their campaign entirely with public funds, removing the need for fund-raising. New York City has multiple matching funds, which magnifies the power of small donors. All these options are feasible . . . and have marked benefits over the current system.[6]

Under a system similar to presidential funding, contributions from individuals would be restricted to no more than $2,600 per candidate per election. Smaller contributions of $250 or less would be matched by government funds, which in federal elections are at least partially funded by a tax check-off system. As with presidential campaigns, strict limits would be placed upon total campaign expenditures, and the news media should be required to provide free airtime (or time bought with government vouchers) for candidate debates. The goal of any public funding system is to ensure that enough funds are available to qualified candidates to get their campaign messages to the voters.

Term Limits

One problem endemic to US government is the advantage of an incumbent running for reelection. In most elections, we vote on the performance of officials in office. When citizens vote to defeat or reelect the president of the United States, they have enough information to cast a reasonable vote. In addition, the opposition party candidate spends hundreds of millions of dollars to criticize the incumbent and present reasons for defeating him. However, for more than 580,000 elected offices in the United States, voters know much less about city, county, and state officials. Generally speaking, unless there is a controversial vote on issues such as tax increases, abortion, gun laws, or same-sex marriage, voters also know less about how officials have performed their public duties.

Incumbents have the advantage of more name recognition and greater acceptance by the media. In addition, they can more easily solicit contributions from wealthy individuals and interest groups wanting government favors. Incumbents spend thousands of government dollars to contact voters in their official government capacity, sending newsletters mailed at government expense to every voter in their districts and creating an attractive government website to tout their achievements. Incumbents also control the redistricting process, which allows them to draw boundaries to select favorable voters rather than voters selecting them. The end result of all these advantages is that incumbents have a 90 percent or better chance of reelection no matter how well they have performed.[7]

One example of the power of incumbency is that in the 2014 primary election in Illinois, 74 of 137 incumbent legislators did not even have an opponent on the ballot. The remaining contested primary districts often did not have a strong opponent from the other party in the general election because gerrymandered districts made election of minority party candidates next to impossible. Even worse, in the local elections outside Chicago in Cook County, Illinois, in 2015, voter turnout was only 14 percent of registered voters because 60 percent of the offices had only incumbents running for reelection with no opponent on the ballot. Uncontested elections undermine democracy.

Even incumbents who do a good job when first elected tend to ossify in office over time. In their first years on the job, they may have been enthusiastic and filled with new ideas. By the first decade, they will have made any progress they are likely to make to carry out their original platform. We are better served by a rotation of people in power because a concentration of power causes constantly reelected officials to disregard public opinion.

As a result of court rulings, limiting terms of members of Congress will require a constitutional amendment. State legislatures or city councils have seldom adopted term limits on their own. Usually, term limits have been instituted by voter initiatives by overwhelming majorities. The latest public opinion poll in Illinois by the Paul Simon Public Policy Institute showed that 80 percent of Illinoisans favored term limits, and 67 percent strongly favored them.[8] Because of this consistent public pressure, more than 100 state and local governments have been forced to adopt term limits since the 1980s, but most others have not.

Instituting term limits would help to restore citizens' faith in government. Recent public opinion surveys show voter approval of Congress at less than 10 percent.[9] The range of trust in state governments varies more. Only 28 percent of Illinois citizens have a great deal or even a fair amount of faith in their government's ability to solve problems. By comparison, 72 percent of Texans have faith in their state government.[10] In general, however, few voters have a high opinion of government officials. Particularly in these circumstances, term limits make government more responsive and more respected.

Standards for Using Analytics

Regardless of how voters or candidates view analytics, the genie is out of the bottle. Campaigns are moving to take advantage of all available voter data in order to win. The best we can strive for is to create standards for the use of analytics.[11] Recently, law professor Paul Schwartz suggested guidelines for companies that can be adapted to political campaigns. When using analytics, campaigns should:

- comply with legal requirements;
- assess the impact of their use on various [citizens];
- use accountable measures, beginning with the acknowledgment that some techniques can have both negative and positive impacts on individuals;
- develop organizational policies that govern information management, training, and oversight;
- implement appropriate safeguards to protect the security of information;
- assess whether analytical data involves sensitive areas and, if so, provide safeguards proportionate to the risk; and
- avoid collecting certain kinds of information.[12]

Campaigns have embraced analytics because they have made targeting voters easier and getting messages to them much less costly. It behooves us now to limit the possible drawbacks of these techniques. Adopting and publicizing standards for analytics use is better than passing new laws or regulations at this stage. It is essential that steps be taken to ensure privacy of individuals' data to the extent possible. This may well require legislation in the future.

Experiments in Democratization

For the last several decades, a great many experiments in democratizing elections and government have been attempted. Some experiments have returned to the older town hall meeting model. Others have attempted to harness modern technology—computers, public opinion polls, and television—in the service of greater citizen participation and influence. Nearly every experiment that has involved citizens more directly has been effective in its limited arena, but almost none of them has been adopted by government, sufficiently funded, and legitimized.

We briefly described the successes of the 44th Ward assembly town hall meetings by which Alderman Dick Simpson involved thousands of Chicago citizens in their local government. The decisions of the assembly were wise, the community was improved, and he became a more effective public official because of citizen advice and direction. Members of the assembly and other units of neighborhood government in the 44th Ward felt empowered and became much more knowledgeable about their government.

Neighborhood governments have also developed in other cities, but they are still not dominant in the United States. Most elected officials are simply not willing to share their power with the people who elected them, and voters do not demand a greater share of government authority. A current example of promoting citizen participation in government decision making is the Participatory Budget Project (PBP) in cities across the United States and around the world. The participatory budget process was first developed in Brazil in 1989, and there are now more than 1,500 participatory budgets around the world. Most of these are at the city level, providing some control over parts of the municipal budget by public meetings and a direct vote of citizens. The process has also been used for counties, states, housing authorities, school systems, universities, and other public agencies. [13]

If permanent town hall meetings with actual governmental authority or participatory budget decision making are neglected by public officials, there are other less demanding alternatives. Modern public opinion polling and Internet voting techniques can be used to discover policies citizens favor. There has been a great variety of experiments in public journalism, citizen agendas, televoting, and Internet voting over the years.

Christa Slaton in *Televote* summarizes the results of several experiments in community television, teleconferencing, and televised town meetings this way:

> These participatory democratic government-affiliated projects have demonstrated the following: (1) Large segments of the population are willing to participate in ways they never have before. (2) Attempts to educate the public on issues processes and functions of government are successful. (3) Citizens not only become better informed through attempts to involve them in public discussion and interaction but begin to understand complexities and approach issues more analytically. (4) When legislators are involved, they become better informed on problems and issues. (5) Legislators become more accountable as public awareness and sophistication grow. (6) Citizens want more, not less, access and responsibility.[14]

Experiments in televoting in Hawaii, San Jose, and Los Angeles developed techniques for involving citizens in government policy making. A representative sample of citizens was chosen using random-digit dialing and asked to participate in a televote on an issue. If they agreed to participate, they were sent a packet of information and asked to discuss the issues with friends and family and then call in their votes (or they were called back and asked their opinions). Citizens were informed about the issue through television news and special television programs designed to provide additional information on the specific policy questions to be voted upon. The process differed from normal polling by presenting citizens further information and encouraging them to discuss the issues before voting. The results of the televote were then presented to public officials charged with making the policy decisions. In each case, experiments in televoting were judged successful by the universities involved and by the government agencies employing them. Unfortunately, like other experiments in democracy, they have not been adopted widely.

In another set of experiments, citizens' conventions of randomly selected voters before the presidential primaries screened the issues and the candidates from both parties. The Center for Deliberative Polling has undertaken twenty-two experiments in the United States and across the globe using similar techniques:

> Each experiment conducted thus far has gathered a highly representative sample together at a single place. Each time, there were dramatic, statistically significant changes in views. The result is a poll with a human face. The process has the statistical representativeness of a scientific sample, but it also has the concreteness and immediacy of a focus group or a discussion group. Taped and edited accounts of the small group discussions provide an opportunity for the public to reframe the issues in terms that connect with ordinary people.[15]

When such experiments have been undertaken with hundreds of voters participating in these discussions of policies, they have been successful, but this methodology has yet to be adopted more broadly.

From these citizen participation experiments of the past four decades, it is clear that greater participation by interested citizens is now possible using modern technology. Unfortunately, government officials remain generally unwilling to use these methods even though such experiments have demonstrated that they improve policy making and citizens' sense of efficacy. They will have to be adopted as a matter of law and become part of the regular governing process if campaigns and government are to be further democratized.

Easier Registration and Voting

Some simple steps can increase access to the polls, achieve higher levels of voter participation, and improve the integrity of elections. The biggest change in registration laws in the past half century was the "motor voter law," which encouraged states to register voters when they obtained or renewed their drivers' licenses. More recently, many states have adopted both online voter registration to streamline the process and same-day voter registration so voters can register even on Election Day. In contrast, because of fears of voter fraud, some states now restrict voting by requiring a government photo-identification (ID) document to register or vote. Minorities and poorer members of society are less likely to have these official documents.

Other than the restrictive voter ID laws, voter registration has generally become easier. Advocates, however, ask why every American cannot be automatically registered at birth to vote or, at least, when they get a Social Security number? This simple reform would solve the voter registration problem.

Unfortunately, higher registration has not always meant higher voting levels. For instance, despite making it possible for eighteen-year-olds to register several decades ago, voter turnout by those between eighteen and twenty-nine years of age has remained low. Less than half, 45 percent in that age range, voted in the highly contested 2012 presidential election and only 21.5 percent in the 2014 nonpresidential elections.[16]

The Center for Information and Research on Civil Learning and Engagement points out that "when young people learn the voting process and vote, they are more likely to do so when they are older. If individuals have been motivated to get to the polls once, they are more likely to return. So, getting young people to vote early could be key to raising a new generation of voters."[17]

Along with easier registration, voting itself has also become easier. The biggest change thus far has been to make absentee or mail voting simpler by no longer requiring proof of absence because of illness or travel on Election Day. Twenty-seven states now permit any qualified voter to vote absentee without requiring an excuse. In addition, thirty-three states and the District of Columbia allow citizens to vote as early as forty-five days before Election Day. Three states conduct all elections by mail, and nineteen others conduct certain elections by mail.[18] However, ease of voting does not guarantee higher voting rates, much less informed voting.

Civic Education and Engagement

The lower rate of voting and citizen participation by youth has caused many to advocate increased civic learning and engagement as well as service learning in schools. This has occurred at the same time that "No Child Left Behind" legislation testing students on fundamentals such as reading and math has caused many schools to drop civics courses.

This trend caused the Illinois Task Force on Civic Education in its 2014 report to recommend that (1) civics should again be a required course for high school graduation, (2) social studies requirements should be revised to provide civic skills, including news literacy, (3) students should be required to do service learning projects in the eighth and twelfth grades, (4) teachers of civics should be licensed and provided continuing professional development, and (5) efforts should be made to encourage high school registration and voting.[19] In 2015 Illinois did pass a law requiring students to take a civics course to be graduated from high school beginning in the 2016 school year. There are many new books on civic engagement that could be used to revitalize these civics courses if they become mandated in other states.[20]

Winning Democracy

Informed voting will not be achieved through legislation or civic education alone, nor can the potential evils of modern political campaigns be curbed by exhortations by political scientists and editorial writers. New cutting-edge campaigns with their modern technology can be made to serve democracy only if the public demands it. We must use the mobilizing possibilities of the Internet and television to elect better candidates. We must volunteer for campaigns and run for office ourselves. As voters, we must reject candidates who spread disinformation about themselves or their opponents. In addition, the candidates we elect must spearhead electoral reforms.

We need to win not only elections but democracy itself. Campaigns using advanced technology have the prospect of either promoting or undermining that democracy. We must build an aware and informed electorate that chooses candidates who use these new techniques to increase democracy and defeat those who would subvert it. We must demand that methods such as participatory budgeting be used to allow us to participate more in government decision making. Winning participatory elections and more participatory government are central to reinventing democracy in the twenty-first century.

Notes

....

Chapter 2. Choosing Sides

1. E. J. Dionne Jr., *Our Divided Political Heart* (New York: Bloomsbury, 2012), 45–48; Kevin Arceneaux and Stephen P. Nicholson, "Who Wants to Have a Tea Party? The Who, What, and Why of the Tea Party Movement," *PS: Political Science & Politics* 45, no. 4 (October 2012): 700–710, accessed June 13, 2015, doi:10.1017/S1049096512000741; "Hundreds of Protesters Descend to 'Occupy Wall Street,'" *CNN Money*, September 17, 2011, accessed June 13, 2015, http://money.cnn.com/2011/09/17/technology/occupy_wall_street/.

2. Jack C. Doppelt and Ellen Shearer, *Nonvoters: America's No-Shows* (Thousand Oaks, CA: Sage, 1999), 220; Paul R. Abramson and John H. Aldrich, "The Decline of Electoral Participation in America," *American Political Science Review* 76, no. 3 (September 1982): 502–521, accessed June 13, 2015, doi:10.2307/1963728; Sidney Verba, Kay Lehman Schlozman, and Henry Brady, *Voice and Equality: Civic Voluntarism in American Politics* (Cambridge, MA: Harvard University Press, 1995, 2001), 1–3, 186–288.

3. See Verba, Schlozman, and Brady, *Voice and Equality,* for a review of the literature relating to personality traits and political participation. Also see Lester Milbrath, *Political Participation* (Chicago: Rand McNally, 1965), Chapter 3.

4. Eric Pultzer, "Becoming a Habitual Voter: Inertia, Resources, and Growth in Young Adulthood," *American Political Science Review* 96, no. 1 (March 2002): 41–56.

5. Thucydides, *History,* in Alfred Zimmern, *The Greek Commonwealth: Politics and Economics in Fifth-Century Athens* (Oxford, UK: Clarendon, 1911).

6. Robert D. Putnam, *Bowling Alone: The Collapse and Revival of American Community* (New York: Touchstone, 2000), 31–47, 412.

7. Max Lerner, "Political Man Is Needed," *Chicago Sun Times,* August 6, 1970, 90.

8. Benjamin I. Page, Larry M. Bartels, and Jason Seawright, "Democracy and the Policy Preferences of Wealthy Americans," *Perspectives on Politics* 11, no. 1 (March 2013): 5 –73; Jennifer Steen, *Self-Financed Candidates in Congressional Elections* (Ann Arbor: University of Michigan Press, 2006), 3–6; Gary Jacobson and Samuel Kernell, *Strategy and Choice in Congressional Elections* (New Haven, CT: Yale University Press, 1981);

Brad Alexander, "Good Money and Bad Money: Do Funding Sources Affect Electoral Outcomes?" *Political Research Quarterly* 58 (2005): 353, accessed June 13, 2015, doi:10 .1177/106591290505800214.

9. William Mahin and Dick Simpson, "Interviews with Campaign Volunteers from the Bernard Weisberg Campaign," in *By the People* (film), Chicago Politics Encyclopedia of Film, Political Science Department, University of Illinois–Chicago, 1969, accessed June 13, 2015, http://pols.uic.edu/political-science/chicago-politics/chicago -politics-encyclopedia-of-film.

10. Richard Wolffe, *Renegade: The Making of a President* (New York: Crown, 2009), 116–118.

11. Beth Fouhy, "2012 Campaign: Obama, Romney Volunteers Hope to Make the Difference in November," *Huffington Post,* July 3, 2012, accessed June 15, 2015, http:// www.huffingtonpost.com/2012/07/03/2012-campaign-obama-romney_n_1647029 .html; Pew Research Center, "Obama Ahead with Stronger Support, Better Image, and Lead on Most Issues," September 12, 2012, accessed June 13, 2015, http://www.people -press.org/files/legacy-pdf/09-19-12%20Political%20release.pdf.

12. John H. Aldrich, *Why Parties? The Origin and Transformation of Political Parties in America* (Chicago: University of Chicago Press, 1995), 181; Steven Rosenstone and John Mark Hanson, *Mobilization, Participants, and Democracy in America* (New York: Macmillan, 1993); Verba, Schlozman, and Brady, *Voice and Equality*, 112–127; Linda L. Fowler, "Who Runs for Congress?" *PS: Political Science & Politics* 29, no. 3 (September 1996): 430–434; Richard L. Fox and Jennifer L. Lawless, "To Run or Not to Run for Office: Explaining Nascent Political Ambition," *American Journal of Political Science* 49, no. 3 (July 2005): 642–659, accessed April 12, 2014, doi:10.1111/j.1540-5907.2005.00147.x; Sidney Verba, Kay Lehman Schlozman, and Henry E. Brady, "Rational Action and Political Activity," *Journal of Theoretical Politics* 12, no. 3 (2000): 243, accessed April 5, 2014, doi:10.1177/0951692800012003001.

13. Rasmus Kleis Nielsen, "Making Room for Volunteers," *Campaigns & Elections* (March–April 2012): 33, accessed June 13, 2015, http://www.campaignsandelections .com/print/313437/making-room-for-volunteers.thtml.

14. Verba, Schlozman, and Brady, *Voice and Equality*, 48, 91.

15. Peter LaChance, "Why Political Party Endorsements Make Sense in Local Races," *Burlington County Times,* February 4, 2012, accessed June 13, 2015, http://www .burlingtoncountytimes.com/blogs/politically-correct/why-political-party-endorse ments-make-sense-in-local-races/article_d0f36f74-72ca-5838-84f1-bfd802d92f3a .html?mode=story.

16. Lawrence Grey, *How to Win a Local Election: A Complete Step-by-Step Guide,* 3rd ed. (New York: M. Evans, 2007), 30.

17. Open Secrets, "2014 Overview: Incumbent Advantage," http://www.opensecrets .org/overview/incumbs.php; Scott Ashworth and Ethan Bueno de Mesquita, "Electoral Selection, Strategic Challenger Entry, and the Incumbency Advantage," *Journal of Pol-*

itics 70 (October 2008): 1006–1025; Stephen Ansolabehere and James M. Snyder Jr., "The Incumbency Advantage in U.S. Elections: An Analysis of State and Federal Offices, 1942–2000," *Election Law Journal* 1, no. 3 (2002): 315–338.

18. Milton Rakove, "Bill Singer: On the Outs with Democrats, He'll Be Heard from Again," *Illinois Issues,* February 19, 1978, accessed June 13, 2015, http://www.lib.niu.edu /1978/ii780218.html; Caroline O'Donovan, "Why Has Chicago Had So Many Democratic Mayors?" WBEZ, October 2, 2012, http://www.wbez.org/series/curious-city /question-answered-why-has-chicago-had-so-many-democratic-mayors-102843.

19. Caroline O'Donovan, "Cook County Regular Democratic Disorganization: Guzzardi and Berrios," *Gapers Block,* March 30, 2012, http://gapersblock.com/mechan ics/2012/03/30/cook-county-regular-democratic-disorganization-guzzardi-and-ber rios/; Quinn Ford, "Guzzardi Beats Berrios in Northwest Side State Rep. Race," *DNAinfo/ Chicago*, March 18, 2014, http://www.dnainfo.com/chicago/20140318/logan-square /northwest-side-state-rep-race-biggest-race-city-of-chicago.

20. Weisberg, quoted in *By the People.*

21. Angus Campbell, Philip E. Converse, Warren E. Miller, and Donald E. Stokes, *The American Voter* (Chicago: University of Chicago Press, 1976); Michael Lewis-Beck, William G. Jacoby, Helmut Norpoth, and Herbert Weisberg, *The American Voter Revisited* (Ann Arbor: University of Michigan Press, 2008), 25, 102.

22. Paul S. Herrnson, *Congressional Elections: Campaigning at Home and in Washington,* 6th ed. (Washington, DC: Congressional Quarterly Press, 2012), 7–9.

23. J. Cherie Strachan, *High-Tech Grass Roots: The Professionalization of Local Elections* (Lanham, MD: Rowman and Littlefield, 2002), 106–108.

24. *Citizens United v. Federal Election Commission,* 558 U.S. 310 (2010); *McCutcheon v. Federal Election Commission,* 12-536 133 S.Ct. 1242 (2013).

25. Jonathan Alter, *The Center Holds: Obama and His Enemies* (New York: Simon and Schuster, 2013), 192, 365.

26. Steven J. Rosenstone, Roy L. Behr, and Edward Lazarus, *Third Parties in America: Citizen Response to Major Party Failure* (Princeton, NJ: Princeton University Press, 1984), 5–6; Shigeo Hirano and James M. Snyder Jr., "The Decline of Third-Party Voting in the United States," *Journal of Politics* 69, no. 1 (February 2007): 1–16.

Chapter 3. Organizing a Campaign

1. William Singer, "Reflections on Campaign Techniques," unpublished paper, Committee on Illinois Government, Chicago, 1969, 8.

2. Catherine Shaw, *The Campaign Manager: Running and Winning Local Elections,* 4th ed. (Boulder, CO: Westview Press, 2010), 22.

3. *By the People* (film, University of Illinois–Chicago, 1969), http://pols.uic.edu/po litical-science/chicago-politics/chicago-politics-encyclopedia-of-film.

4. Donald Page Moore, in ibid.

5. Shaw, *Campaign Manager*, 11–12.

6. Lawrence Grey, *How to Win a Local Election: A Complete Step-by-Step Guide*, 3rd ed. (New York: M. Evans, 2007), 99, 101.

7. Joseph Napolitan, *The Election Game and How to Win It* (New York: Doubleday, 1972), 16–17.

8. Shaw, *Campaign Manager*, 26.

9. June Rosner, in *By the People*.

10. Bob Houston, "What Every *Great* Coffee Chairman Has to Know," unpublished instructions, Bruce Dumont for State Senate Campaign, Chicago, 1970.

11. Angus Campbell, Philip E. Converse, Warren E. Miller, and Donald E. Stokes, *The American Voter* (New York: Wiley, 1960); William H. Flanigan, Nancy H. Zingale, Elizabeth Theiss-Morse, and Michael W. Wagner, *The Political Behavior of the American Electorate*, 13th ed. (Washington, DC: Congressional Quarterly Press, 2014).

12. See Campbell et al., *American Voter;* Norman H. Nie, Sidney Verba, and John R. Petrocik, *The Changing American Voter* (Cambridge, MA: Harvard University Press, 1976); Benjamin Page and Robert Shapiro, *The Rational Public* (Chicago: University of Chicago Press, 1992).

13. Paula McClain and James Stewart, *"Can We All Get Along?" Race and Ethnic Minorities in American Politics*, 4th ed. (Boulder, CO: Westview Press, 2005).

14. Community Media Workshop, "Chicago Is the World," accessed June 13, 2015, http://chicagoistheworld.org/ethnic-media.

15. Jackie Calmes, "Obama Campaign Banks on High-Tech Ground Game to Reach Voters," *New York Times,* June 26, 2012, accessed June 13, 2015, http://www.nytimes.com/2012/06/27/us/politics/obama-campaign-banks-on-a-high-tech-ground-game.html?pagewanted=all&_r=0; Charu C. Aggarwal, ed., *Social Network Data Analytics* (New York: Springer Science and Business Media, 2011).

16. Jonathan Alter, *The Center Holds: Obama and His Enemies* (New York: Simon and Schuster, 2013), 100.

17. Ibid., 84.

18. Ibid., 109; Flanigan et al., *Political Behavior of the American Electorate*, 13th ed., 88.

19. Flanigan et al., *Political Behavior of the American Electorate*, 87; Donald P. Green and Alan S. Gerber, "The Effects of Canvassing, Telephone Calls, and Direct Mail on Voter Turnout: A Field Experiment," *American Political Science Review* 94, no. 3 (September 2000): 653–663, http://www.jstor.org/stable/2585837.

20. Calmes, "Obama Campaign Banks on High-Tech Ground Game."

Chapter 4. Raising Money

1. Herbert Alexander, *Reform and Reality: The Financing of State and Local Campaigns* (New York: Twentieth Century Fund, 1991), 2.

2. James A. Thurber, "Understanding the Dynamics and the Transformation of

American Campaigns," in *Campaigns and Elections American Style,* 3rd ed., ed. James A. Thurber and Candice J. Nelson (Boulder: Westview Press, 2010).

3. Lawrence Grey, *How to Win a Local Election: A Complete Step-by-Step Guide,* 3rd ed. (New York: M. Evans, 2007), 126.

4. Ibid., 128.

5. Hank Parkinson, *Winning Your Campaign: A Nuts-and-Bolts Guide to Political Victory* (Englewood Cliffs, NJ: Prentice-Hall, 1970), 77.

6. Donald Page Moore, in *By the People* (film, University of Illinois–Chicago, 1969), http://pols.uic.edu/political-science/chicago-politics/chicago-politics-encyclopedia -of-film.

7. Grey, *How to Win a Local Election,* 130.

8. David Himes, "Strategy and Tactics for Campaign Fund-Raising," in *Campaigns and Elections American Style,* ed. James A. Thurber and Candice J. Nelson (Boulder, CO: Westview Press, 1995), 62.

9. Ibid., 63.

10. Americans for Campaign Reform, "Money in Politics: Who Gives," http://www .acrreform.org/research/money-in-politics-who-gives/.

11. Peter Olsen-Phillips, Russ Choma, Sarah Bryner, and Doug Weber, "The Political One Percent of the One Percent: Megadonors Fuel Rising Cost of Elections in 2014," Sunlight Foundation, accessed June 13, 2015, http://sunlightfoundation.com /blog/2015/04/30/the-political-one-percent-of-the-one-percent-megadonors-fuel-ris ing-cost-of-elections-in-2014/.

12. Himes, "Strategy and Tactics for Campaign Fund-Raising," 65.

13. Tamara Holder, "Why Rahm Has Raised Millions of Dollars from Out-of-State Donors," *Daily Caller,* National Louis University, February 22, 2011, http://dailycaller .com/2011/02/22/why-rahm-has-raised-millions-of-dollars-from-out-of-state-do nors/#ixzz3mEmw0zLM.

14. "Legislative Candidates, Groups Dole Out $16.9 Million in 2014 Elections," Wisconsin for Democracy Campaign, accessed September 5, 2015, http://www.wisdc.org /pr030415.php.

15. Ibid., 65–66, emphasis added.

16. Ibid., 67, emphasis added.

17. "4 Best Tools for Creating a Financial Statement," businessbee.com, accessed June 13, 2015, http://www.businessbee.com/resources/profitability/4-best-tools-for-creat ing-a-financial-statement/.

18. *Citizens United v. Federal Election Commission,* 558 U.S. 310 (2010); "*Citizens United v. Federal Election Commission,*" Wikipedia.org, accessed June 13, 2015, https:// en.wikipedia.org/wiki/Citizens_United_v._FEC.

19. Alexandra Duszak, "Donor Profile: George Soros," Center for Public Integrity, May 19, 2014, accessed June 13, 2015, http://www.publicintegrity.org/2012/12/21/11975 /donor-profile-george-soros.

20. Steve Kraske, "When It Comes to Political Donations, the Koch Brothers Trump

All," *Kansas City Star,* December 5, 2013, http://www.kansascity.com/news/local/news
-columns-blogs/the-buzz/article333248/When-it-comes-to-political-donations-the
-Koch-Brothers-trump-all.html.

21. Nina Kasniunas and Mark Rozell, "Interest Groups and the Future of Campaigns," in *Campaigns on the Cutting Edge,* 2nd ed., ed. Richard Semiatin (Washington, DC: Congressional Quarterly Press, 2013), 132.

22. Michael J. Malbin, Peter Brusoe, and Brendan Glavin, "Public Financing of Elections after *Citizens United* and *Arizona Free Enterprise*: An Analysis of Six Midwestern States Based on the Elections of 2006–2010, Campaign Finance Institute," July 2, 2011, accessed June 13, 2015, http://www.cfinst.org/pdf/ state/CFI_Report_Small-Donors-in -Six-Midwestern-States-2July2011.pdf.

Chapter 5. Sending Your Message

1. Susan A. MacManus, with Renee Dabbs and Mary L. Moss, "Women and Campaigns: Growing Female Activism," in *Campaigns on the Cutting Edge,* 2nd ed., ed. Richard Semiatin (Washington, DC: Congressional Quarterly Press, 2013), 200.

2. Theodora Blanchfield, "Superficial Significance: Tailoring the Perfect Female Candidate," *Campaigns and Elections (1996)* 28, no. 1 (January 2007): 35. Also quoted in MacManus, Dabbs, and Moss, "Women and Campaigns," 199.

3. See, for example, Joe McGinniss, *The Selling of the President 1968* (New York: Penguin, 1989, first published by Trident Press, 1969).

4. See Gary Selnow, *High-Tech Campaigns: Computer Technology in Political Communication* (Westport, CT: Praeger, 1994); "Explaining the 'Dark Magic' of Microtargeting," *Campaigns and Elections (2010)* 31, no. 294 (2010): 36–41; David Talbot, "Personalized Campaigning," *Technology Review* 112, no. 2 (March 2009): 80–82.

5. Selnow, *High-Tech Campaigns,* 19.

6. Ibid., 102, 106.

7. Ibid., 172.

8. Much of the information in this section was provided by Mac Hansbrough, NTS, www.ntsdc.com.

9. Kirby Goidel, "Public Opinion in the Digital Age: Meaning and Measurement," in *Political Polling in the Digital Age: The Challenge of Measuring and Understanding Public Opinion,* ed. Kirby Goidel (Baton Rouge: Louisiana State University Press, 2011), 11–12.

10. Steven Yaccino, Robert Hutton, and Margaret Talev, *Chicago Tribune,* October 4, 2015, 28. The original research on this issue was published by Kirby Goidel, ed., *Political Polling in the Digital Age: The Challenge of Measuring and Understanding Public Opinion.*

11. Chad Merda, "Gallup Admits Defeat, Pulls Plug on Primary Polling," October 7, 2015, http://national.suntimes.com/national-world-news/7/72/1951017/gallup-ad mits-defeat-pulls-plug-election-polling.

12. Movement for a New Congress, *Vote Power: The Official Activist Campaigner's Handbook,* (Englewood Cliffs, NJ: Prentice-Hall, 1970), 14–15, 27. See also 14–15.

13. Ibid., 18.

14. David Orr, "Questions and Answers on Motor Voter," unpublished document, July 1995, 2.

15. National Council of State Legislatures, "History of Voter ID," October 16, 2014, accessed June 14, 2015, http://www.ncsl.org/research/elections-and-campaigns/voter-id -history.aspx.

16. "New Rules Make Illinois Voting Easier," *Chicago Tribune,* October 31, 2014, accessed June 14, 2015, http://www.chicagotribune.com/news/ct-illinois-voting-changes -20141031-story.html.

17. E. E. Schattschneider, *The Semi-Sovereign People* (New York: Holt, Rinehart, and Winston, 1960), 4.

18. Movement for a New Congress, *Vote Power,* 17.

19. State Board of Elections, "Registering to Vote in Illinois," accessed June 14, 2015, http://www.elections.il.gov/downloads/electioninformation/pdf/registervote.pdf.

20. Jerry Murray, in *By the People* (film), Chicago Politics Encyclopedia of Film, Political Science Department, University of Illinois at Chicago, http://pols.uic.edu/po litical-science/chicago-politics/chicago-politics-encyclopedia-of-film.

21. William Grimshaw, *Bitter Fruit: Black Politics and the Chicago Machine, 1931– 1991* (Chicago: University of Chicago Press, 1992), 163.

22. Ibid., 163.

23. Ibid., 171–173.

24. These themes are adapted from William Grimshaw's analysis in "Is Chicago Ready for Reform?" in *The Making of the Mayor: Chicago, 1983,* ed. Melvin Holli and Paul Green (Grand Rapids, MI: Eerdmans, 1984).

25. Grimshaw, *Bitter Fruit,* 174.

26. Ibid., 177.

27. Paul Kleppner, *Chicago Divided: The Making of a Black Mayor* (DeKalb: Northern Illinois University Press, 1985), 165–169.

28. R. Darcy, Susan Welsh, and Janet Clark, *Women, Elections, and Representation* (Lincoln: University of Nebraska Press, 1994), xiii.

29. Data from the Center for American Women and Politics, Rutgers University, accessed June 14, 2015, http://www.cawp.rutgers.edu/; Women and Politics Institute, School of Public Affairs, American University, accessed June 14, 2015, http://www .american.edu/spa/wpi/.

30. Seth Motel, "Who Runs for Office? Profile of the 2%," Pew Research Center, September 3, 2014, accessed June 14, 2015, http://www.pewresearch.org/fact-tank/2014 /09/03/who-runs-for-office-a-profile-of-the-2/.

31. Darcy, Welsh, and Clark, *Women, Elections, and Representation,* 73.

32. Jennifer L. Lawless, Richard L. Fox, and Gail Baitinger, "Women's Underrepresentation in U.S. Politics: The Enduring Gender Gap in Political Ambition," in *Women*

and Elective Office, ed. Sue Thomas and Clyde Wilcox (Oxford, UK: Oxford University Press, 2014), 42.

33. MacManus, Dabbs, and Moss, "Women and Campaigns," 198.

34. Ibid., 208.

35. Atiya Kai Stokes-Brown, "Minority Candidates and the Changing Landscape of Campaigns in the Twenty-First Century," in *Campaigns on the Cutting Edge,* 2nd ed., ed. Richard Semiatin (Washington, DC: Congressional Quarterly Press, 2013), 211.

36. 2011 Directory of Latino Elected Officials, http://www.naleo.org./directory /html.

37. Stokes-Brown, "Minority Candidates," 212–213.

38. Ricardo Vasquez, "Number of Asian American Public Officials Has Reached Historic Levels, UCLA Study Shows," UCLA Newsroom, June 2, 2014, accessed June 14, 2015, http://newsroom.ucla.edu/releases/number-of-asian-american-public-officials -has-reached-historic-levels-ucla-study-shows.

Chapter 6. Winning the Traditional Media War

1. Joe McGinness, *The Selling of the President, 1968* (New York: Penguin, 1989, first published by Trident Press, 1969).

2. Ibid., 34, 39.

3. Gary Selnow, *High-Tech Campaigns: Computer Technology in Political Communications* (New York: Praeger, 1993), 42, emphasis added.

4. William R. Hamilton, "Political Polling: From the Beginning to the Center," in *Campaigns and Elections American Style,* ed. James A. Thurber and Candice J. Nelson (Boulder, CO: Westview Press, 1995), 178.

5. Alex Stambaugh, "Getting the Most out of Focus Groups," *Campaigns and Elections,* March 25, 2012, http://www.campaignsandelections.com/magazine/1869/get ting-the-most-out-of-focus-groups.

6. Ibid.

7. Sean J. Miller, "Passing the Ad Test," *Campaigns and Elections,* February 11, 2013, http://www.campaignsandelections.com/magazine/1797/passing-the-ad-test.

8. Abacus Associates, "Conducting Surveys and Focus Groups," 2001, accessed June 14, 2015, http://www.abacusassoc.com/articles/SurveysandFocusGroups.pdf; Jeff Anderson Consulting, "What You Can Expect for Your Focus Group Investment, http:// www.jeffandersonconsulting.com/marketing-research.php/focus-group/focus-group -costs.

9. NSON Opinion Strategy, "Political Polling," 2013, accessed June 14, 2015, http:// nsoninfo.com/political-polling/.

10. Hamilton, "Political Polling," 170.

11. Glen Bolger and Trip Mullen, "There's an App for That," *Campaigns and Elections,* January 6, 2014, accessed June 10, 2015, http://www.campaignsandelections.com /magazine/1722/there-s-an-app-for-that.

12. Ibid.

13. Don Rose, in *By the People* (film), Chicago Politics Encyclopedia of Film, Political Science Department, University of Illinois at Chicago, http://pols.uic.edu/politi cal-science/chicago-politics/chicago-politics-encyclopedia-of-film.

14. Ibid.

15. See Sydney Blumenthal, *Pledging Allegiance: The Last Campaign of the Cold War* (New York: HarperCollins, 1990), 300–301; Museum of the Moving Image, "The Living Room Candidate: Presidential Campaign Commercials, 1952–2012—1988: Bush v. Dukakis, the Willie Horton Ad," accessed June 13 2015, http://www.livingroomcandi date.org/commercials/1988/willie-horton; Boston Harbor ad, accessed June 13, 2015, http://www.livingroomcandidate.org/commercials/1988/harbor; Dukakis tank ad, accessed June 13, 2015, http://www.livingroomcandidate.org/commercials/1988/tank -ride; Josh King, "Dukakis and the Tank," Politico.com, November 17, 2013, accessed June 15, 2015, http://www.politico.com/magazine/story/2013/11/dukakis-and-the -tank-99119.html#.VGkWUoeO7fY.

16. *The War Room* (film directed by Chris Hegedus and D. A. Pennebaker), 1993.

17. Jonathan Alter, *The Center Holds: Obama and his Enemies* (New York: Simon and Schuster, 2013), 187, 216, 245.

18. Joel C. Bradshaw, "Who Will Vote for You and Why: Designing Strategies and Theme," in *Campaigns and Elections American Style*, 2nd ed., ed. James A. Thurber and Candice J. Nelson (Boulder CO: Westview Press, 2004), 42–43.

19. Ibid.

20. Ibid., 44.

21. Ibid.

22. Joseph Napolitan, *The Election Game and How to Win It* (New York: Doubleday, 1972), 2–3.

23. Hank Parkinson, "Publicity Is Inexpensive and Neglected," *Campaign Insight* 1, no. 3 (June 1970), 35–36.

24. Adlai Stevenson III for U.S. Senate Campaign, *Stevenson for Illinois Campaign Manual*, (1970), 35–36.

25. Dennis McGrath and Dane Smith, *Professor Wellstone Goes to Washington* (Minneapolis: University of Minnesota Press, 1995), 148.

26. NorthWoods Ads, "Fast-Paced Paul," uploaded July 13, 2009, accessed June 15, 2015, https://www.youtube.com/watch?v=aTiW0YCMM0g.

27. McGrath and Smith, *Professor Wellstone Goes to Washington*, 149.

28. Todd Blair and Garrett Biggs, "Cable Advertising: An Underrated Medium for Local Elections," *Campaigns and Elections* 26, no. 8 (September 12, 2005): 40.

29. Stephen C. Brooks, "Discovering Campaign Messages in Political Fliers," poster presented at the annual meeting of the American Political Science Association, Chicago, Illinois, August 2013.

30. Alan Gerber and Donald P. Green, "The Effects of Canvassing, Telephone Calls, and Direct Mail on Voter Turnout: A Field Experiment," *American Political Science Re-*

view 94, no. 3 (September 2000), 653–663; http://www.jstor.org/stable/2585837; David Broockman and Joshua Kalla, "Experiments Show This Is the Best Way to Win Campaigns. But Is Anyone Actually Doing It?" Vox.com, November 13, 2014, http://www.vox.com/2014/11/13/7214339/campaign-ground-game.

31. Bryan Sistler, "Political Action in Action," *IVI Bellringer* (March 1969): 6.

32. Broockman and Kalla, "Experiments Show."

33. Sistler, "Political Action in Action," 6.

Chapter 7. Getting the Word Out in the Digital Age

1. CSpan2, "The Jesse Ventura Campaign," December 1, 1998, Program ID: 116012-1, http://www.c-span.org/video/?116012-1/jesse-ventura-campaign.

2. Alison Stateman, "Wrestling with Stereotypes," *Public Relations Tactics* 6, no. 3 (March 1999): 1; Lisa Mascaro, "Candidates Peddle as They Run," *Chicago Tribune*, May 10, 2015, 23.

3. Dean Lacy and Quin Monson, "Anatomy of a Third-Party Victory: Electoral Support for Jesse Ventura in the 1998 Minnesota Gubernatorial Election," paper presented at the Annual Meeting of the Midwest Political Science Association, Chicago, Illinois, April 28, 2000, 14, 20.

4. Paul S. Herrnson, *Congressional Elections: Campaigning at Home and in Washington* (Washington, DC: Congressional Quarterly Press, 2012), 23.

5. Pew Research Center, "Internet: The Mainstreaming of Online Life," *Trends 2005*, 2005, accessed June 14, 2015, http://www.pewresearch.org/files/old-assets/trends/trends2005-internet.pdf.

6. Internet Live Stats, "United States Internet Users," accessed June 14, 2015, http://www.internetlivestats.com/internet-users/united-states/.

7. Ron Faucheux, "How Campaigns Are Using the Internet: An Exclusive Nationwide Survey." *Campaigns & Elections (1996)* 19, no. 9 (1998): 22.

8. LaCrystal D. Ricke, *The Impact of YouTube on U.S. Politics* (London: Lexington, 2014), 4–5.

9. Kathryn Coombs, "Online Voter Mobilization: The Gilmore Model," *Campaigns & Elections (1996)* 20, no. 1 (1999): 26; Mike Allen, "Legislature to Focus on Tax Cut," *Washington Post*, January 11, 1998, B01, accessed June 15, 2015, http://www.washingtonpost.com/wpsrv/local/longterm/library/vastateleg/issues/legis1.htm.

10. Ricke, *Impact of YouTube on U.S. Politics*, 5–6; Dave Gram, "Howard Dean Presidential Campaign Remembered Fondly by Former Staffers," *Huffington Post*, June 20, 2013, http://www.huffingtonpost.com/2013/06/20/howard-dean-presidential-campaign_n_3473785.html?view=print&comm_ref=false.

11. "Internet Campaigning," *Campaigns & Elections (1996)* 24, no. 10 (2003): 51–54.

12. Pew Research Center, "Social Networking Factsheet," http://www.pewinternet.org/fact-sheets/social-networking-fact-sheet/; Eileen Brown, *Working the Crowd: So-*

cial *Media Marketing for Business*, 2nd ed. (Swindon, UK: British Informatics Society, 2012), 1, accessed June 14, 2015, http://site.ebrary.com/id/10582853?; Herrnson, *Congressional Elections*, 237.

13. Leonard Steinhorn, "The Selling of the President in a Converged Media Age," in *Campaigns and Elections American Style*, 3rd ed., ed. James A. Thurber and Candice J. Nelson (Boulder, CO: Westview Press, 2010), 150–151.

14. Darren Lilleker and Nigel A. Jackson, "Towards a More Participatory Style of Election Campaigning: The Impact of Web 2.0 on the UK 2010 General Election," *Policy and Internet* 2, no. 3 (August 10, 2010): 71, doi:10.2202/1944-2866.1064; Steinhorn, "Selling of the President," 141–155; Jose Antonio Vargas, "Politics Is No Longer Local. It's Viral." *Washington Post*, December 28, 2008, accessed June 15, 2015, http://www.washingtonpost.com/wp-dyn/content/article/2008/12/26/AR2008122601131.html.

15. Thomas H. Davenport and Jinho Kim, *Keeping Up with the Quants: Your Guide to Understanding and Using Analytics* (Boston, MA: Harvard Business Review Press, 2013), 2–7; Charu C. Aggarwal, "An Introduction to Social Network Data Analysis," in *Social Network Data Analytics*, ed. Charu C. Aggarwal (New York: Springer Science and Business Media, 2011), 3; Rob Brown, Stephen Waddington, and Brian Solis, *Share This Too: More Social Media Solutions for PR Professionals* (Somerset, NJ: Wiley, 2013); Sharon Meraz, "The Fight for 'How to Think': Traditional Media, Social Networks, and Issue Interpretation," *Journalism* 12 (January 2011): 107–127, doi:10.1177/1464884910385193.

16. Thomas Edsell, "Let the Nanotargeting Begin, Campaign Stops," *New York Times*, April 15, 2012, http://campaignstops.blogs.nytimes.com/2012/04/15/let-the-nanotargeting-begin/?_php=true&_type=blogs&_r=0.

17. Ibid.; Craig Varoga, "Small-Time Microtargeting?" *Campaigns & Elections (2010)* 319 (2013): 60.

18. Michael M. Franz, "Targeting Campaign Messages: Good for Campaigns but Bad for America?" *New Directions in American Politics*, ed. Travis N. Ridout (Florence, KY: Taylor and Francis, 2013): 114; John Sides and Jake Haselswerdt, "Campaigns and Elections," *New Directions in Public Opinion*, ed. Adam Berinsky (New York: Routledge, 2012): 241–257.

19. Franz, "Targeting Campaign Messages," 117.

20. Kristen McQueary, "A Revolution in Canvassing among Voters," *New York Times*, November 19, 2011, http://www.nytimes.com/2011/11/20/us/a-revolution-in-canvassing-among-voters.html; "Bill Brady Runs from Pet Euthanasia, Despite His Record," *Huffington Post*, October 20, 2010, http://www.huffingtonpost.com/2010/10/20/bill-brady-runs-from-pet-_n_770093.html.

21. Josh Richman, "In 2012, Mining Data about Voters, and Then 'Nanotargeting' Message, Is the New Way to Campaign," MercuryNews.com, October 20, 2012, http://www.mercurynews.com/presidentelect/ci_21811375/2012-mining-data-about-voters-and-then-nanotargeting.

22. Natch Greyes, "The Untapped Potential of Social Media: A Primer for Savvy

Campaigners," *Campaigns & Elections (2010)* 32, no. 300 (2011): 44–47, http://www
.campaignsandelections.com/magazine/us-edition/175967/the-untapped-potential
-of-social-media-a-primer-for-savvy-campaigners.thtml.

23. Jake Williams, "4 Tactics Your Campaign Should Explore in 2014," *Campaigns
& Elections* (February 12, 2014), accessed June 14, 2015, http://www.campaignsandelec
tions.com/magazine/1714/4-tactics-your-campaign-should-explore-in-2014.

24. Steve Pearson and Ford O'Connell, "Down-Home Digital: Campaigning on the
Web—What's Next?" *Campaigns & Elections (2010)* 32, no. 298 (January 14, 2011):
51, accessed June 14, 2015, http://www.campaignsandelections.com/magazine/us-edi
tion/255063/down-home-digital-campaigning-on-the-web-what-s-next.thtml; Colin
Delany, *How to Use the Internet to Win in 2014: A Comprehensive Guide to Online Politics for Campaigns and Advocates*, Version 2.0, Kindle ed. (Epolitics.com, 2014), Kindle
Locations 347–357; Williams, "4 Tactics Your Campaign Should Explore in 2014."

25. Nick Moschella, quoted in Colin Delany, "You're Already Behind Online,"
Campaigns & Elections (August 26, 2013): 43–45, accessed June 15, 2015, http://www
.campaignsandelections.com/magazine/us-edition/397787/youand39re-already-be
hind-online.thtml.

26. Roger Alan Stone, "The Internet as a Get Out the Vote Tool," *Campaigns & Elections (1996)* 25, no. 8 (2004): 35–36.

27. Colin Delany, "Getting Your Campaign Website Right: Campaign Websites—
The Red-Headed Stepchildren of Digital Politics," *Campaigns & Elections (2010)* 32,
no. 308 (February 16, 2012): 15, accessed June 14, 2015, http://www.campaignsandelec
tions.com/magazine/us-edition/298737/getting-your-campaign-website-right.thtml;
Herrnson, *Congressional Elections,* 238.

28. Steve Pearson and Ford O'Connell, "Down-Home Digital: Minding Your Social Media," *Campaigns & Elections (2010)* 3, no. 293 (July 19, 2010): 44–45, accessed
June 15, 2015, http://www.campaignsandelections.com/magazine/us-edition/255123
/down-home-digital-minding-your-social-media.thtml.

29. Ibid.; Delany, "Getting Your Campaign Website Right"; Eileen Brown, *Working
the Crowd: Social Media Marketing for Business,* 2nd ed. (Swindon, UK: British Informatics Society, 2012), 235.

30. Herrnson, *Congressional Elections,* 238; Beth Butler, "Democracy for America
Night School: Developing an Online Strategy—Strategy 101 Presentation," Democracyfor
America.com; Pearson and O'Connell, "Down-Home Digital: Campaigning on the Web."

31. Brown, *Working the Crowd,* 135–136; Kate Tummarello, "Mastering the Mystery
of SEO," *Campaigns & Elections (2010)* 33, no. 312 (July 13, 2012): 50–52, accessed June
14, 2015, http://www.campaignsandelections.com/magazine/us-edition/324362/mas
tering-the-mystery-of-seo.thtml; Pearson and O'Connell, "Down-Home Digital: Campaigning on the Web"; Laura Packard, "Simple Search Engine Optimization Techniques
for Non-Profits and Political Campaigns," Epolitics.com, February 18, 2014, accessed
June 14, 2015, http://www.epolitics.com/2014/02/18/simple-search-engine-optimiza
tion-techniques-for-non-profits-and-political-campaigns/.

32. Dotty Lynch, "How the Media Covered the 2008 Election," in *Campaigns and Elections, American Style: Transforming American Politics,* 3rd ed., ed. James A. Thurber and Candice J. Nelson (Boulder, CO: Westview Press, 2010), 183.

33. Meraz, "Fight for 'How to Think'"; Lynch, "How the Media Covered the 2008 Election," 181–183; Alan Rosenblatt, "Dimensions of Campaigns in the Age of Digital Networks," in *Campaigns and Elections American Style: Transforming American Politics,* 3rd ed., ed. James A. Thurber and Candice J. Nelson (Boulder, CO: Westview Press, 2010), 220–221.

34. Lynch, "How the Media Covered the 2008 Election," 181–183; Rosenblatt, "Dimensions of Campaigns in the Age of Digital Networks," 220.

35. Rosenblatt, "Dimensions of Campaigns in the Age of Digital Networks," 220–221.

36. Justin Kutner, "Instagram Gets Political: Social Media Photography on the Campaign Trail," Epolitics.com, August 1, 2012, accessed June 14, 2015, http://www.epolitics.com/2012/08/01/instagram-gets-political-social-media-photography-on-the-campaign-trail/; Pew Research Center, "Social Media Update, 2014," January 9, 2015, accessed June 14, 2015, http://www.pewinternet.org/2015/01/09/social-media-update-2014/; Beth Butler, "Pinterest for Politics: Not Just a Shiny New Toy," Epolitics.com, February 23, 2012, accessed June 14, 2015, http://www.epolitics.com/2012/02/23/pinterest-for-politics-not-just-a-shiny-new-toy/.

37. Jeffrey Gottfried and Michael Barthel, "How Millennials' Political News Habits Differ from Those of Gen Xers and Baby Boomers," *Pew Research* (June 1, 2015), accessed June 20, 2015, http://pewrsr.ch/1d9mxF2.

38. Brown, *Working the Crowd,* 73; "Facebook Tops for Political Engagement," *Campaigns & Elections (2010)* 32, no. 305 (2011): 10; Pew Research Center, "Social Media Update, 2014."

39. Williams, "4 Tactics Your Campaign Should Explore in 2014."

40. Brown, *Working the Crowd,* 77–80. Dave Nyczepir, "50 Consultants You Should Be Following on Twitter," *Campaigns & Elections (2010)* 34, no. 316 (2013): 14–15; Delany, *How to Use the Internet to Win in 2014;* Delany, "Twitter Expands Its Advertising Menu," *Campaigns & Elections* (July 2, 2014): 12–14, accessed June 15, 2015, http://www.campaignsandelections.com/magazine/1698/twitter-expands-its-advertising-menu; Andrew Clark, "The Art of Hashtagging," *Campaigns & Elections (2010)* 319 (2013): 54–55.

41. Ricke, *Impact of YouTube on U.S. Politics,* 3, 36–37.

42. Craig Smith, "By the Numbers: 80+ Amazing YouTube Statistics," May 9, 2015, http://expandedramblings.com/index.php/youtube-statistics/.

43. Jake Batsell, "In Plano Mayor's Race, Web Ads Are a Sure Hit: Candidates Put a Little Cash and a Lot of Faith in Efficient E-videos," *Dallas Morning News,* May 11, 2006, Metro Section, 1B.

44. Varoga, "Small-Time Microtargeting?" 60.

45. Ward, "The Behind the Scenes Story of the RNC's Quest for Data Supremacy,"

Huffington Post, April 18, 2014; David Magleby, "Continuity and Change in the 2008 Federal Elections," in *The Change Election: Money, Mobilization, and Persuasion in the 2008 Federal Elections,* ed. David Magleby (Philadelphia, PA: Temple University Press, 2010), 292; Steven Levy, "Campaigns Get Personal," *Newsweek* (April 19, 2008), accessed June 14, 2015, http://www.newsweek.com/levy-campaigns-get-personal-85655; Kate Kaye, "Obama's Data Too Much to Handle for Many," *Advertising Age* 85, no. 8 (2014): 26.

46. Shane D'Aprile, "On the Hill: Amelia Showalter," *Campaigns & Elections (2010)* 34, no. 316 (April 5, 2013): 57, http://www.campaignsandelections.com/magazine/us -edition/366607/on-the-hill-amelia-showalter.thtml; Lizzie Kendrick, "The Role of a Digital Political Consulting Firm," *Campaign Workshop,* July 21, 2014, accessed June 14, 2015, http://thecampaignworkshop.com/digital-role-political-consulting-firm/#sthash .shw4he0V.dpuf.

47. Virginia Department of Elections, "Official Results: Primary Election, June 10, 2014," accessed June 15, 2015, http://elections.virginia.gov/Files/ElectionResults/2014 /June-Primaries/resultsSW7217.html?type=CON&map=CTY._

48. Jonathan Martin, "Eric Cantor Defeated by David Brat, Tea Party Challenger, in G.O.P. Primary Upset," *New York Times,* June 10, 2014, accessed June 15, 2015, http:// www.nytimes.com/2014/06/11/us/politics/eric--loses-gop-primary.html?_r=0.; Dave Kabaservice, "Dave Brat and the Rise of Right-Wing Populism," Politico.com, June 12, 2014, http://www.politico.com/magazine/story/2014/06/dave-brat-and-the-rise-of -right-wing-populism-107803.html#.U9bU_KhidO0; see also John Sides, "The Expert on Congressional Primaries Weighs in on Cantor's Loss," *Washington Post,* June 12, 2014, accessed June 14, 2015, http://www.washingtonpost.com/blogs/monkey-cage/wp /2014/06/12/the-expert-on-congressional-primaries-weighs-in-on-s-loss/; Ezra Klein, "Eric Cantor Wasn't Beaten by the Tea Party," Vox.com, June 11, 2014, accessed June 14, 2015, http://www.vox.com/2014/6/11/5799710/Eric--beaten-tea-party.

49. Steve Adler, "How a Tiny GOP Data Firm Helped David Brat Win," *Campaigns & Elections,* June 25, 2014, accessed June 14, 2015, http://www.campaignsandelections .com/magazine/us-edition/446397/how-a-tiny-gop-data-firm-helped-david-brat-win .thtml; Darren Samuelson, "Cochran Whizzed, Cantor Fizzed," Politico.com, June 26, 2014, accessed June 14, 2015, http://www.politico.com/story/2014/06/eric--thad-co chran-midterm-primaries-108355.html; Kabaservice, "Dave Brat and the Rise of Right-Wing Populism."

50. Joe Piasecki, field director of Julie Morrison for State Senate campaign, interview with author, July 9, 2014; Dave Nyczepir, "The Challenge of Analytics," *Campaigns & Elections (2010)* 33, no. 314 (December 17, 2012): 33–35; Pearson and O'Connell, "Down-Home Digital: Tapping Online Insights to Target Voters," *Campaigns & Elections (2010)* 32, no. 301 (April 1, 2011): 49; "Explaining the 'Dark Magic' of Microtargeting," *Campaigns & Elections (2010)* 31, no. 294 (August 23, 2010): 36–41, accessed June 14, 2015, http://www.campaignsandelections.com/magazine/us-edition/256278 /explaining-the-dark-magic-of-microtargeting-.thtml.

51. Delany, *How to Use the Internet to Win*, Kindle locations 858–866; Google Analytics, "Case Study: Obama for America Uses Google Analytics to Democratize Rapid, Data-driven Decision Making," accessed June 14, 2015, http://static.googleusercontent.com/media/www.google.com/en/us/analytics/customers/pdfs/obama-2012.pdf; Nyczepir, "Challenge of Analytics."

52. Colin Delany, "Microsites on the March," *Campaigns & Elections (2010)* 32, no. 308 (February 16, 2012): 16, http://www.campaignsandelections.com/magazine/us-edition/298747/microsites-on-the-march.thtml.

53. Richman, "In 2012, Mining Data about Voters."

54. Greyes, "Untapped Potential of Social Media," 44–47.

55. D'Aprile, "On the Hill," 57.

56. Steve Pearson and Ford O'Connell, "Online Metrics: What's the Conversion?" *Campaigns & Elections (2010)* 313 (September 2012): 60.

57. Pear Analytics, "Twitter Study" (August 2009), accessed June 14, 2015, http://www.scribd.com/doc/18548460/Pear-Analytics-Twitter-Study-August-2009; Girish Gulati and Christine Williams, "The Evolution of Online Campaigning in Senate Elections, 2000–2004," paper presented at the Annual Meeting of the Midwest Political Science Association, Chicago, Illinois, April 20, 2006; accessed December 17, 2013, http://citation.allacademic.com/meta/p137057_index.html; C. Williams and G. Gulati, "What Is a Social Network Worth? Facebook and Vote Share in the 2008 Presidential Primaries," paper presented at the Annual Meeting of the American Political Science Association, Boston, Massachusetts, 2008, 1–17; J. DiGrazia, K. McKelvey, J. Bollen, and F. Rojas, "More Tweets, More Votes: Social Media as a Quantitative Indicator of Political Behavior," *PLoS ONE 8(11):e79449* (2013): 2–4, accessed June 14, 2015, http://www.plosone.org/article/fetchObject.action?uri=info%3Adoi%2F10.1371%2Fjournal.pone.0079449&representation=PDF; Andrea Ceron, Luigi Curini, Stefano M. Iacus, and Giuseppe Porro, "Every Tweet Counts? How Sentiment Analysis of Social Media Can Improve Our Knowledge of Citizens' Political Preferences with an Application to Italy and France," *New Media and Society* 16, no. 2 (2014): 340–358.

58. Christine B. Williams, Jeff Gulati, and Rob DeLeo, "The Dissemination of Social Media to Campaigns for State Legislature: The 2012 New England Case," paper presented at the Annual Meeting of the American Political Science Association, Chicago, Illinois, 2013, 13–16, accessed June 14, 2015, http://papers.ssrn.com/sol3/papers.cfm?abstract_id=2301245; Piasecki interview.

59. Eric Schmidt and Jared Cohen, *The New Digital Age: Reshaping the Future of People, Nations, and Business* (New York: Knopf, 2013): 11, 132–133.

60. Daniela V. Dimitrova, Adam Shehata, Jesper Strömbäck, and Lars W. Nord, "The Effects of Digital Media on Political Knowledge and Participation in Election Campaigns: Evidence from Panel Data," *Communication Research* 41, no. 1 (2014): 95–118, Communication and Mass Media Complete, http://crx.sagepub.com/content/41/1/95, doi:10.1177/0093650211426004.

61. Michael Heany, Matthew E. Newman, and Dari E. Sylvester, "Campaigning in the

Internet Age," in *The Electoral Challenge: Theory Meets Practice,* ed. Stephen C. Craig, David B. Hill (Washington, DC: Congressional Quarterly Press, 2011), 167; Natalie Stroud, "Media Use and Political Predispositions: Revisiting the Concept of Selective Exposure," *Political Behavior* 30, no. 3 (2008): 358–361.

62. Chris Casey, "The Political Professionals Respond, Campaigning in the Internet Age," in *The Electoral Challenge: Theory Meets Practice,* ed. Stephen C. Craig and David B. Hill (Washington, DC: Congressional Quarterly Press, 2011), 189–193.

63. Meraz, "Fight for 'How to Think,'" 120–127.

64. Elizabeth Housholder and Heather LaMarre, "Examining the Use of Facebook for Participatory Behavior," paper presented at the Annual Meeting of the International Communication Association, Phoenix, Arizona, May 24, 2012, http://citation.allaca demic.com/meta/p553007_index.html, 1, 14–19.

65. Lilleker and Jackson, "Towards a More Participatory Style of Election Campaigning," 93.

Chapter 8. Canvassing the Voters and Election Day

1. Movement for a New Congress, *Vote Power: The Official Activist Campaigner's Handbook* (Englewood Cliffs, NJ: Prentice-Hall, 1970), 28.

2. "How to Win Elections," mimeographed instructions developed originally by Sherwin Swartz and Barbara O'Connor of the Independent Voters of Illinois (IVI); used and revised many times since the 1960s.

3. Movement for a New Congress, *Vote Power,* 29.

4. Catherine Shaw, "Conducting a Comprehensive Precinct Analysis," *Campaigns & Elections* (May–June 2014), 15–19. See also Catherine Shaw, *The Campaign Manager: Running and Winning Local Elections,* 4th ed. (Boulder, CO: Westview Press, 2010), Chapter 1.

5. These tactics are discussed by Ed Lawrence, Handbook for Independent Precinct Workers (mimeographed manual for IPO and IVI precinct workers in the 42nd Ward, Chicago, 1970), 3.

6. The problem of First Amendment rights and the ability of campaigns to reach voters with their messages are covered in Evan McKenzie, *Privatopia* (New Haven, CT: Yale University Press, 1994); McKenzie, *Beyond Privatopia* (Washington, DC: Urban Institute Press, 2011).

7. James Kessler reports spending less than $3,000 in a successful primary battle to become the Republican candidate for state senate in a rural district in Indiana in 1963. Half of the funds were his own, and half were raised from some thirty-eight contributors. James Kessler, "Running for State Political Office," in *Practical Politics in the United States,* ed. Cornelius Cotter (Boston: Allyn and Bacon, 1969), 126. In the same era, Jim Nowlan reports spending only $4,000 (the equivalent of about $30,000 today) to run as a Republican in an Illinois primary in 1966 and again in 1968. Quoted in Dick Simp-

son, James D. Nowlan, and Betty O'Shaughnessy, *The Struggle for Power and Influence in Cities and States* (New York: Pearson, 2011), 164–165.

8. Katy Brunett, "Rethinking Rural Campaign Strategies for Progressives," *Florida Squeeze*, June 27, 2014, accessed July 11, 2014, http://thefloridasqueeze.com/2014/06/27/rethinking-rural-campaign-strategies-for-progressives/.

9. Dennis J. McGrath and Dane Smith, *Professor Wellstone Goes to Washington* (Minneapolis: University of Minnesota Press, 1995), 92–93.

10. Ibid., 93.

11. Ibid., 103.

12. Ibid., xvi.

13. Will Robinson, "Organizing the Field," in *Campaigns and Elections American Style*, ed. James A. Thurber and Candice J. Nelson (Boulder, CO: Westview Press, 1995), 183.

14. Grace Jewell, team leader for 2012 Obama for America campaign, telephone interview with author, December 14, 2014.

15. "How to Win on Election Day," mimeographed instructions developed originally by Sherwin Swartz and Barbara O'Connor.

16. Robinson, "Organizing the Field," 147.

17. According to Illinois law, workers may campaign no closer than 100 feet from the polls. However, laws differ on Election Day work in other states.

18. Sandye Wexler, "So You're a Poll Watcher?" Mimeographed manual for poll watchers developed for the Bernard Weisberg campaign, Chicago, 1969.

19. J. B. Wogan, "The Looming Crisis in Voting Tech," *Governing* (July 2014): 11.

20. Presidential Commission on Election Administration, *The American Voting Experience: Report and Recommendations of the Presidential Commission on Election Administration,* January 2014, accessed July 7, 2014, https://www.supportthevoter.gov/files/2014/01/Amer-Voting-Exper-final-draft-01-09-14-508.pdf.

21. The quote is from a science fiction novel by Karen Traviss, *Gears of War: Coalition's End* (New York: Gallery Books, 2011), 428. Although the quote is about action in war, it fits many campaign experiences as well.

Chapter 9. The Campaign to Elect Will Guzzardi

1. Illinois State Board of Elections, "Election Results General Election—11/4/2008," http://www.elections.il.gov/ElectionResultsStateHouseSet2.aspx?ID=22; Illinois State Board of Elections, "Election Results General Election—11/2/2010," http://www.elections.il.gov/ElectionResultsStateHouseSet2.aspx?ID=29.

2. Caroline O'Donovan, "Out of Turn: The Story of the Will Guzzardi Campaign, Election 2012," *Gapers Block,* March 9, 2012, http://www.gapersblock.com/mechanics/2012/03/09/out-of-turn-the-story-of-the-will-guzzardi-campaign/.

3. A 2002 federal court decision upheld a challenge that found the new redistricting

did not violate the voting rights of Latino/as in Illinois, a ruling that favored Berrios. See *Campuzano v. Illinois State Board of Elections*, No. 01 C 50376 (N.D. Ill. May 3, 2002).

4. Ibid.

5. Ibid.

6. Elias Cepeda, "Primary Election in Latino-Heavy IL. District Rolls on through Discovery Recount," *Hoy Chicago*, April 11, 2012, http://www.vivelohoy.com/noticias/8085299/primary-election-in-latino-heavy-il-district-rolls-on-through-discovery-re count.

7. Carol Felsenthal, "Will Guzzardi on His Plans for the Recount (and After)," *Chicago Magazine*, April 10, 2012, http://www.chicagomag.com/Chicago-Magazine/Felsenthal-Files/April-2012/Will-Guzzardi-on-His-Plans-for-the-Recount-and-After/.

8. Erica Sagrans, "Op-ed: Rage against the Machine—Lessons from Guzzardi-Berrios Race," *Illinois Observer*, May 15, 2014, www.illinoisobserver.net/author/ericasa grans/. See also Ray Long and Maura Zurick, "A House Challenge to Bosses' Power," *Chicago Tribune*, March 19, 2014, 10; Dan Mihalopoulous and Matt McKinney, "Clout, but Out: Berrios Defeated," *Chicago Sun-Times*, March 19, 2014, 6; Ellyn Fortino, "Election Preview: A Look at the 39th District State Representative Race," *Progress Illinois* at http://progressillinois.com/posts/content/2014/03/electionpreview; Erin Hegarty, "Toni Berrios, Will Guzzardi Race for 39th District," *LoganSquarist*, http://logansquar ist.com/2013/11/06/guzzardiberrios-39th-district; Rachel Anspack, "Guzzardi Victory Gives Chicago Progressives Hope," *Gapers Block*, http://gapersblock.com/mechan ics/2014/04/09/in-whatwasperhaps-chicagos.

9. Sagrans, "Op-ed: Rage against the Machine."

10. Alan S. Gerber, Donald P. Green, and Christopher W. Larimer, "Social Pressure and Voter Turnout: Evidence from a Large-Scale Field Experiment," *American Political Science Review* 102 (2008): 40–45, doi:10.1017/S000305540808009X.

11. Elise Doody-Jones, interview with author, 2014.

12. Sagrans, "Op-ed: Rage against the Machine."

13. Ibid.

14. Ibid.

15. Sagrans, "Op-ed: Rage against the Machine." Our list of lessons is similar to the ones in her articles and borrows from her analysis.

Chapter 10. Challenges to Democracy

1. Sasha Issenberg, *The Victory Lab: The Secret Science of Winning Campaigns* (New York: Broadway Books, 2012), 152–155, 294–296; for a more comprehensive discussion of the relationship between politician's decisions and public opinion, see Brandice Canes-Wrone, *Who Leads Whom? Presidents, Policy, and the Public* (Chicago: University of Chicago Press, 2006); E. E. Schattschneider, *The Semisovereign People* (New York: Holt, Rinehart, and Winston, 1960), 10; V. O. Key, *The Responsible Electorate: Ratio-*

nality in Presidential Voting, 1936–1960 (Cambridge, MA: Harvard University Press, 1966), 6–7; John Zaller, *The Nature and Origins of Mass Opinion* (Cambridge, UK: Cambridge University Press, 1992); Nicholas J. O'Shaughnessy, *The Phenomenon of Political Marketing* (New York: St. Martin's, 1990), 1, 2, 7. Two other excellent books are Larry Sabato, *The Party's Only Just Begun* (Glenview, IL: Scott Foresman, 1988); Stephen Frantiach, *Political Parties in the Technological Age* (New York: Longman, 1989). The concluding chapters of both books are worth reading along with the later books on the same topics.

2. Randall Rothenberg, "Politics on TV: Too Fast, Too Loose?" *New York Times*, July 15, 1990, Section 4, 1, 4.

3. *Citizens United v. Federal Election Commission*, 558 U.S. 310 (2010), http://www.scotusblog.com/case-files/cases/citizens-united-v-federal-election-commission/.

4. *McCutcheon v. Federal Election Commission*, 572 U.S. ___ (2014), http://www.scotusblog.com/case-files/cases/mccutcheon-v-federal-election-commission/.

5. Fredreka Shouten, "Unlimited Money Swamps Mayors' Races," *USA Today*, July 25, 2014, accessed June 15, 2015, http://www.usatoday.com/story/news/politics/2014/07/25/super-pacs-mayors-chicago-newark-san-diego-rahm-emanuel/ 13122613/.

6. Illinois Campaign for Political Reform, "Campaign Finance Reform," accessed June 15, 2015, http://www.ilcampaign.org/issues-and-legislation/campaign-finance-reform/.

7. David R. Mayhew, *Congress: The Electoral Connection* (New Haven, CT: Yale University Press, 1974), 205; James E. Campbell, "The Return of the Incumbents: The Nature of Incumbency Advantage," *Western Political Quarterly* 36 (September 1983): 434–444.

8. Paul Simon Public Policy Institute, "The 2014 Simon Poll: Voter Opinions on Term Limits in Illinois," results released at the symposium Term Limits for Illinois: Will They Work?, April 7, 2014.

9. Justin McCarthy, "No Improvement for Congress' Job Approval Rating," Gallup Poll, April 10, 2014, accessed June 15, http://www.gallup.com/poll/168428/no-improvement-congressional-approval.aspx?version=print.

10. John Tierney, "Do You Trust Your State Government?" *Atlantic*, May 12, 2014, http://www.theatlantic.com/politics/archive/2014/05/trust-your-state-government/362044/.

11. Franz, "Targeting Campaign Messages," 129.

12. Paul M. Schwartz, "Privacy, Ethics, and Analytics," *Privacy Interests: The IEEE Computer and Reliable Societies* (2011): 67–68, accessed June 15, 2015, http://ieeexplore.ieee.org.proxy.cc.uic.edu/stamp/stamp.jsp?tp=&arnumber=5772964.

13. Participatory Budgeting Project (PBP), "What Is PB?" Accessed June 14, 2105, http://www.participatorybudgeting.org/about-participatory-budgeting/what-is-pb/.

14. Christa Daryl Slaton, *Televote: Expanding Citizen Participation in the Quantum Age* (New York: Praeger, 1992).

15. James Fishkin, "Deliberative Polling®: Executive Summary," Center for Deliber-

ative Democracy, Stanford University, accessed July 30, 2014, http://cdd.stanford.edu /polls/docs/summary/.

16. Center for Information and Research on Civil Learning and Engagement, "UP-DATE: 21.5% Youth Turnout—Two-Day Estimate Comparable to Recent Midterm Years," accessed March 8, 2015, http://www.civicyouth.org/21-3-youth-turnout-pre liminary-estimate-comparable-to-recent-midterm-years/.

17. Center for Information and Research on Civil Learning and Engagement, "Why Youth Voting Matters," accessed March 8, 2015, http://www.civicyouth.org/quick-facts /youth-voting/.

18. National Council of State Legislatures, "Absentee and Early Voting," February 11, 2015, accessed June 14, 2015, http://www.ncsl.org/research/elections-and-campaigns /absentee-and-early-voting.aspx.

19. Members of the Illinois Task Force, "Illinois Task Force on Civic Education Report," May 2014, accessed June 14, 2015, http://www.isbe.net/reports/il-civic-ed-task -force2014.pdf; Alison Rios Millett McCartney, Elizabeth A. Bennion, and Dick Simpson, eds., *Teaching Civic Engagement* (Washington, DC: American Political Science Association, 2013); Association of American Colleges and Universities, *A Crucible Moment: College Learning and Democracy's Future* (Washington, DC: AACU, 2012).

20. Anne Colby, Elizabeth Beaumont, Thomas Ehrlich, and Josh Corngold, *Educating for Democracy* (San Francisco: Jossey-Bass/Carnegie Foundation for Teaching, 2003).

Selected Bibliography

Abramson, Paul R., and John H. Aldrich. "The Decline of Electoral Participation in America." *American Political Science Review* 76, no. 3 (September 1982): 502–521. doi:10.2307/1963728

Adams, Bryan. "Financing Local Elections: The Impact of Institutions on Electoral Outcomes and Democratic Representation." Symposium. *PS: Political Science & Politics* 44 (2011): 111–112. doi:10.1017/S1049096510001988

Aggarwal, Charu C., ed. *Social Network Data Analytics.* New York: Springer Science and Business Media, 2011.

Aldrich, John H. *Why Parties? The Origin and Transformation of Political Parties in America.* Chicago: University of Chicago Press, 1995.

Alexander, Brad. "Good Money and Bad Money: Do Funding Sources Affect Electoral Outcomes?" *Political Research Quarterly* 58 (2005): 353–358. doi:10.1177/106591290505800214

Alexander, Herbert. *Reform and Reality: The Financing of State and Local Campaigns.* New York: Twentieth Century Fund, 1991.

Alter, Jonathan. *The Center Holds: Obama and His Enemies.* New York: Simon and Schuster, 2013.

Andersen, Kristi. "What I Learned (and Re-Learned) When I Ran for Local Office." *PS: Political Science & Politics* 40 (July 2007): 507–510. doi:10.1017/S104909650707076X

Arceneaux, Kevin, and Stephen P. Nicholson. "Who Wants to Have a Tea Party? The Who, What, and Why of the Tea Party Movement." *PS: Political Science and Politics* 45 (October 2012): 700–710. doi:10.1017/S1049096512000741

Ashworth, Scott, and Ethan Bueno de Mesquita. "Electoral Selection, Strategic Challenger Entry, and the Incumbency Advantage." *Journal of Politics* 70, no. 4 (October 2008): 1006–1025. doi:10.1017/S0022381608081024

Association of American Colleges and Universities. *A Crucible Moment: College Learning and Democracy's Future.* Washington, DC: AACU, 2012.

Ayala, Louis J. "Trained for Democracy: The Differing Effects of Voluntary and Involuntary Organizations on Political Participation." *Political Research Quarterly* 53 (March 2000): 99–115. http://www.jstor.org/stable/449248

Bari, Anasse, and Mohamed Chaouchi. *Predictive Analytics for Dummies.* Somerset, NJ: Wiley, 2014.

Blumenthal, Sydney. *Pledging Allegiance: The Last Campaign of the Cold War.* New York: HarperCollins, 1990.

Broersma, Marcel, and Todd Graham. "Social Media as Beat: Tweets as a News Source during the 2010 British and Dutch Elections." *Journalism Practice* 6, no. 3 (2012): 403–419. doi:10.1080/17512786.2012.663626

Brown, Eileen. *Working the Crowd: Social Media Marketing for Business.* 2nd ed. Swindon, UK: British Informatics Society, 2012.

Brown, Rob, Stephen Waddington, and Brian Solis. *Share This Too: More Social Media Solutions for PR Professionals.* Somerset, NJ: Wiley, 2013.

Burns, Nancy, Kay Lehman Schlozman, and Sidney Verba. *Private Roots of Public Action: Gender, Equality, and Political Participation.* Cambridge, MA: Harvard University Press, 2001.

Butler, Beth. "Democracy for America Night School: Developing an Online Strategy—Social Media Strategy 101 Presentation." June 2014. Accessed June 10, 2015. https://s3.amazonaws.com/static.democracyforamerica.com/public/asset/file/UP/UPDATEDDFANightSchoolJune2014.pdf

Camaj, Lindita, and David H. Weaver. "Need for Orientation and Attribute Agenda-Setting during a U.S. Election Campaign." *International Journal of Communication* 7 (2013): 1464–1485. http://ijoc.org/index.php/ijoc/article/view/1921

Campaigns & Elections. http://campaigns&elections.com

Campbell, Angus, Philip E. Converse, Warren E. Miller, and Donald E. Stokes. *The American Voter.* New York: Wiley, 1960.

Campbell, James E. "The Return of the Incumbents: The Nature of Incumbency Advantage," *Western Political Quarterly* 36 (September 1983): 434–444. http://www.jstor.org/stable/448401

Canes-Wrone, Brandice. *Who Leads Whom? Presidents, Policy, and the Public.* Chicago: University of Chicago Press, 2006.

Carey, John M., Richard G. Niemi, and Lynda W. Powell. *Term Limits in State Legislatures.* Ann Arbor: University of Michigan Press, 2000.

Carsey, Thomas M. *Campaign Dynamics: The Race for Governor.* Ann Arbor: University of Michigan Press, 2001.

Center for Information and Research on Civil Learning and Engagement. "Youth Voting." Jonathan M. Tisch College of Citizenship and Public Service, Tufts University. Accessed June 10, 2015. http://www.civicyouth.org/quick-facts/youth-voting/

Ceron, Andrea, Luigi Curini, Stefano M. Iacus, and Giuseppe Porro. "Every Tweet Counts? How Sentiment Analysis of Social Media Can Improve Our Knowledge of Citizens' Political Preferences with an Application to Italy and France." *New Media & Society* 16, no. 2 (2014): 340–358. doi:10.1177/1461444813480466

Citizens United v. Federal Election Commission, 558 U.S. 310 (2010).

Colby, Anne, Elizabeth Beaumont, Thomas Ehrlich, and Josh Corngold. *Educating for Democracy.* San Francisco: Jossey-Bass/Carnegie Foundation for Teaching, 2003.

Committee on State Voter Registration Databases, National Research Council. *Im-*

proving State Voter Registration Databases: Final Report. Washington, DC: National Academies Press, 2010.

Crew Jr., Robert E., "The Political Scientist as a Local Campaign Consultant." *PS: Political Science & Politics* 44 (April 2011): 273–278. doi:10.1017/S1049096511000047

C-Span2, *The Jesse Ventura Campaign* (film). December 1, 1998. http://www.c-span.org /video/?116012-1/jesse-ventura-campaign

Darcy, R., Susan Welsh, and Janet Clark. *Women, Elections, and Representation.* Lincoln: University of Nebraska Press, 1994.

Davenport, Thomas H., and Jinho Kim. *Keeping Up with the Quants: Your Guide to Understanding and Using Analytics.* Boston: Harvard Business Review Press, 2013.

Delany, Colin. *How to Use the Internet to Win in 2014: A Comprehensive Guide to Online Politics for Campaigns and Advocates.* Version 2.0. Kindle ed. Epolitics.com, 2013.

Dimitrova, Daniela V., Adam Shehata, Jesper Strömbäck, and Lars W. Nord. "The Effects of Digital Media on Political Knowledge and Participation in Election Campaigns: Evidence from Panel Data." *Communication Research* 41, no. 1 (2014): 95–118. doi:10.1177/0093650211426004

Dionne Jr., E. J. *Our Divided Political Heart.* New York: Bloomsbury, 2012.

Doppelt, Jack C., and Ellen Shearer. *Nonvoters: America's No-Shows.* Thousand Oaks, CA: Sage, 1999.

Eliasoph, Nina. "Measuring the Grassroots: Puzzles of Cultivating the Grassroots from the Top." *Sociological Quarterly* 55 (Summer 2014): 467–492. doi:10.1111/tsq.12063

Engage Research. "Inside the Cave: An In-Depth Look at the Digital, Technology, and Analytics Operations of Obama for America." Accessed July 15, 2014. http://engage .stage.enga.ge/dl/Inside_the_Cave.pdf

Enjolras, Bernard, Kari Steen-Johnsen, and Dag Wollebæk. "Social Media and Mobilization to Offline Demonstrations: Transcending Participatory Divides?" *New Media Society* 15 (2013): 890–908. doi:10.1177/1461444812462844

Fishkin, James. "Deliberative Polling®: Executive Summary," Center for Deliberative Democracy, Stanford University, http://cdd.stanford.edu/polls/docs/summary/.

Flanigan, William H., Nancy H. Zingale, Elizabeth Theiss-Morse, and Michael W. Wagner. *The Political Behavior of the American Electorate.* 13th ed. Washington, DC: Congressional Quarterly Press, 2014.

Fowler, Linda. "Who Runs for Congress?" *PS: Political Science & Politics* 29, no. 3 (September 1996): 430–434.

Fox, Richard, and Jennifer Lawless. "To Run or Not to Run for Office: Explaining Nascent Political Ambition." *American Journal of Political Science* 49, no. 3 (July 2005): 642–659.

Frantiach, Stephen. *Political Parties in the Technological Age.* New York: Longman, 1989.

Gilmore, Jason. "Ditching the Pack: Digital Media in the 2010 Brazilian Congressional Campaigns." *New Media and Society* 14, no. 4 (2012): 617–633. Communication and Mass Media Complete. doi:10.1177/146144481142242

Goidel, Kirby, ed. *Political Polling in the Digital Age: The Challenge of Measuring and Understanding Public Opinion.* Baton Rouge: Louisiana State University Press, 2011.

"GOP Data Center Software Guides." N.d. http://gopdatacenterguide.com/c/GOP _Data_Center#guideList

Graf, Joseph. "Nonpartisan and Political Websites." *National Civic Review* 94, no. 1 (March 28, 2005): 36–42. doi:10.1002/ncr.81

Green, Donald P., and Alan S. Gerber. "The Effects of Canvassing, Telephone Calls, and Direct Mail on Voter Turnout: A Field Experiment." *American Political Science Review* 94, no. 3 (September 2000): 653–663. http://www.jstor.org/stable/2585837

———. *Get Out the Vote: How to Increase Voter Turnout.* 2nd ed. Washington, DC: Brookings Institution, 2008.

Grey, Lawrence. *How to Win a Local Election: A Complete Step-by-Step Guide.* 3rd ed. New York: M. Evans, 2007.

Grimshaw, William. *Bitter Fruit: Black Politics and the Chicago Machine, 1931–1991.* Chicago: University of Chicago Press, 1992.

Hegedus, Chris, D. A. Pennebaker, R. J. Cutler, Wendy Ettinger, Frazer Pennebaker, James Carville, George Stephanopoulos, and Bill Clinton, eds. *The War Room.* Film. 1993.

Herrnson, Paul S. *Congressional Elections: Campaigning at Home and in Washington.* 6th ed. Washington, DC: Congressional Quarterly Press, 2012.

Hirano, Shigeo, and James M. Snyder Jr. "The Decline of Third-Party Voting in the United States." *Journal of Politics* 69, no. 1 (February 2007): 1–16. doi:10.1111 /j.1468-2508.2007.00490.x

Hogan, Robert E. "Candidate Perceptions of Political Party Campaign Activity in State Legislative Elections." *State Politics and Policy Quarterly* 2, no. 1 (April 2002): 66–85. doi:10.1177/153244000200200105

Housholder, Elizabeth, and Heather LaMarre. "Examining the Use of Facebook for Participatory Behavior." Paper presented at the annual meeting of the International Communication Association, Phoenix, Arizona, May 24, 2012. http://citation.allac ademic.com/meta/p553007_index.html

Houston, J. Brian, Joshua Hawthorne, Matthew L. Spialek, Molly Greenwood, and Mitchell S. McKinney. "Tweeting during Presidential Debates: Effect on Candidate Evaluations and Debate Attitudes." *Argumentation and Advocacy* 49, no. 4 (2013): 301–311. Communication and Mass Media Complete. doi:10.1080/10510974.201 3.832693

Howard, Philip. *New Media Campaigns and the Managed Citizen.* New York: Cambridge University Press, 2006.

Issenberg, Sasha. *The Victory Lab: The Secret Science of Winning Campaigns.* New York: Broadway Books, 2012.

Jamieson, Kathleen. *Electing the President 2008: The Insiders' View.* Philadelphia: University of Pennsylvania Press, 2009.

———. *Electing the President 2012: The Insiders' View.* Philadelphia: University of Pennsylvania Press, 2013.

Johnson, Dennis. *Campaigning in the Twenty-First Century.* New York: Routledge, 2011.

Judd, Nick. "Republican Party's Technology Revival Hopes Hinge on Data and Data Analysis." Techpresident.com. February 7, 2013. http://techpresident.com/news /23479/republican-partys-technology-revival-hopes-hinge-more-just-skype

Jurkowitz, Mark. "The Growth in Digital Reporting: What It Means for Journalism and News Consumers." Pew Research Center, Journalism and Media. March 26, 2014. http://www.journalism.org/2014/03/26/the-growth-in-digital-reporting/

Kaufmann, Karen M. *Urban Voter: Group Conflict and Mayoral Voting Behavior in American Cities.* Ann Arbor: University of Michigan Press, 2004.

Key, V. O. *The Responsible Electorate: Rationality in Presidential Voting, 1936–1960.* Cambridge, MA: Harvard University Press, 1966.

Kleppner, Paul. *Chicago Divided: The Making of a Black Mayor.* DeKalb: Northern Illinois University Press, 1985.

Kreiss, Daniel. "The Virtues of Participation without Power: Campaigns, Party Networks, and the Ends of Politics." *Sociological Quarterly* 55, no. 3 (Summer 2014): 537–554. doi:10.1111/tsq.12068

Kurtz, Karl, Bruce Coin, and Richard G. Niemi. *Institutional Change in American Politics: The Case of Term Limits.* Ann Arbor: University of Michigan Press, 2007.

Lawless, Jennifer L., Richard L. Fox, and Gail Baitinger. "Women's Underrepresentation in U.S. Politics: The Enduring Gender Gap in Political Ambition." In *Women and Elective Office.* Edited by Sue Thomas and Clyde Wilcox. Oxford, UK: Oxford University Press, 2014.

Lepore, Meredith. "Fashion Can Be a Woman in Politics' Craftiest Weapon and Her Downfall." Grindstone.com, September 12, 2012. Accessed June 12, 2015. http://www.thegrindstone.com/2012/09/12/career-management/fashion-clothes-poli tics-285/2/

Lewis, Raymond. "VoteBuilder 101: An Introduction to the Software VoteBuilder." April 2, 2014. Prezi presentation. http://prezi.com/xofvvuktbzvz/votebuilder-101/

Lewis-Beck, Michael S., Helmut Norpoth, William G. Jacoby, and Herbert F. Weisberg. *American Voter Revisited.* Ann Arbor: University of Michigan Press, 2009.

MacManus, Susan A., with Renee Dabbs and Mary L. Moss. "Women and Campaigns: Growing Female Activism from the Grass Roots to the Top." In *Campaigns on the Cutting Edge.* 2nd ed. Edited by Richard J. Semiatin. Washington, DC: Congressional Quarterly Press, 2013, 193–210.

Magleby, David, ed. *The Change Election: Money, Mobilization, and Persuasion in the 2008 Federal Elections.* Philadelphia, PA: Temple University Press, 2010.

Marschall, Melissa, Paru Shah, and Anirudh Ruhil. "The Study of Local Elections: Editors' Introduction: A Looking Glass into the Future." *PS: Political Science and Politics* 44 (January 2011): 97–100. doi:10.1017/S1049096510001940

Mayhew, David R. *Congress: The Electoral Connection.* New Haven, CT: Yale University Press, 1974.

McAtee, Andrea, and Jennifer Wolak. "Why People Decide to Participate in State Politics." *Political Research Quarterly* 64 (March 2011): 45–56. http://www.jstor.org /stable/41058321

McCartney, Alison Rios Millett, Elizabeth A. Bennion, and Dick Simpson, eds. *Teaching Civic Engagement.* Washington, DC: American Political Science Association, 2013.

McClain, Paula, and James Stewart. *"Can We All Get Along?" Race and Ethnic Minorities in American Politics.* 4th ed. Boulder, CO: Westview Press, 2005.

McGinniss, Joe. *The Selling of the President 1968.* New York: Penguin, 1989. First published 1969 by Trident Press.

McGrath, Dennis, and Dane Smith. *Professor Wellstone Goes to Washington.* Minneapolis: University of Minnesota Press, 1995.

McKelvey, Karissa, Joseph DiGrazia, and Fabio Rojas. "Twitter Publics: How Online Political Communities Signaled Electoral Outcomes in the 2010 US House Election." *Information, Communication, and Society* 17, no. 4 (2014): 436–450. doi:10.1371 /journal.pone.0079449

McKenzie, Evan. *Beyond Privatopia.* Washington, DC: Urban Institute Press, 2011.

———. *Privatopia.* New Haven, CT: Yale University Press, 1994.

Medina, Rocío Zamora, and Cristina Zurutuza Muñoz. "Campaigning on Twitter: Towards the 'Personal Style' Campaign to Activate the Political Engagement during the 2011 Spanish General Elections/La Campaña en Twitter: El 'Estilo Personal' como Estrategia para Activar la Participación Política durante las Elecciones Generales Españolas de 2011." *Comunicación y Sociedad* 27, no. 1 (2014): 83–106.

Meraz, Sharon. "The Fight for 'How to Think': Traditional Media, Social Networks, and Issue Interpretation." *Journalism* 12 (January 2011): 107–127. doi:10.1177 / 1464884910385193

Movement for a New Congress. *Vote Power: The Official Activist Campaigner's Handbook.* Englewood Cliffs, NJ: Prentice-Hall, 1970.

Murakami, Michael H. "Divisive Primaries: Party Organizations, Ideological Groups, and the Battle over Party Purity." *PS: Political Science & Politics* (October 2008): 918–923. doi:10.1017/S104909650838127X

Napolitan, Joseph. *The Election Game and How to Win It.* New York: Doubleday, 1972.

Nickerson, David W., Ryan D. Friedrichs, and David C. King. "Partisan Mobilization Campaigns in the Field: Results from a Statewide Turnout Experiment in Michigan." *Political Research Quarterly* 59, no. 1 (March 2006): 85–97. http://www.jstor .org/stable/4148077

Olsen, Marvin E. "Three Routes to Political Party Participation." *Western Political Quarterly* 29, no. 4 (December 1976): 550–562. http://www.jstor.org/stable/448137

Orbell, John M., Robyn M. Dawes, and Nancy J. Collins. "Grass Roots Enthusiasm and the Primary Vote." *Western Political Quarterly* 25, no. 2 (June 1972): 249–259. http:// www.jstor.org/stable/447195

O'Shaughnessy, Nicholas J. *The Phenomenon of Political Marketing.* New York: St. Martin's, 1990.

Page, Benjamin I., Larry M. Bartels, and Jason Seawright. "Democracy and the Policy Preferences of Wealthy Americans." *Perspective on Politics* 11, no. 1 (March 2013): 51–73. doi:10.1017/S153759271200360X

Pariser, Eli. *The Filter Bubble: What the Internet Is Hiding from You.* New York: Penguin, 2011.

Parkinson, Hank. *Winning Your Campaign: A Nuts-and-Bolts Guide to Political Victory.* Englewood Cliffs, NJ: Prentice-Hall, 1970.

Perry, Anthony. "Practicing Politics: The National Student Issues Conventions." In *Teaching Civic Engagement.* Edited by Alison Rios Millett McCartney, Elizabeth A. Bennion, and Dick Simpson. Washington DC: American Political Science Association, 2013, 189–202.

Pew Research Center. *Beyond Red vs. Blue: The Political Typology—Fragmented Center Poses Challenges for Both Parties.* June 26, 2014. http://www.people-press.org/2014/06/26/the-political-typology-beyond-red-vs-blue/

Polletta, Francesca. "Is Participation without Power Good Enough? Introduction to 'Democracy Now: Ethnographies of Contemporary Participation.'" *Sociological Quarterly* 55, no. 3 (2014): 453–466. doi:10.1111/tsq.12062

Presidential Commission on Election Administration. *The American Voting Experience: Report and Recommendations of the Presidential Commission on Election Administration.* January 2014. Accessed July 7, 2014. https://www.supportthevoter.gov/files/2014/01/Amer-Voting-Exper-final-draft-01-09-14-508.pdf

Putnam, Robert D. *Bowling Alone: The Collapse and Revival of American Community.* New York: Touchstone, 2000.

Ricke, LaCrystal D. *The Impact of YouTube on U.S. Politics.* London: Lexington, 2014.

Rosenblatt, Alan. "Dimensions of Campaigns in the Age of Digital Networks." In *Campaign and Elections American Style.* 3rd ed. Edited by James A. Thurber and Candice J. Nelson. Boulder, CO: Westview Press, 2010, 207–226.

Sabato, Larry. *The Party's Only Just Begun.* Glenview, IL: Scott Foresman, 1988.

Schattschneider, E. E. *The Semisovereign People.* New York: Holt, Rinehart, and Winston, 1960.

Schmidt, Eric, and Jared Cohen. *The New Digital Age: Reshaping the Future of People, Nations, and Business.* New York: Knopf, 2013.

Schweitzer, Eva Johanna. "The Mediatization of E-Campaigning: Evidence from German Party Websites in State, National, and European Parliamentary Elections, 2002–2009." *Journal of Computer-Mediated Communication* 17, no. 3 (2012): 283–302. Communication and Mass Media Complete. doi:10.1111/j.1083-6101.2012.01577.x

Selnow, Gary. *High-Tech Campaigns: Computer Technology in Political Communication.* Westport, CT: Praeger, 1994.

Semiatin, Richard J., ed. *Campaigns on the Cutting Edge.* 2nd ed. Washington, DC: Congressional Quarterly Press, 2013.

Shaw, Catherine. *The Campaign Manager: Running and Winning Local Elections.* 5th ed. Boulder, CO: Westview Press, 2014.

Sides, John, Daron Shaw, Matt Grossman, and Keena Lipsitz. *Campaigns and Elections.* 2nd ed. New York: Norton, 2015.

Sigelman, Lee, and Emmett H. Buell Jr. "Avoidance or Engagement? Issue Convergence in U.S. Presidential Campaigns, 1960–2000." *American Journal of Political Science* 48, no. 4 (October 2004): 650–661. http://www.jstor.org/stable/1519925

Slaton, Christa Daryl. *Televote: Expanding Citizen Participation in the Quantum Age.* New York: Praeger, 1992.

Steckler, Paul. "Vote for Me: Politics in America." *PS: Political Science & Politics* 29 (September 1996): 419–422. doi:10.2307/420816

Steen, Jennifer A. *Self-Financed Candidates in Congressional Elections.* Ann Arbor: University of Michigan Press, 2006.

Strachan, J. Cherie. *High-Tech Grass Roots: The Professionalization of Local Elections.* Lanham, MD: Rowman and Littlefield, 2002.

Talbot, David. "Personalized Campaigning." *Technology Review* 112, no. 2 (March 2009): 80–82.

Thurber, James A. "The Transformation of American Campaigns." In *Campaigns and Elections American Style.* Edited by James A. Thurber and Candice J. Nelson. Boulder, CO: Westview Press, 1995, 1–13.

Thurber, James A., and Candice J. Nelson, eds. *Campaigns and Elections American Style.* Boulder: Westview Press, 1995.

———. *Campaign and Elections American Style.* 2nd ed. Boulder, CO: Westview Press, 2004.

———. *Campaign and Elections American Style.* 3rd ed. Boulder, CO: Westview Press, 2010.

———. *Campaigns and Elections American Style.* 4th ed. Boulder, CO: Westview Press, 2014.

Turk, Michael. "Social and New Media: An Evolving Future." In *Campaigns on the Cutting Edge.* 2nd ed. Edited by Richard J. Semiatin. Washington, DC: Congressional Quarterly Press, 2013, 48–63.

Verba, Sidney, Kay Lehman Schlozman, and Henry E. Brady. *Voice and Equality: Civic Volunteerism in American Politics.* Cambridge, MA: Harvard University Press, 1995.

Wankel, Charles. *Teaching Arts and Science with the New Social Media.* Bradford, UK: Emerald, 2011.

Wojcieszak, Magdalena, and Briar Smith. "Will Politics Be Tweeted? New Media Use by Iranian Youth in 2011." *New Media and Society* 16, no. 1 (2014): 91–109. Communication and Mass Media Complete. doi:10.1177/1461444813479594

Wolffe, Richard. *Renegade: The Making of a President.* New York: Crown, 2009.

Yamamoto, M., and M. J. Kushin. "More Harm Than Good? Online Media Use and Political Disaffection among College Students in the 2008 Election." *Journal of Computer-Mediated Communication* 19 (2014): 430–445. doi:10.1111/jcc4.12046

Zaller, John. *The Nature and Origins of Mass Opinion.* Cambridge, UK: Cambridge University Press, 1992.

Index